Contents

Chapter 3
The World of Business 44

You can serve, plan, transact, build, advise, or market. Whatever your interests and skill, you'll find something just for you among these forty-one careers.

Chapter 4
The World of Communications 70

Communication has never been more important or easier than it is today. From selling newspapers to creating sophisticated computer programs, the forty-six jobs described here offer something for everybody.

Chapter 5
The Creative World 92

People who are creative cannot be happy doing routine work. The twenty-five jobs listed here are perfect for them, but there are positions that support creative individuals, such as sales and marketing, representation, supply, and other activities.

Chapter 6
The Fashion World 101

The world of fashion has always suggested success and glamour. Here are forty-two career possibilities for people who yearn to be part of it.

CREATE THE JOB YOU LOVE (and Make Plenty of Money)

More than 550 Ways to Escape the 8 to 5 Grind

BARBARA JOHNSON WITCHER

PRIMA PUBLISHING

For my husband, Harvey North Witcher,
with love and gratitude for
a wonderful life.

Library of Congress Cataloging-in-Publication Data

Witcher, Barbara Johnson.
Create the job you love : and make plenty of money / Barbara Johnson Witcher.
p. cm.
Includes index.
ISBN 0-7615-0811-2
1. Vocational guidance. 2. Career development. I. Title.
HF5381.W777 1996 96-25773
650.14—dc20 CIP

97 98 99 HH 10 9 8 7 6 5 4 3 2 1
Printed in the United States of America

How to Order

Single copies may be ordered from Prima Publishing, P.O. Box 1260, Rocklin, CA 95677; telephone (916) 632-4400. Quantity discounts are also available. On your letterhead, include information concerning the intended use of the books and the number of books you wish to purchase.

CHAPTER 7
The World of Foods: Gourmet and Simple 122

Everyone needs and is interested in food. Thirty-seven opportunities in this industry are featured—and they're not limited to cooks.

CHAPTER 8
The World of Houses and Homes 139

Just as everyone needs food, everyone needs a place to live. So if you are attracted to the housing industry, there's a niche for you—from building to selling to decorating to repairing. Examine these sixty-nine careers and adopt the one that fits you.

CHAPTER 9
The Legal World 171

As our society becomes more complex, we become more dependent on laws to protect us. Therefore, people who are interested in this field have many choices. Litigation and private investigation are the glamorous fields, but fifteen others can be equally fulfilling.

CHAPTER 10
The World of Money Matters 180

If you're money-minded, there's a world of opportunity for you. Banking is only the most obvious career; twenty-two other possibilities await you.

CHAPTER 11
The Nature Lover's World 193

Why are people who work with nature happier and calmer than the rest of us? Because they've exchanged concrete jungles for the beauty of a mountain, brook, flower, or animal. If this is the world you yearn for, here are forty-two jobs that will get you there.

CHAPTER 12
The World of Entertainment 217

Do you want to live in the spotlight? Make people laugh, cry, be moved in a special way? Then the field of entertainment is for you. However, it's also for those who support the entertainers and help people bring entertainment into their lives. You might find what you're interested in among the fifty-five choices listed here.

CHAPTER 13
The World of Caring for People 247

Among the sixty-three career opportunities listed here, you'll find medical, counseling, and caretaking professions—plus much more.

CHAPTER 14
The World of Religion 280

Work done by and for religious groups involves more than just standing behind a pulpit. The work done by churches and religious organizations and businesses offers good jobs to millions of people. Check out these twenty-four prospects.

CHAPTER 15
The Sports World 293

You don't have to be a famous sports figure to work in this field. There are plenty of great careers for ordinary people. Twenty-five are highlighted here.

CHAPTER 16
The World of Travel 306

The travel industry offers jobs for people who like to visit different worlds and help others do the same. Some of the twenty-two possibilities here will really surprise and thrill you.

CHAPTER 17
The World of Wheels, Wings, and Water 318

Transportation—by road, air, water—offers career opportunities to people with various skills and abilities. You're certain to find something that fits you perfectly in the thirty-seven careers listed here.

CHAPTER 18
Keep the Job You Have but Work When You Want 339

How do you convince your employer to let you escape the 8-to-5 grind and work *your* way? Try these suggestions.

Introduction

Can You Really Work When You Want and Still Make Money?

It's 6 A.M. Monday morning. You're snuggled cozily in your soft bed as your mind delights in a lovely dream. Suddenly a horrible shrieking clang assaults you. Your body is jarred into instant alert as the idyllic scene of a second ago shatters. You know immediately what has happened. The same thing happens to you almost every weekday of your life. Your alarm clock is reminding you that in two hours you will have to be at the office, and you will have to stay there for eight long, dreary hours. As you stare at your bedroom ceiling before crawling out of bed, you wonder, "Is there no escaping this awful grind?"

Maybe your form of bondage is different. Spring break is approaching, and you'd love to spend some daylight hours with your daughter. You can manage that only if you use some of your precious vacation days. But if you do—well—you have only two weeks. You'll have to give up part of your much-needed summer vacation at the beach.

"My job owns me," you tell yourself as you grimly arrange for a baby-sitter to care for your daughter during the week that she is home.

Or maybe you're busy at both work and home. And since you devote five long days a week to the job, you have only two days to run household and personal errands, clean, launder, iron, cook, shop, entertain, and . . .

If only—*if only,* you think, I had one more day to "do my thing."

Does any of this sound familiar?

It did to me until I discovered that I *could* work when I wanted and still make money. Lots of it.

I'm not alone. Hundreds of thousands of ordinary people like you and me have jobs that allow them the time and flexibility to live their lives and not just exist in them. (I do mean "like you and me"; I'm not talking about those millionaire entrepreneurs who obviously can do what they want when they want.)

Would you like to join us? No matter how old you are or how long you have been stuck in that 8-to-5 prison, this book can set you free by giving you more than 500 job/career options that lend themselves to flexible work schedules. (I use the words *job* and *career* interchangeably.) They range from positions requiring little education, such as being a waiter or housecleaner, to professions such as medicine and law. (Yes, Mr. Doctor and Ms. Lawyer—you too can earn wonderful incomes and not be slaves to your practices.)

In this book, I have categorized these flexible careers according to sixteen areas of interest, each having its own chapter. I've listed the jobs alphabetically in each chapter. Examine the ones you're passionate about and match a job with your skills. After all, since you're going to change your work lifestyle, you might as well do something you like and something that interests you. You'll probably be surprised to discover that your present position is listed even though you've probably never even considered that it could be turned into a flexible job. Chapter 18 will show you how to talk that tough boss of yours into letting you put some flexibility in your life.

Each job description consists of four parts. First is a brief general description of the job, followed by the type of time schedule involved, the requirements you will need to get the job or start the business, and the compensation you can expect. By *compensation,* I don't mean specific dollar figures because pay structures vary so much in all the places where this book will be read. However, I will tell you whether the position pays commissions, salaries, flat hourly rates, minimum wage—or whether it offers several different kinds of compensation. I will also describe the kinds of benefits it includes. Based on this information, you can then investigate whether a similar job in your town would meet your financial needs.

Frequently, the description of a particular profession will refer you to a number in Chapter 1. Many of the more than 500 jobs listed in this book fall into the same basic category, such as sales or teaching. To keep the book from becoming too large and repeating information, I have given in Chapter 1 a detailed general explanation of those jobs that fall into the same category. Each category discussion includes an in-depth description of the basic job, time schedule, requirements, and general compensation as well as any applicable advancement opportunities. And finally, under each category, I include "personal profiles"—descriptions of real people who hold down these jobs in a unique way. If they can do well—why not you?

This general information can then be applied to the specific job in the category that catches your interest. For example, you may wish to sell giftware to retail stores, while your friend wants to sell auto supplies to auto stores. Although the products are very different, the time schedule, requirements, and compensation for these outside sales positions are basically the same. Consequently, you could both look up the generic information concerning a sales career in Chapter 1 and then apply it to your specific interest.

Once you have identified the position (or positions) that appeal to you, then you can learn more about the job by reading books on the subject in your library, interviewing people in the field, checking into training through your local school, and interviewing with companies that are offering such a position through the classified advertisements in the newspaper. The limits of this book do not allow me to write a "how-to-get-this-job" manual for each of the jobs, but you should be able to glean enough information about the career so that you can determine whether or not to pursue it.

About now you're probably getting a bit cynical. This book is just so much blue-sky hype, you think. *Not so!*

This is probably a good time to introduce you to my career history so that you can see that I do indeed "practice what I preach."

At one time, early in my life, I was just like you—assuming that work meant giving up all freedom. I learned this lesson from my parents. When I was young, we lived in Chicago, and every day Mom and Dad rushed off to work by 7 A.M. Their routines never changed. They would stand on crowded, jostling elevated trains to get to "the Loop" and their 8 A.M. jobs. Then in the evening they would reverse the whole process. Packed into noisy trains, they would stand bleary-eyed, hoping to get home by six—where meal preparations and household chores awaited them. Occasionally, during school breaks, I accompanied them, and I can still remember thinking dismally, "How awful!"

Yet when I started working, I did the same thing.

Having moved from Chicago to Los Angeles, I exchanged the crowded trains my parents rode for a bumpy bus that belched exhaust fumes back into its interior through open windows. Every morning I allowed it to jostle me to my clerical job at an engineering firm. As if that weren't bad enough, I had to endure this torture at the ungodly hour of six in the morning because I had to clock in by seven every day.

This schedule almost killed me because I am not a morning person. I am one of those people whose internal clock does not even start ticking, much less swing into high gear, until around 9 A.M. Then I perk away brilliantly until around two in the afternoon, die down and fall practically flat around four, and then become revitalized again by six. After that I can whiz along until midnight.

I am not alone. Many people are like me, and we are called "Owls" because we start later and keep going into the night. Our opposites—those people who bounce out of bed bright-eyed, eager, and energetic—are "Larks." A Lark would not have had my difficulties getting to a 7 A.M. job. I, however, did.

Then, to make matters worse, the tasks of filing and typing statistical reports bored me. Each day dragged by, inflicting upon me a mental torture that literally made me ill. When I became pregnant and medical complications forced me to quit my job, I was ecstatic.

The next time I went job hunting, I was a mother with three children. Quite by accident I stumbled upon a flexible job when I took a sales position for a company that didn't provide an office. When I was asked if I would "mind" working out of my home, I jumped at the chance because that meant that I could be home when my children returned from school (and so save baby-sitting costs). If I arranged my schedule correctly, I could even go to the school in late afternoon and watch my son play ball. That I did, and I rarely missed any of my children's activities. Of course, I also often did paperwork at midnight; but that was fine with me because I thought I had a wonderful arrangement. And wonder of wonders—I was even making money when and how I wanted.

That was more than thirty years ago, and I'm still enjoying a flexible work schedule. During those years I have run my own businesses, including a very busy retail gift store. (Yes, even there I worked when I wanted because I hired reliable, efficient people to help me.)

Today, employed by a national marketing company, I am responsible for nine sales managers and more than a hundred salespeople in nine western states. It is certainly a demanding job, and I never see an end to the work. Yes, I spend much time traveling. But do you know what? Last Thursday my granddaughter was in a school play at 10 A.M. Grandma was there. And when my daughter Linda and her children visited from Massachusetts for a week last April, I limited my field work and devoted most of my work week to catching up on the avalanche of paperwork that covered my desk in my home office. When did I do this? Late at night after spending the day with the branch of the family I don't often see.

Did I give the company that employs me its very significant money's worth that week? You bet I did. Because you see, the company really doesn't care at what time I write the memos, evaluate the sales figures, read the reports, and so on. What's important is only that it is done during a certain time frame and that my markets are producing the desired results. They are, and I have never missed a deadline.

In addition, since my office is in my home (my company's headquarters are in a southern state), I can live and work in the beautiful mountain resort of Big Bear Lake, California. My fax machine, telephone, voice mail, and computer make me just as efficient as I'd be working in a Wall Street high-rise. Consequently, I can work looking out at the blue sky, tall pines, and sparkling lake. When I take a break, my dog Finnigan Flynn and I go for a quick stroll in the national forest within steps from my house.

You might think that this is wonderful (in fact, you probably envy me). But, you may be asking yourself, is it really possible for me?

Actually it is, if you will do what I did and make the demands of your job fit into your lifestyle. When I have to catch a plane, I simply schedule my flights for afternoons in order to allow the necessary time to drive leisurely down the mountain to the airport in Ontario, California. When I work with my sales team in Southern California, I stay with my other daughter and her five children or with my mother. That way I can incorporate family time into work time. Yes, it does take some creativity and planning to make my work and personal needs mesh, but the flexibility is worth it.

Yet with all this freedom, I'm still a top producer for my company. Don't think that working when you want to means not working or shirking your career responsibilities. Rather, it simply means readjusting them so that you and the company that pays your wages (whether it is your own business or an outside employer) both win.

You can work when you want and still make money. All you have to do is read this book with an open mind, use your imagination, and don't be afraid to change your work life so that, at last, you really can start living.

Henry David Thoreau described the alternative best: "The mass of men [and women] lead lives of quiet desperation."

Don't you be one of them.

Chapter 1

Basic Jobs That Offer a World of Freedom, Fun, and Financial Security

Most jobs fall into a category whose descriptions, time schedules, requirements, and compensation potential apply to many different positions. These categories are the core or the foundation upon which any specialized position builds.

Take sales, for example. All of us know what it feels like to have someone attempt to sell us something. If you're in sales, you also know what it feels like to be the person doing the selling.

Anyone who wants to be a salesperson should have certain characteristics. A salesperson needs to like people and to be able to communicate easily with others; someone in sales also needs to be able to persevere in the face of rejection (not everyone will want to buy the product being sold). A salesperson also needs to be able to deal with extended hours and should understand and enthusiastically support the product or service being sold.

If Pete wants to sell auto parts to auto parts stores, Mary wants to sell jewelry to jewelry stores, and John wants to sell real estate to potential homeowners, they all will need the basic characteristics of a salesperson. But they all will have to meet requirements specific to the product they sell—or the market they sell to—as well. For example, John should have specific knowledge about the methods of selling real estate and should understand the laws that govern real estate sales; Mary must be an expert on gems; Pete should know the jargon that goes with automobile repair and should feel comfortable with people who love cars.

In Chapters 2 through 17, the descriptions for sales jobs will offer requirements specific to selling a particular product—like jewelry. The descriptions will also refer you to this chapter, which will give you, in great detail, the basics that apply to all sales positions.

Eleven basic job categories are described in this chapter. For each, I give general requirements that will apply to many specific positions. The best way for you to find a job that you will love among the more than 500 included in this book is to first identify the job categories that fit your background, temperament, income, and time needs. Once you have done that, then turn to the chapters that describe your interests. Maybe you have discovered that you would like a sales job. You also know that you love beautiful things and want to work around and with them. And you also know without a moment's hesitation that you definitely are not interested in anything that pertains to the world of transportation.

How, then, would you find the job that you could love?

You would explore the many jobs described in Chapter 2, "The World of Beautiful Things." Several jobs listed there involve the sale of beautiful objects. When you find positions that most interest you, read the specific details concerning them, add that knowledge to the general information given in this chapter, and you should know enough to seriously set out finding or creating that career or job.

You might also wonder how you'll be able to find employment in those positions you have selected as the ones that you think you would love.

In addition to the suggestions outlined under the specific description, a good way to learn about any job is to talk with people in your community who are already doing it. If you explain to them that you want to get into the business and are not going to compete with them, most people are happy and even flattered to help you. Local colleges have career guidance programs and job placement services that can be most helpful in offering suggestions on how to get a job. Additionally, I strongly suggest that you go to the personnel offices of large companies and answer ads in newspapers so that you will be able to speak to someone about what skills and experience they would require of you if you were to be hired.

I once answered a large department store's ad for an assistant buyer of coats. I knew nothing about being a clothing buyer, but I wanted to find out what experience and knowledge I would need to get that job. After the interview, when I had obtained the information I needed, I was offered a "head of stock" position where I could work as the assistant to an assistant buyer. I took the job and six months later was promoted to an assistant buyer.

This tactic works! Don't be afraid to try it.

Here then, are eleven positions that can give you everything you need so that you can find the job you love and make plenty of money. Lest you think that they sound too good to be true or that they are for only a privileged few, I have also included "real people" who are making a living in these positions and loving every minute of it.

You can be just like them—really you can!

So start now finding the job you love. This chapter and the ones that follow provide the directions. All you have to do is start the journey.

1. ARTIST/CRAFTSPERSON

Description: Creates something that can be used or appreciated by another. You might sell your product directly to the consumer through special orders; or you might go to craft shows or sell through gift and craft stores on a consignment basis.

Time Schedule: Your time is totally your own. However, if you are making products for a particular show, you may have to work long hours to make enough merchandise for a large inventory. And if someone commissions you to make a craft item, then you will have to deliver the goods *on time.*

Requirements: You will need the knowledge and ability to create something unique and more attractive than the average person could make. These qualities will make your product marketable. Use your imagination and keep current on what is popular with the general public.

Compensation: You'll be paid outright for the item. Consequently, you must be sure to charge enough for it. To do so, determine what your time is worth by the hour and then add all material and marketing costs to your price.

For example, suppose you make and sell wooden trucks for children. Your wood and other materials plus the ads you run to attract customers cost you $5. This is the raw cost of your product. It takes you two hours to produce one truck. You feel that your time is worth $7 per hour. Two hours' time equals $14 plus the $5 raw product cost. That totals $19 minimum that you must charge for your finished craft item. If you charge too little, you will not enjoy your business and will soon leave it. However, you must also be cautious not to overcharge. The best way to avoid doing so is by checking out your competition. If your competition makes wooden trucks and you don't think there's a market for "more of the same," then make wooden airplanes or ships or trains instead.

There are many ways of selling your goods besides selling each one individually to a customer. One of the most popular is to place your merchandise in a "consignment" shop that takes your item, prices it, and sells it for you—and then receives a percentage of the sale price in exchange. This can be 10 percent to 40 percent; the percentage might seem high, but remember that the store bears the cost of a retail establishment—clerks, rent, and so on. You can also participate in crafts fairs. Here you pay rent for your space and then sell your crafts. This is a particularly good way to get exposure and take custom orders.

Personal Profile: Debbie Smith of California makes teddy bears and sells them only at crafts fairs. It takes about six hours to make one 8-inch bear, complete with clothing. No two bears are ever alike, and she will design custom bears for her customers. She prices her bears from $300 to $800 each. Working an average of twenty-four hours a week making bears and an additional twenty days per year appearing at crafts shows, Debbie cleared over $50,000 last year. And she worked while caring for her small children.

2. CONSULTANT/COUNSELOR

Description: Gives "advice" or counsel to individuals or businesses on specific subjects. This category can also include other professionals (such as accountants) who are similar to consultants in the way they interact with clients.

Time Schedule: Consultants set their own schedules but also have to be available to meet with clients at their convenience. Consultants can, however, block out days, weeks, and maybe even months between assignments to do what they choose to.

Requirements: First, you must have formal education and degrees in the specific field you are consulting in. You must have gained expertise and have a successful track record—often through previous work experience with prestigious companies. Then you must have the ability to communicate that knowledge and tailor it to fit the clients' needs. Finally, you must know how to market your service; such marketing usually includes attendance at trade shows and membership in organizations where your potential clients might be found.

Compensation: You will usually be paid a flat fee for a specific project; if the project is very long or ongoing, you can negotiate an hourly fee. Expenses are generally paid too.

It is customary to be paid a retainer of at least 30 percent of the projected cost of your service "up front"—before the project begins and right after the contract has been signed.

When writing a contract for your services, be sure to itemize everything the client expects of you to avoid any expectation that you will deliver more than what is agreed upon for the contracted price.

Personal Profiles: Robert Schafer, who owns Creative Culinary Consultants of Mission Viejo, California, is a food consultant who develops new products, menus, and recipe ideas for restaurant chains and major food manufacturers. When he travels, as he often must, his hours are long. However, he enjoys flexibility in scheduling that allows him to attend his children's sports and school activities and to balance job-related stresses with relaxation. He graduated from the Culinary Institute of America and spent twenty-two years in the food and beverage industry. His income is approximately $125,000 per year.

Carl Meisner, president and owner of the West Coast advertising agency Creative Edge, has spent thirty years designing total advertising campaigns for businesses. Now he averages a three- to four-day work week. Because he meets his clients at their locations, he can run his business from his home office, where he interacts with his network of creative professionals. This flexible lifestyle gives Carl more time to enjoy his wife, children, and grandchildren while still maintaining a six-figure annual income.

3. CRITIC

Description: Gives a personal opinion about and judgment of something that interests the public; this critique can be made through the written word or via radio, television, or both. A critic might review fashions, restaurants, books, concerts, recordings, films, and so on.

Time Schedule: You usually set your own hours if your critique is written, unless you have to meet a daily newspaper deadline. Once you evaluate the event or subject and write about it, then all you have to do is turn it in to whoever publishes it. If you appear on a television or radio show, you'll have to work your schedule around the program unless you tape your appearance in advance.

Requirements: You'll need expertise (through an extensive education and business-related background) in whatever you are critiquing plus the ability to be at least somewhat fair and objective. It is also important to be knowledgeable and experienced in writing or broadcasting. Finally, know how to market yourself and have a vast network of friends and associates who will help you get started.

Compensation: You are usually paid by the written piece or appearance. When setting your rate or deciding whether to accept what you're offered for the critiquing, consider your hourly worth. All costs (such as meals in restaurants, tickets to shows, and so on) should be added to your rates if you have to pay for them. Books and tickets to concerts, plays, and movies are often offered to reviewers at no charge.

Personal Profile: Marcie Edwards is a book critic for several magazines. She works out of her home and reads all the new books (supplied to her free by the publishers), then writes her critiques as she feels the magazines' various readers might relate to them. She works about twenty hours a week and earns approximately $25,000 a year.

4. "EXPO" OR SHOW PRODUCER

Description: Puts on an exposition or show around a certain theme in a public place, such as a convention center. Some shows are aimed at the general public (such as a new car show); other shows are aimed at specific members of the public who have a special or professional interest in the show's subject (like the wholesale gift show for retailers who need to buy giftware for their stores).

Time Schedule: You set your own schedule during the planning and organizing of the event. However, the days or weeks prior to the show and shortly thereafter are usually very long and hectic.

Requirements: You must have the ability to foresee what show themes would appeal to the public. You also need imagination, daring, and a flair for promotion. Organization is necessary too because of the many details involved in such an undertaking. For a show to be successful, the producer must succeed in finding and renting the expo location, identifying and "selling" businesses on participating in the expo (and collecting their money), negotiating with the decorators who set up the booth spaces and the carpeting, setting up the utilities in the hall, and arranging the advertising and promotion for the event (it's the planner's great responsibility to bring the public to the expo); in addition, the producer must arrange for the ticket-takers, security, food vendors, and emergency medical staff. And because of all the "up-front" charges, having some money to invest in the beginning is an absolute must.

Compensation: You make money in two ways: from "renting" booth space to the show's participants (who want to sell something to the people who attend your event) and from admissions paid by the public.

The first should pay for all of your production costs, including building rental, utilities, decorators, and advertising.

The second, referred to as the "gate," should bring in your income. That's one of the reasons why it is so critical that you spend enough money on advertising to bring in attendees. (If you are producing a "trade show," where people will not pay to attend, then your income also comes from booth rentals. However, trade shows do not require advertising: those attending usually know about the event because it is part of their business.)

Personal Profile: A producer I will call J. T. (since he has asked that I not reveal his real name) yearly puts on a three-day bridal expo in a large Midwestern city. He rents space to stores selling wedding gowns, florists, photographers, musical groups—anyone and everyone wishing to sell their services to brides and grooms. The rental spaces usually cost an average of $1,000 for the three days, and J. T. generally has about 100 exhibitors participating. His rents cover all his costs of putting on the show (as outlined above), and he spends a great deal of money on advertising. He nets about $150,000 from the 30,000+ attendees, who pay $5 each to enter the show. He estimates that he works 60 to 75 days a year. The rest of his time he travels with his wife.

5. INSTRUCTOR/TEACHER

Description: Teaches something specific to people, usually in a classroom setting.

Time Schedule: To some extent, as a teacher, you can set your own schedule, particularly if you are running your own business or freelancing. But if you work for a school that hires you to teach a specific subject or subjects, you may have to work around the school schedule. However, in most cases, you can still request certain times off—especially if there are many classes and instructors.

Requirements: Teaching requires patience and an understanding of, if not expertise in, your subject. You will also need good public speaking skills if you are going to teach a group, and you must be able to make what is complicated easy to learn and understand. Depending on what you teach and for whom, you might need to have special training and to hold the credentials or licenses required by the state you live in.

Compensation: If you are a freelancer, you will be paid for each class you teach. The amount you can earn depends on the course and who is employing you. If you are considered an employee, you will probably be paid a salary.

If you teach crafts, you may earn additional money by selling the supplies that your students will need. Many teachers pick up significant extra money this way.

Advancement Opportunities: You may start out as a teacher and then decide to start your own school. Your compensation will then be generated from what you charge for your classes, minus all the expenses you incur giving them (such as classroom rent, teachers' pay, advertising, and so on). The more people your school educates, the more money you make.

Personal Profiles: When my husband Harvey decided to retire from the insurance business, he accepted a teaching position with a school that prepared people to pass the state test to become licensed insurance salespeople. He taught three classes, each of which was four hours in length, during weekday mornings and one evening. He was paid $100 for each class, which gave him $300 per week. It was a nice addition to his other retirement income, and he loved it. Because the school had many instructors available, Harvey could trade his classes for others in order to have a certain day free.

Paul Miller, a graduate of UCLA with a bachelor's degree in English, taught conversational English to the Japanese in Osaka, Japan. Working through a company specializing in these classes, he was there for a year and worked from noon to 9 P.M. Paul, in his late twenties, enjoyed the job because it gave him a wonderful opportunity to travel and learn about another culture firsthand; in addition, he had every morning off to pursue a writing career. There are similar opportunities in almost all countries, but Paul tells me that Japan has a reputation for paying the most—about $30,000 a year.

6. PHOTOGRAPHER

Description: Takes pictures of specific subjects—people, objects, scenery, animals—anything. Photographers usually work from a studio or on site at an event—or sometimes at the subject's convenience.

Time Schedule: If you work for yourself (and most photographers do), you can block out certain days, weeks, or even months when you don't wish to work at all. Otherwise, you must work around your subjects' or clients' needs in order to get the business. Frequently, this also means being available during seasons when your services will be most needed (such as wedding seasons if you are a wedding photographer).

Requirements: To start, you need a professional's skill in taking pictures. Some specialized education is usually necessary, and it may include learning to develop the pictures from film. Also required is empathy, patience (with difficult subjects like wiggly children), and special ability to enhance your subject's attractiveness. You must also know how to market yourself and your service. One photographer told me that he was an artist who uses photography as his medium. If you are that, you will be successful.

Compensation: Photographers normally charge a fee for taking the photographs, plus a very high markup on the pictures sold.

For instance, it might cost you $1 to develop an 8- by 10-inch photograph, but you could easily charge $10 for it. Add frames, keychains, and other accessories, and photography can be a very good business. Usually discounts are given if more than one picture is purchased. This is why most photography studios sell "packages."

Personal Profile: Bonnie specializes in taking wedding pictures. She works from her home and usually secures her clients from booths at "bridal fairs" and through recommendations from satisfied clients. She has several bridal packages, which include an hourly rate plus numbers of photographs.

The average wedding *commitment* (the amount she knows she will make before she goes to the wedding because it is the minimum package the couple has agreed to buy) is $600, and she gets half of that up front. Usually additional pictures and albums are purchased, not only by the bridal couple but also by their relatives and friends. This increases her average income per wedding to around $1,000.

7. RETAILER

Description: Sells some type of merchandise to the public from a retail store. This category can also include any type of business or professional practice that is open to the public.

Time Schedule: Everyone knows that running or owning a retail store or publicly accessed business can be demanding, and the hours can be long. However, with careful planning and organization, you too can love your job, work it when you want—and still make money.

The secret is in hiring and training some of your employees to "run the store" in your absence. You might want your employees to do no more than spell you for a few hours every day, or you might want them to open and close the business so that you can take several days, or even weeks, off.

You start by identifying which of your responsibilities you would like to eventually share with someone else. Once you know what they are, you then try to hire someone with experience in those tasks or someone who can be trained to perform them. For example, if you want to hire someone who can decorate your store's windows, you will choose someone with artistic ability or experience in decorating or both. If you want someone to handle your bookkeeping, give a test of mathematical aptitude. If you do find people with the specific skills you want, you'll probably have to pay them more for taking on extra responsibility, but the freedom you gain will be worth it.

It should also be noted that the hours you must keep depend on where your business is located. If you are in a mall, you will have to be open during the hours established by the mall owners or managers. Most of them are open (and expect you to be) from 10 A.M. to 9 P.M. The hours you'll need to be open should be considered when you choose your location.

Something that is enabling more people to enjoy ownership of a retail store without the headaches of long hours is renting space in "retail malls," which are generally large buildings or stores specializing in a certain type of merchandise (such as antiques or crafts or giftware). The mall owner provides clerks who walk throughout the store, show your items, and sell them. The mall also handles all credit card transactions and provides any advertising that might be necessary to bring in the customers. For this service you pay rent for your space plus a percentage of your sales. You can also work in your part of the store, interacting with customers, as much as you want. This method of retailing truly gives you the best of all worlds.

If you work in the retail store but do not own it, you will generally find that most managers will give you a flexible schedule if that is what you want. Most stores are open all day and evening, seven days a week. This makes the work ideal for parents who need to work around their children's schedules, students with school responsibilities, and retirees who want to work only when they wish.

Requirements: What you need most is a "passion" for what you sell and patience in dealing with people. You also need to be an expert businessperson because you will be dealing with tasks that include controlling inventory, handling payroll, managing employees, negotiating your contracts with your landlord and other vendors, and handling advertisement and promotion. On top of all of this, you still have to be very good at selling merchandise or performing whatever service you offer. Fortunately, there are consultants and organizations (such as the Small Business Administration) that can help you get started. And if you can learn about a business that you eventually want to own by working in it, that would be the best education you could get.

Compensation: Your income is derived from the markup you charge on the merchandise that you sell, minus all expenses of doing business. If you sell a service and not merchandise, then your income would come from the fees you charge, minus your business costs. Therefore you would need to make certain that you charge per hour what you must make to be successful.

However, let's assume that you are a retailer who sold $4,000 worth of merchandise in a month. If you purchased those items from wholesalers for $2,000, you made $2,000 from your sales (deduct the cost of the merchandise). If your store's monthly rent, insurance, utilities, and employees' costs are $1,500, you have to subtract this from the $2,000 you made from the markup of your merchandise. This leaves you with $500 as your net income. Retailers try to buy merchandise at a price low enough so that they can charge more than a 100 percent markup. Ideally, those $2,000 items at wholesale could bring in $4,500 or $5,000—or because you buy large quantities or make special deals, you get items that normally would cost you $2,000 for $1,500. This greatly increases your net.

If you simply work for the store or business, you will generally be paid a salary or hourly wage.

Advancement Opportunities: If you work for the business or store, you can be promoted to manager. In this position you will obviously make a better wage and you might even make a percentage (usually in the form of a bonus) of the profits you make for the business. This greater responsibility generally pays benefits such as medical insurance too.

Personal Profiles: In Big Bear Lake (where I live), there is a wonderful store called "Wild Wings Unlimited." It is owned and operated by Bill Strickler, who took his hobby of bird watching and turned it into a business that sells bird seed, bird houses and feeders, books, and everything else that would interest bird enthusiasts. He and his wife work together six days a week—10 to 5—and often they spell each other so that one can get away. Known as an expert in his field, Bill frequently gives bird seminars to attract new customers. As Bill says, "I'm doing something that I enjoy. This is not work." If you're going to be in the retail business, this is the best attitude to have.

When attorney Kenneth Marapese of Hawthorne, California, decided to cut back on hours to enjoy life more, he established a 9:30 A.M. to 2:30 P.M. time schedule and hired a part-time secretary. Limiting his involvement in handling cases, he uses other lawyers and investigators and concentrates primarily on negotiation and property management. While he doesn't make the large income he used to, he still enjoys one in the six-figure bracket—and he's enjoying life more!

8. SALESPERSON (OUTSIDE)

Description: Makes sales calls to customers within a certain geographical "territory." Customers can be individuals in homes, retail outlets of all types, factories, and so on. Products sold this way can be anything that someone or some organization might want or need.

Time Schedule: Great flexibility is possible because you set your own schedules. However, the more customers and potential customers you see, the more money you make. To utilize time and travel wisely, most outside salespeople arrange several appointments within a certain geographical area for the same day. Many salespeople devote four days a week to being "out in the field" and the fifth day to handling paperwork and making telephone calls. Paperwork can be done anytime—nights, early in the morning, or weekends.

Requirements: You need to be outgoing with new people, to be able to talk to them and motivate them (through an understanding of their needs) to buy your product. You need a belief in what you're selling, and you need to enjoy traveling (in whatever form you use to get to your customers, usually by driving an automobile which must be reliable). The ability to work alone is especially important. Most salespeople report that the hardest door for them to go through is their own as they start a new day. Remember that you'll have to go out and call on your customers even when you don't feel like it. For this reason, being an outside salesperson requires great discipline. You must also have a persistent and optimistic personality.

Compensation: Almost every salesperson receives some pay through commissions (making a percentage of the dollar amount sold). However, depending on the company, you could also earn a base salary or a "draw against commission." A draw has to be paid out of your commissions. The key thing to consider is when, if, or how often the draw is erased. If it never is, then two or three poor months can build up so much draw that when you do start making commissions, they will all be used in paying back the draws or advances. A fair advance program is one that erases advances at least quarterly or semiannually.

You should know that many outside salespeople are treated as independent contractors. This means that the company does not withhold any money from their paycheck (for social security, federal taxes, and so on). This means that you will have to pay these and be responsible for the paperwork yourself. Nor will you usually receive any benefits, such as vacations, holiday pay, and so on. This can work to your advantage because you can take many tax deductions as an independent businessperson. You also have much more freedom because the company usually doesn't interfere in when or how you do your work.

Other businesses hire you as an employee, with all the benefits and supervision of an employee-employer relationship. If this is what is offered to you, be sure that you get the appropriate remuneration for using your own automobile or that you get a company car (the latter is preferable).

Advancement Potential: It is possible to become a sales manager, who supervises other salespeople. In addition to all of the requirements and successes of a salesperson, you will also need to know how to teach and motivate the people who work for you to successfully sell your company's products.

Your compensation, while usually including a higher salary, will also include a commission or override on what your salespeople sell.

Personal Profiles: Kathleen Widdison, of Sell-Thru-Services, started with the company eight years ago as a part-time merchandiser who worked about twenty hours a week representing a candy manufacturer in small stores. This schedule enabled her to work around her children's school schedule.

Now most of them are grown, and last year she was promoted to service manager. Supervising twenty-one representatives who do the same thing she did, she now has a weekly schedule that averages 40 hours a week. But, to a great extent, she can still set up her own schedule to accommodate her family's needs. She earns $24,000 a year, plus a bonus and profit sharing.

A friend I shall call Bob sells real estate three and a half days a week (which includes weekends, when most people have the time to look for a new house). From straight commissions, he made over $40,000 last year in an area that suffered economically.

9. SERVICE PROVIDER

Description: Provides a service to a person or business. This service can be anything that is valued and needed by another—from hairstyling, accounting, and chauffeuring to pumping out a septic tank.

Time Schedule: If you work for yourself, you set your own schedule; however, you do have to accommodate the needs of your customers. As an employee, you may have to work around the schedule your company sets up. (See Chapter 18 for information on how to get your employer to let you have a flexible schedule.)

Requirements: You have to know how to perform the particular service you are providing. You might need considerable education and skill, plus state or federal licensing. If you are running your own business, it is important to know how to market yourself and your service. You might need to do considerable networking in your community and within your industry.

Compensation: No matter what service you are performing, you must consider your hourly worth. If you have to provide materials as part of the service (such as hair dye for a beautician's work), the cost of that has to be built into what you charge.

For example, if you are a barber and need to make $12 an hour and if it takes you 45 minutes to give someone a haircut, you might charge $9.00 for the haircut. What you also need to consider in setting your fees is where you do your business, what your competition charges, and how much business you have. If you are a barber who averages eight or fewer customers a day, even though it takes you only 45 minutes (or three-fourths of an hour) to cut someone's hair, you may elect to charge your hour's rate—in this example, $12.

Obviously the more specialized and unique your service, the more you can charge for it.

Personal Profiles: Gail Stickels is a licensed beautician in California. She rents her station in a beauty salon with other hairdressers and manicurists and works only during the week, Monday through Friday. Because she is a single mother she chooses not to work on weekends when her daughter is home from school. She thinks this is a wonderful profession for a mother.

Darlynn Stephens, of C & D Interprizes Billing & Follow Up, owns and operates a medical claims processing business for physicians. While she averages six to ten hours a day four to five days a week, she still enjoys a flexible schedule that allows her to schedule her personal appointments and responsibilities when she desires. To prepare for her business, which brings in a yearly income close to $100,000, she worked for several years as an office manager and consultant for physicians.

Gary Johnson of Arizona also wanted a career that would allow him time to be involved with his sons in Indian Guides and sports. As an insurance inspector and auditor, his hours are his own. He calls on businesses to audit their books and inspect their property for the insurance companies, and then he fills out very specialized paperwork. The hours, including considerable driving, are long, but they are still very flexible.

10. SHOPPER

Description: Shops for specific products for individuals or businesses. This can be done as an independent businessperson or as an employee of a department store.

Time Schedule: If you work as a freelancer, you can arrange somewhat flexible hours, but you must accommodate the needs and schedules of your clients. During holiday seasons, the hours can be very long and stressful. As an employee of a store you might be expected to work regular hours. Refer to Chapter 18 for suggestions on how to turn traditional employment into a flexible job.

Requirements: You must enjoy shopping and know where to find specific items. Excellent taste and the ability to get your clients their money's worth is also extremely important as is patience and having good marketing skills to promote your service. Marketing this kind of business includes a great deal of "cold calling" on potential customers and networking within your community and among those who might be attracted to your service.

Compensation: You are usually paid by the hour and reimbursed for travel and other expenses. If you are purchasing expensive items, you might improve your compensation by charging a percentage of the purchase. When determining your fee, you must be sure to identify what you must make per hour to warrant being in this business. If you don't or if you lower your prices considerably, you will find yourself making a very poor income. Also try wherever possible to shop in the same places at the same time for several clients. This practice maximizes your income per hour.

If you are working as an employee for a department or specialty store, try to get a commission on what you sell as well as a salary and employee benefits.

Personal Profile: Marcel Morgan is a personal fashion shopper who works for a famous upscale New York department store. She started her career as a salesclerk, then became an assistant buyer. She decided to accept this new position because it seemed to be "more fun." It also pays very well, earning her "close to six figures" in commissions, salary, and benefits. Her hours are four long days a week, and they always include Saturdays.

11. WRITER

Description: Creates something specific for others to read. You could write fiction, nonfiction, or technical books; newsletters; magazine or newspaper articles; radio or television commercials; screenplays; and so on.

Time Schedule: As a freelancer, you have total control of your schedule. However, you will have to meet the deadlines of your publisher or whoever buys what you write.

Requirements: You'll need an ability to write and a knowledge of spelling, grammar, and the particular requirements of your market (books, magazines, screenplays, grant proposals, and the like). It helps if you enjoy the writing process, and you must also have patience for research and rewrites. Obviously, you need an imagination to write fiction, but creativity is also useful in writing nonfiction. Writers *have to write* in order to be happy—it is practically a compulsion. If you don't have this drive and dedication, don't select this profession.

Compensation: Writers are sometimes paid outright for their work, through either a "flat fee" ($500 for a magazine article, for example) or an hourly rate ($50 an hour to write press releases for a Fortune 500 company). Sometimes they are paid with a percentage of what their work earns in the marketplace. The latter is true in mainstream publishing, where authors get commissions called royalties on their book sales. In most instances, advances are paid against royalties. The advances are then deducted from the royalties before the writer receives them.

Once you have been published, you should be able to get an agent who will market your work for you. The agent gets a percentage (usually 15 percent) of what your work sells for; but because the agent usually can negotiate a better contract, with more money, than you can negotiate on your own, these services are worth paying for. If you write screenplays, you must go through an agent because the movie industry won't even look at unagented material.

Personal Profile: A friend of mine, whom I shall call Gladys, since she wishes to remain anonymous, just sold a screenplay "thriller"; she received $200,000 when the contract was signed and an additional $300,000 after two rewrites. On top of that, she will earn a percentage of the movie's box office take. This is the first screenplay of her career, although she has written books and magazine articles.

Chapter 2

The World of Beautiful Things

Although most of us prefer to be surrounded by things that are pleasing to the eye, for some it is an absolute necessity. They can't endure drabness or ugliness. They must surround themselves with the beautiful things humans create; these are as essential to their survival as food and water. (We shall discuss natural beauty in another chapter.)

This description may seem a bit extreme, but if you are such a person, you know exactly what I mean. As you try to find a job or create a career that you will love, the first requirement is that you will be involved with beauty—the kind that fits your personality.

Although other chapters include positions that involve other kinds of beautiful objects, this chapter concentrates on those things we find in gift shops, collectible and jewelry stores, art galleries, and museums.

ANTIQUES APPRAISER

Description: Appraises antiques for individuals and businesses. Appraisals are needed by insurance companies, collectors, estates, and others.

Time Schedule: If you are working as a self-employed appraiser, your time is usually your own; however, you will have to accommodate your clients' schedules too. If you are hired by an appraisal company as an employee, refer to Chapter 18 for suggestions on turning your job into a flexible one.

Requirements: You must have an extensive background in antiques, particularly in how to distinguish reproductions from the real thing. The knowledge required can be gained from both education and work experience, usually with dealers or museums. If you are in business for yourself, you must know how to market your services and network with people who would hire you.

Compensation: You will usually charge a flat fee. Refer to #2 and #9 in Chapter 1 for suggestions on pricing your services. If you are an employee, you'll be paid a salary. The amount depends on your credentials.

✪ ANTIQUES DEALER

Description: Buys and sells antiques, usually from a retail store. You might specialize in a particular type of antique (such as dishes, furniture, or figurines), or you might deal in anything that fits the definition.

Time Schedule: There are two ways to own and run an antiques store. If you choose to run your store yourself and still want a flexible schedule, refer to #7 in Chapter 1 for advice on delegating some of your responsibilities to employees. Another method of running an antiques store, which is gaining in popularity, is to rent space in an antiques mall. These are large buildings that have been divided into booths of various sizes. You rent the size you need, move in your merchandise, and then display and price it as you would in an individual shop. But in an antiques mall, neither you nor an employee need be in attendance. Instead, the mall supplies salespeople who help shoppers make purchases. They handle all your sales. When your merchandise is sold, the mall collects your price, which includes any applicable taxes. The mall managers also handle all transactions involving credit cards. Once a month, they give you a statement of what items were sold, plus a check representing your sales. Frequently, a mall will charge a percentage of sales plus rent. This is an excellent way to make extra money and enjoy the benefits and fun of having a store without all the everyday work.

Requirements: You need to be able to distinguish true antiques from good, often misleading, reproductions. You also need an expert knowledge of the value of antiques.

Compensation: Refer to #7 in Chapter 1 for general information regarding making money in a retail store. However, the markup on antiques can be very large if you find your merchandise at garage sales or estate liquidations. People who are getting rid of what they see as "old junk" often don't know its true value and usually sell the merchandise at ridiculously low prices. Smart antiques dealers, knowing the worth of their finds, buy such items and resell them at their true value. A friend of mine who dealt in a certain kind of antique crystal that hasn't been made in over a hundred years bought a vase at a swap meet for 50 cents. It was in perfect condition, and she sold it for $300. That's quite a profit and not at all unusual in the antiques business.

ANTIQUES REPAIRPERSON

Description: Repairs antique furniture of all kinds; the work can vary from repairing a broken table leg to mending torn or burned upholstery.

Time Schedule: Refer to #9 in Chapter 1.

Requirements: This career requires a professional knowledge and appreciation of antique furniture and how to repair it. Being able to sell yourself and your abilities to antique dealers is also necessary if your business is to be successful.

Compensation: Refer to #9 in Chapter 1.

✪ ANTIQUES REPRODUCER

Description: Millions of people would like an antique look for their household furnishings but cannot afford the high cost of the real thing. In addition, antique furniture is often not as comfortable or as strong as more modern furniture. Consequently, good antique reproductions are very popular. And they have to be designed and made—possibly by you.

Time Schedule: If you work for a manufacturer of antique reproductions as an employee, please refer to Chapter 18 for advice on making a full-time job more flexible. You might also work as a freelancer, selling designs to manufacturers. Then you have total control over your time.

Requirements: To be successful in this field you need knowledge of antiques and skill in designing furniture. Both education and experience will help.

Compensation: If you are an employee, you will be paid a salary and benefits. If you are a freelancer, you might be paid outright for the design. Be sure that your fee is large enough not only to cover your time in making the design but also to take into account the potential popularity of the design. If possible, negotiate a royalty agreement which guarantees that you will be paid for every piece sold or manufactured.

ART APPRAISER

Description: Evaluates the worth of original works of art for individuals, businesses, and museums. Appraisals are done for insurance companies as well as estates interested in selling art collections.

Time Schedule: As a freelancer, you can usually organize your time schedule as outlined in #2 in Chapter 1.

Requirements: You must have a professional knowledge of what art is worth on the secondary market. It is essential that you be able to distinguish good copies from true originals because only the latter have value. You can learn this skill through education and experience working for art appraisers. Networking and having a good reputation in the industry are important too.

Compensation: Refer again to #2 in Chapter 1 for suggestions on establishing fees.

ART AUCTIONEER

Description: Auctions original artwork or very good framed copies or both. Other *objets d'art* might also be included in an auction. An auctioneer might work for individual collectors who wish to sell some or all of their artwork, for an auction house, or for a fund-raising company that auctions good, moderately priced original art to benefit schools or nonprofit organizations.

Time Schedule: If you are a freelancer, you can schedule your own hours. Even as an employee, you should be able to control your schedule most of the time.

Requirements: In addition to having all the salesmanship requirements outlined in #8 of Chapter 1 and a knowledge of art, you must be a convincing entertainer who can excite an audience into doing what you want them to do—which is to buy your wares.

Compensation: An auctioneer is usually paid a commission on sales. The percentage depends on both location and employer.

✪ ART CONSULTANT

Description: Advises private collectors (both individual and corporate) or art museums about art investments.

Time Schedule: Refer to #2 in Chapter 1.

Requirements: If you're interested in this career, you need an obvious knowledge about and education in art plus the ability to recognize the potential value of works by new artists. An art consultant has to be an astute businessperson with a good understanding of investments.

Compensation: Refer to #2 in Chapter 1. You may also be compensated by earning a percentage of the purchase price.

✪ ART DEALER

Description: Sells paintings and good reproductions, usually from a retail environment.

Time Schedule: Refer to #7 in Chapter 1.

Requirements: You need to know about paintings and their value, how to use them in decorating, and how to frame them properly. Many art dealers also do or arrange framing.

Compensation: Refer to #7 in Chapter 1. In addition, if you can discover new artists and buy their works before they become famous, then your investment will possibly increase many times.

ART SALESPERSON (WHOLESALE)

Description: Sells artwork to stores at wholesale and might also sell to the end user at less than retail. This is usually an outside sales position.

Time Schedule: Refer to #8 in Chapter 1.

Requirements: A love and understanding of your merchandise is a must, as is networking with interior decorators for additional business. Also refer to #8 in Chapter 1.

Compensation: Refer to #8 in Chapter 1.

ART TEACHER

Description: Teaches art, in its many forms, either through a school or privately.

Time Schedule: Refer to #5 in Chapter 1.

Requirements: In addition to those requirements listed in #5 (Chapter 1), you will need to be an artist yourself, with professional training.

Compensation: Refer to #5 in Chapter 1.

CHRISTMAS GOODS RETAILER

Description: Sells Christmas merchandise, such as ornaments, wreaths, lights, Christmas character figurines, nativity sets, and the like, from a retail environment.

Time Schedule: In addition to what is described in #7 of Chapter 1, this business can be seasonal, which means you open no later than September and close by January 15. Of course, with Christmas decorating becoming more popular, many Christmas stores are now open year-round.

Requirements: The greatest requirement is a love for Christmas and the ability to infect your customers with your enthusiasm.

Compensation: Consult #7 in Chapter 1.

COLLECTIBLE DOLL DEALER

Description: Buys and sells collectible dolls. You can do so from a retail store or your own home, via mail order, and even by the "party plan."

Time Schedule: Selling dolls from your home, by mail order, or through direct sales in home party settings offers you complete freedom. If you choose to sell collectible dolls from a retail setting, refer to #7 in Chapter 1.

Requirements: Obviously you need to love collectible dolls. But that's not enough. You also must know about the various grades of porcelain, who the top doll designers are, the importance of the right costumes, and—if you're dealing in antique dolls—about that segment of the antiques business. Knowing how to use dolls for home decorating is another plus.

Compensation: It depends on how you buy the dolls. If you buy them at wholesale and sell at retail, you'll make the standard profit. If you make either the dolls or their clothes, your profit might be more. However, the greatest money-making opportunity is found on the secondary market. This means that you buy the first issue series of a specific doll produced by a popular doll artist, hold it until it is no longer made (until "the mold is broken"), and then resell it at a very inflated price because only a limited number of dolls were made and they've all been sold. Therefore, a collector's only hope of acquiring that particular doll is to buy one from someone who has it. If that's you, you can make significant money.

DOLLHOUSE DEALER

Description: Sells not only the dollhouse but also the paint, wallpaper, floor and window coverings, furniture, and accessories that go into the house—plus the tiny dolls who will live there. Just as dolls are popular, so are dollhouses; people love to decorate them. Very large and expensive, these dollhouses are not purchased for children but by and for adults.

Time Schedule: Refer to #1 and #7 in Chapter 1.

Requirements: It's essential that you know how to decorate dollhouses. You also should be able to teach people how to wallpaper the small walls and make draperies as well as wire the houses with electricity. The best person for this job would feel passionate about collecting dollhouses and all that is involved with the hobby.

Compensation: Refer to #1 and #7 in Chapter 1. Another way to earn money is to teach classes on decorating dollhouses. Not only will you make a profit from what you sell but you can also charge for the instruction. Refer to #5 in Chapter 1.

ESTATE APPRAISER AND LIQUIDATOR

Description: Appraises—and then helps liquidate—all furniture and other items held by estates. The appraiser is usually hired by the heirs or executors of wills, and the liquidation is often done in conjunction with an auction house.

Time Schedule: To some degree, you can control your own hours; however, you will also be very much at the mercy of others' time schedules.

Requirements: You must be an expert in the value of furnishings, especially if antiques or art objects are involved. If you also have a sense of what the public will buy, you should be successful.

Compensation: You'll usually receive a fee; but if you're involved in selling the items for the estate, you should also earn a commission on the sales.

GIFT RETAILER

Description: Sells a large variety of gift items from a retail environment.

Time Schedule: Refer to #7 in Chapter 1.

Requirements: Refer to #7 in Chapter 1.

Compensation: Refer to #7 in Chapter 1.

GIFT SALESPERSON (WHOLESALE)

Description: Sells wholesale giftware to retail stores; might sell one line for one manufacturer or represent several lines created by many manufacturers. This is an outside sales job.

Time Schedule: Refer to #8 in Chapter 1.

Requirements: Refer to #8 in Chapter 1.

Compensation: Refer to #8 in Chapter 1.

JEWELRY DEALER

Description: Sells jewelry in the form of precious gems or pure gold and silver, usually from a retail setting.

Time Schedule: Refer to #7 in Chapter 1.

Requirements: A knowledge of jewelry, especially precious gems, is mandatory. You need to be interested in helping people select jewelry that is the right size and style for them. Good taste is essential. Also consult #7 in Chapter 1.

Compensation: Refer to #7 in Chapter 1.

JEWELRY REPAIRPERSON

Description: Someone in this position repairs jewelry, usually in a retail store.

Time Schedule: Refer to #7 and #9 in Chapter 1.

Requirements: A professional knowledge and ability to repair jewelry are essential. The ability to repair jewelry is like an art. Training in gemology will contribute to success.

Compensation: Refer to #7 and #9 in Chapter 1.

MUSEUM CURATOR

Description: Puts the collections together, catalogues them, handles all administrative details, arranges public relations, and recruits and trains volunteers who work at the museum.

Time Schedule: A curator's schedule is often quite flexible, depending on the size of the museum and its staff.

Requirements: It is necessary to understand the museum's displays and to be educated in history, science, or art (depending on the museum's focus). Being well-organized and creative is also essential.

Compensation: Because most museums are nonprofit organizations, you will never make what you could in a purely commercial venture. But if the museum is located in a big city and is renowned, your income could be substantial. Spin-offs from this position, such as giving lectures or writing and publishing books about items featured in the museum or related subjects, are also possible and could prove to be very profitable.

STAMP DEALER

Description: Sells to and buys stamps from collectors in a retail store.

Time Schedule: Refer to #7 in Chapter 1.

Requirements: A love for and knowledge of stamps and their history is essential; also refer to #7 of Chapter 1.

Compensation: Refer to #7 in Chapter 1.

STATUARY DEALER

Description: Sells statuary from a retail store. The merchandise might include unpainted ceramic statues; in this case, the dealer would also sell the supplies needed to paint the items.

Time-Schedule: Refer to #7 in Chapter 1.

Requirements: In addition to those requirements outlined in #7 of Chapter 1, refer to #5 as well if you are planning on teaching classes on painting statuary.

Compensation: Refer to #5 and #7 in Chapter 1.

Chapter 3

The World of Business

Since the beginning of history, commerce has enabled civilizations to grow and prosper. Those attracted to the world of business can choose from a variety of money-making opportunities that allow flexible time schedules.

ACCOUNTANT

Description: Handles all bookkeeping and accounting for individuals, small businesses, and corporations. The work done for clients includes handling payroll, paying bills, creating profit-and-loss statements, balancing the books, and preparing taxes and making the necessary payments.

Time Schedule: If you are an employee, refer to Chapter 18. If you are a freelancer, you can schedule your own time. Refer to #2 and #9 in Chapter 1 for suggestions on handling your time.

Requirements: To start on this career, you will need a degree in accounting and a tax preparer's license. Also essential is an ability to network with others and sell your services. An extensive knowledge of marketing is crucial. Before you call yourself an "accountant," check your state's laws; some require you to be a Certified Public Accountant with the necessary credentials and licensing in order to use "accountant" by your name. In most jurisdictions, you can always generally perform the functions outlined above without being a CPA if you use the title of bookkeeper.

Compensation: Refer to #2 and #9 in Chapter 1 for advice on how to set your fees. If you are going to be balancing your clients' accounts and checks, be sure to look over the last three months' worth of check activity before establishing a price because generally you will charge a flat monthly fee based on the specific number of checks used. It is important that you allocate enough time to do the work when you first accept the job, because it is generally impossible to charge your client for more time later on.

ADVERTISING AGENCY HEAD

Description: Plans and oversees the advertising for businesses or professionals who require it. The responsibilities include establishing and working within a budget, designing whole campaigns (print and media), and handling public relations. Much of the actual work is hired out, but the advertising agency head has the ultimate responsibility for putting it all together.

Time Schedule: If you have a large office full of employees, obviously you will spend more time at your business. However, refer to #7 in Chapter 1 for advice on finding employees to help you. Working out of your home (which is becoming more common) allows you to be the master of your own hours but you do still have to be available when your clients want to meet with you.

Requirements: You'll need an education in advertising, business, and marketing. An extensive network of advertising professionals you can work with and the ability to market your own business are also essential.

Compensation: You will be paid a fee or retainer as well as percentages of whatever advertising is purchased through the various media. The latter is arranged with the media at the agency rate.

ADVERTISING COUNSELOR

Description: Counsels companies and small businesses on the most effective type of advertising for promoting their business, product, or service, within a specified budget. Actual advertising campaigns are not usually created by an advertising counselor but are handled by an advertising agency.

Time Schedule: Refer to #2 in Chapter 1.

Requirements: To work in this field, you'll need experience and education in advertising and an understanding of many different kinds of businesses and what it will take to attract customers to them.

Compensation: Refer to #2 in Chapter 1.

ADVERTISING SALES

ADVERTISING SALESPERSON—BILLBOARD

Description: Sells advertising on billboards in certain geographical locations for specific periods of time.

ADVERTISING SALESPERSON—DIRECTORIES

Description: Sells advertising in various kinds of directories, from telephone books to specialty directories (such as directories that consist entirely of Christians, women business owners, members of a particular profession, alumni of a certain school, and so on).

ADVERTISING SALESPERSON—MOTION PICTURES

Description: Sells advertising that is seen on screens during intermissions or before the movie starts in theaters or, now, on videocassettes. This is a new field just opening up.

ADVERTISING SALESPERSON—NEWSPAPERS

Description: Sells the two kinds of advertising included in newspapers. Large trade ads, located throughout most of the newspaper, promote businesses, products, and store merchandise. Pictures are frequently included in these ads. Classified ads, located in a special section, are smaller and advertise employment opportunities, real estate, rentals, and almost anything individuals wish to sell or promote. Pictures are almost never included in these small advertisements.

ADVERTISING SALESPERSON—PERIODICALS

Description: Someone in this field sells advertisements that are placed in magazines which appeal to the products' users; the ads are similar to those that run in newspapers. For example, ads for women's cosmetics would appear in magazines aimed at women but not in those aimed at men.

ADVERTISING SALESPERSON—RADIO/TV

Description: Companies buying commercials on radio and television contract for a certain number of time slots (the times when and programs in which the commercials are aired) and frequencies (the number of times the commercial is aired). Just as periodical advertising is specialized, so also are radio and television stations. They too offer specific audiences that would be receptive to particular products or business establishments (local radio stations frequently advertise local businesses). For example, if you were selling a newsletter about world affairs, you would advertise on a station whose format was primarily news, not rock and roll.

ADVERTISING SALESPERSON—SPECIALTY ITEMS

Description: Sells merchandise of all kinds (pens, key-chains, T-shirts, luggage, and the like) that bears the name, address, and telephone number of a business or the logo of a company or product.

Time Schedule for All Types of Advertising Sales: Refer to #8 in Chapter 1, which deals with outside sales.

Requirements for All Types of Advertising Sales: Refer to #8 in Chapter 1. In order to succeed in selling any of these advertising resources, you must also have enthusiasm for that media. If you never listen to the radio or hate rock and roll, you can hardly be convincing when you try to sell advertising for a radio station, especially for one that plays rock and roll all day. You will also find it easier to sell advertising if you understand the concerns of your customers and can participate with them in planning effective messages.

Compensation for All Types of Advertising Sales: Refer to #8 in Chapter 1.

BALLOON ADVERTISER

Description: Provides large balloons that sit on top of commercial buildings and display logos or signs pertaining to businesses. This type of advertising gains attention readily and can be used for a short period of time (as opposed to billboards or most other kinds of advertising).

Time Schedule: You own the balloon and the business; therefore, you can choose to be unavailable when you want.

Requirements: You will need the necessary equipment, which includes not only the balloons (you should have more than one so that you can have several working for you in different locations at the same time) but also the truck to transport them and the equipment to inflate them. Knowledge of marketing is also very crucial for your success.

Compensation: You will charge a flat fee for each balloon, which depends on how long the balloon will be in the location and what will be on it. Refer to #1 and #9 in Chapter 1 for suggestions on how to charge for your services.

BILLING SERVICE PERSON

Description: Processes medical claims for physicians—including Medicare, personal injury, HMO, PPO, group health, and worker's compensation claims. A billing service might also handle billing for other professionals, such as attorneys, although medical offices most often utilize such services.

Time Schedule: If you are an independent operator, your time is your own. Refer to #2 and #9 in Chapter 1 for advice on this type of business. Although you do have control of your time, most people who run billing services find that they cannot be gone from their business for more than ten consecutive days because the cash flow for clients will drop (and so will their own).

Requirements: The best way to get started is through experience in physicians' offices; you will need a computer, the appropriate software, and the training to use both. You must be able to market yourself. Many franchises deal in this type of business.

Compensation: You receive a percentage of what you bill, so the more clients you have and the higher their volumes, the more money you make.

BUSINESS BROKER

Description: Sells businesses the way a real estate broker sells houses or property. For example, an independent businessperson ready to retire might need help selling his or her business. Part of the job is advising the client on appropriate pricing and finding qualified buyers.

Time Schedule: Refer to #8 in Chapter 1.

Requirements: You will need the appropriate state license (usually a real estate license) and sales ability. (Again refer to #8 in Chapter 1.) It also helps to be very active in your town's business community and to be able to understand the basics of many different types of businesses so that you can match the right buyers and sellers.

Compensation: You will make a percentage of the sale. This is a straight commission business that can be very lucrative.

BUSINESS EXPO PLANNER

Description: Creates fairs or expos where franchisers, direct-selling companies, and others offering money-making opportunities can gather under one roof (usually a convention center) to talk to the public—their potential business colleagues.

Time Schedule: Refer to #4 in Chapter 1.

Requirements: Refer to #4 in Chapter 1.

Compensation: Refer to #4 in Chapter 1.

BUSINESS LICENSE INSTRUCTOR

Description: Teaches people what they need to know to pass state or city licensing tests. These may include real estate, insurance, construction, mutual fund, and stocks and bond sales licenses. It does not include professional licenses, such as medical or legal licenses, which require specific education and apprenticeships.

Time Schedule: Refer to #5 in Chapter 1.

Requirements: Refer to #5 in Chapter 1.

Compensation: Refer to #5 in Chapter 1.

BUSINESS LOAN BROKER

Description: Arranges such financial transactions as start-up loans for new businesses, temporary loans against accounts receivable to cover cash-flow shortages, and building or expansion loans.

Time Schedule: As an independent broker, you can generally set your own schedule; however, you do have to be available when your clients need to meet with you. If you work full-time for a lending institution, refer to the advice in Chapter 18.

Requirements: You need a background in business loans, which you can get from working in a lending institution; in addition, you'll need to network with your community's business people. Knowing how to market your services is also necessary, and you will need access to several different lending institutions.

Compensation: Your commission will be a percentage of the loan.

EFFICIENCY EXPERT

Description: Evaluates the efficiency of specific positions within a company and then recommends ways to achieve greater efficiency and cost-effectiveness.

Time Schedule: An efficiency expert works as a consultant; refer to #2 in Chapter 1.

Requirements: Education in business and marketing is necessary. Experience in many different phases of the business world is required so that you will be able to accurately analyze the productivity of every position. Refer to #2 in Chapter 1 for more information.

Compensation: Refer to #2 in Chapter 1.

EMPLOYEE ASSISTANCE COUNSELOR

Description: Counsels a business's employees regarding personal, substance-addiction, family, and financial problems—any kind of problem that can interfere with an employee's productivity. Unless the business is very large, most contract with firms that can supply a counselor when needed.

Time Schedule: If you have this kind of job, your schedule can be very flexible, even part-time.

Requirements: An education and license in social work, psychology, or family counseling is needed.

Compensation: Your compensation will depend on how much responsibility you take. If you manage a client company and have a master's degree, you will earn more than if you do not. I spoke to one company that provides counselors in Orange County, California, and learned that full-time counselors can earn from $24,000 to $40,000 per year. Part-time compensation is altered accordingly.

✪ EMPLOYEE BENEFIT AND COMPENSATION CONSULTANT

Description: Counsels businesses on setting up employee benefit programs that are part of the compensation package.

Time Schedule: Refer to #2 in Chapter 1.

Requirements: You will need a background in the human resources aspect of business as well as the other requirements outlined in #2 (Chapter 1).

Compensation: Consult #2 in Chapter 1.

✪ EMPLOYMENT COUNSELOR

Description: Matches employers' job openings with potential employees who have been screened for work experience and ability to perform the job's tasks. A counselor might try to fill jobs that are clerical, mid-management, sales, or blue collar, as well as jobs in specific fields, such as medical or legal.

Time Schedule: Most of the activities of an employment counselor are done from an office because applicants usually come in to register and conduct a preliminary interview. However, flexible time schedules are still possible. See Chapter 18 for pointers on achieving a flexible schedule.

Requirements: You should have at least a basic understanding of what each job order you receive requires so that you can fill it correctly. Good telephone communication skills are also very important because most of your interaction with client companies will be done over the phone. An ability to judge people is another must because you will be selecting the applicants to send to your clients. Obviously, if you don't do a good job of evaluating applicants, you won't keep your position for long.

Compensation: You are usually paid by both salary and commission. Commissions can generate an excellent income, because client companies pay a significant percentage of the new employee's salary to the employment agency or counselor.

EXECUTIVE SEARCH CONSULTANT

Description: Matches companies with people through an extensive network of large companies who need top management personnel. Usually the consultant knows people who may or may not be job hunting and approaches them, "searching them out" to determine if they have an interest in discreetly interviewing for the position. This is frequently how the top corporate jobs are filled.

Time Schedule: It's generally the same as for an employment counselor, but occasionally an executive search consultant may travel to conferences where potential candidates may be or to visit one individual.

Requirements: You must have many contacts on both sides of the corporate world and enjoy the "networking" that goes along with it. It's also important to be as bright and accomplished as the executives and clients with whom you interact.

Compensation: You will be compensated with a salary and commission. Because the salaries you deal with are very high, your commissions obviously will be larger than those an employment counselor would make.

FRANCHISE CONSULTANT

Description: Advises businesses on how to create franchising programs that will expand their operations. The advice given includes the best way to handle all the legalities and the best approach to marketing franchises and training franchisees.

Time Schedule: Refer to #2 in Chapter 1.

Requirements: You will need education and experience in business and marketing. Legal knowledge is also helpful. Many attorneys become franchise consultants.

Compensation: Refer to #2 in Chapter 1.

HAZARDOUS WASTE CONSULTANT

Description: Counsels businesses (usually manufacturers) and medical establishments on how to properly eliminate hazardous wastes, according to city, state, and federal laws and guidelines.

Time Schedule: Refer to #2 in Chapter 1.

Requirements: In addition to the requirements outlined in #2 in Chapter 1, you may need a scientific degree as well as extensive knowledge and an established reputation in this very complicated field. The best way to establish your credentials is to work for a hazardous waste consultant or government agency dealing with environmental issues.

Compensation: Refer to #2 in Chapter 1.

MAIL LIST BROKER

Description: Sells lists of names and addresses (and frequently telephone numbers) of businesses or individuals. These lists are compiled according to various demographic categories. Businesses may be listed according to size, products manufactured or sold, customer base, gross sales, net worth, and the like. Facts about individuals might include gender, age, race, occupation, income, and personal interests (sometimes inferred from their magazine subscriptions). Consequently, if you wanted to send information about your product to white female executives who earn from $40,000 to $60,000 per year, subscribe to women's business magazines, and live in certain zip code areas, a mail list broker would be able to sell you such a list. Examples of what mail list brokers provide are in your mailbox almost daily: every time you receive an advertisement that describes a product like one you've already ordered through the mail or a product tied to specialty magazines you subscribe to (say, a canoeing magazine), chances are that a mail list broker sold the advertiser your name.

Time Schedule: Your time is your own. Most mail list brokers work by telephone and mail, so you can choose your own hours.

Requirements: No special training is required. You do need a computer system and printer as well as access to the sources that will provide you with lists for your customers. Mail-order businesses are just one valuable resource for these.

Compensation: Your revenue is generated from the sale of your lists. Each name is worth a few cents; but since you sell in bulk (several hundred or thousand at a time), you can earn many dollars from each transaction. The more lists you sell, the more money you make. (A word of caution: be sure that your lists are constantly updated and accurate because your business is only as good as your lists.)

MAIL-ORDER SALESPERSON

Description: Sells just about anything (from stamps to yachts to residences) through mail order. You find your customers by mailing catalogues, descriptive letters, or brochures to people who might be potential users of the product you are selling. You could also attract customers through small ads in the back of magazines that would appeal to potential customers.

Time Schedule: Because your biggest job is going to the post office to get the mailed-in orders and then filling them, you can choose to do that any time that you wish—morning, noon, night, midnight! But you *do* have to fill the orders in a timely manner and give good value for the money received.

Requirements: You will need some money to get started, advertising acumen that will enable you to create and evaluate your ads and mailings, and the ability to either produce or find products that people will want to buy through the mail. There are many excellent books on how to succeed in the mail-order business. Study them before launching your business.

Compensation: Because the markup on what you sell is generally slightly higher than it would be if you sold it from a retail environment, you might assume that your profit would be greater. That's not usually the case, because many costs come out of the selling price. They include advertising, packaging, storing, and processing orders. Usually you charge your customers for the postage costs along with any appropriate taxes. Money is made in this business from volume sales and sales generated from additional products inexpensively advertised on a flyer included in the package with the original purchase.

MANAGEMENT CONSULTANT

Description: Counsels businesses in what management positions they need and develops management training programs.

Time Schedule: Refer to #2 in Chapter 1.

Requirements: You will need an education and experience in business, especially management, and a knowledge of the field and business of your clients.

Compensation: Refer to #2 in Chapter 1.

MANUFACTURER'S REPRESENTATIVE ("REP")

Description: Sells the company's products to whatever kind of establishment will eventually get them to the end user. For example, a greeting card manufacturer would instruct his rep to sell the line to greeting card, gift, drug, grocery, department, or other specialty stores; a hardware manufacturer's rep would sell its products to hardware stores. This is usually an outside sales job.

Time Schedule: Refer to #8 in Chapter 1.

Requirements: Refer to #8 in Chapter 1.

Compensation: Refer to #8 in Chapter 1.

MARKETING CONSULTANT

Description: Gives advice to businesses on the best way to market their products or services. The consultant also helps the business establish a marketing budget.

Time Schedule: Refer to #2 in Chapter 1.

Requirements: This career requires education and experience in marketing. Good experience would be working for (and preferably heading) the marketing department for a major corporation.

Compensation: Refer to #2 in Chapter 1.

✪ MARKET RESEARCHER

Description: Collects information from the public concerning its reaction to products, companies, people, and so on. This can be done by asking questions over the telephone or in person at locations where people who fit the description of the product's users might be found. For example, if questions are being asked regarding new ski gear, the market researcher would talk to people at ski resorts. Market research covers many subjects, from food products to ideas.

Time Schedule: If you are an employee of one of the large market research companies located in major regional malls, you will probably have to work during specific hours, although you can probably choose them. If you are a freelancer, your time will be your own.

Requirements: You must like people and not be afraid to initiate a conversation. You must be willing to pay attention to details, because you will need to accurately fill out lengthy questionnaires. You must be punctual in meeting deadlines and be able to handle rejection because many people will not want to talk to you.

Compensation: Compensation varies by job and by the company hiring you; you might be paid hourly or by the project. A good way to determine that you're getting paid well is to seek an hourly rate if the questionnaire you will be filling out as you interview someone is long or detailed. A long questionnaire generally means that you will spend at least an hour with each person. If the questions are short, lasting just a few minutes, and you are able to move easily from one respondent to another, then you'd probably do better accepting a flat amount for each questionnaire completed.

MERCHANDISER

Description: Calls on different kinds of retail outlets (supermarkets, drug stores, convenience stores, mass merchandisers, specialty stores) for manufacturers whose products are used (or eaten) by consumers. Merchandising activities include bringing products out of the back room and properly positioning them on the shelf, resetting shelves, building displays, and selling the company's new products to the store. Frequently these jobs are provided by brokers, service or merchandising companies who represent various manufacturer clients as well as the manufacturing companies themselves.

Time Schedule: Refer to #8 in Chapter 1. In addition, many of these positions are part-time and so offer still more flexibility.

Requirements: You must enjoy physical work and not be afraid of getting dirty; stores (and their back rooms) are not clean. Being self-motivated and attentive to detail is also necessary; obviously, you should also like people and the products you represent. Refer to #8 in Chapter 1.

Compensation: What you will be paid varies greatly according to the job and company. Many full-time positions (40 hours per week) offer excellent salaries, with such perks as company cars. Part-time merchandisers are usually paid above-average hourly wages, plus expenses, which include mileage.

NETWORK MARKETER

Description: Sells a consumer product to people and then recruits them to sell the same product to others and to convince those users to do the same. The success of this business lies in signing up as many people as possible beneath you (known as a "downline") so that you can earn commissions (or overrides) on what they and their downlines sell.

Time Schedule: The schedule is strictly your own. But to be successful in this business you must constantly be introducing your company and product to people who will become both customers and recruits. Therefore, many highly successful networkers have spent much more time, in the beginning, building their businesses than they ever would have devoted to a job. The payoff comes later when there are hundreds in their downline whose sales are generating commissions every month—whether the original networker is working or not!

Requirements: Perseverance, patience, and a willingness to talk to everyone about this business opportunity are absolute musts. If you are thin-skinned or easily discouraged, this venture is not for you. You also need sufficient spare time to work this business and some money to invest in products, recruiting literature, and the like. The amount of money you'll need depends on the marketing programs of the company you work for; some require you to stockpile inventories, others do not. Initial start-up financial requirements are usually considerably smaller than they are for other business opportunities. A dedication to the company's products and philosophy are also necessary.

Compensation: The networking company will always present their top producers as role models; because of enormous downlines, these producers make commissions from the sales made by thousands of other people. Certainly six-figure incomes are possible, but they are rare. Many more people who get into network businesses make decent second or part-time incomes and get discounts on the products, which they like, but do not get rich from this business. Still others burn out quickly and end up quitting the business and using the products.

OFFICE DECORATORS/DESIGNERS

Description: Designs or decorates offices or does both.

Time Schedule: Refer to #2 and #9 in Chapter 1.

Requirements: You must have experience and education in designing efficient and yet attractive office settings. You need an understanding of the specific needs of various office workers.

Compensation: Refer to #2 and #9 in Chapter 1; also look at how to figure markup in #7 if your service includes selling furnishings to your clients.

PERSONNEL CONSULTANT

Description: Advises businesses on personnel needs. The job may include acting as an independent human resources consultant who can advise and even handle special human resources needs and problems.

Time Schedule: Refer to #2 in Chapter 1.

Requirements; You will need a degree in business and experience in human resources. Also refer to #2 in Chapter 1.

Compensation: Refer to #2 in Chapter 1.

PUBLIC RELATIONS ADVISOR

Description: Creates positive public images for corporations and sometimes for individuals in the public eye. The job includes writing press releases, staging publicity events, and aiding in marketing strategies and advertising. A public relations advisor frequently participates in writing advertising copy, newsletters, stockholder reports, and the like.

Time Schedule: If you are a freelancer, you control your own hours. In most cases, you do have to consider your clients' schedules, but this doesn't mean you'll have no flexibility. If you are working for one company in its corporate office, you will need to negotiate flex time just as you would in any other corporate position. Refer to Chapter 18 for advice.

Requirements: A degree in business communications is a definite plus because you will be doing a lot of writing. You should be able to get along with the media and know how to utilize their services as well as be able to speak in public. Imagination is very important as is an ability to anticipate situations that could put the company or person you represent in a negative light. You'll also need to know how to offset any negative portrayals with positive ones. If you have all these skills, you should do well in this field.

Compensation: Remuneration can be very good. Usually you are paid by the project or via a retainer. Refer to #1, #2, and even #9 in Chapter 1 for suggestions that will help you price yourself correctly.

QUALITY-CONTROL INSPECTOR

Description: Inspects products as they come off an assembly line to be certain that they have been manufactured correctly. This is usually a position within the company. There are also "secret shoppers," who are freelancers. They visit stores and restaurants, ride on airplanes (yes! all the airlines have them), stay in hotels, purchase products, and so on to determine how the public is being treated. A report is submitted to the company, explaining the inspector's findings.

Time Schedule: If you are a freelancer, your time is your own, but most assignments must be completed within a specific time frame.

Requirements: You will need an eye for detail because nothing good or bad should be overlooked (otherwise the report is useless). A good memory is important because you cannot carry your report into the establishment you are checking. You must remember the questions and then fill out the questionnaire once you have left.

Compensation: Depending on the level of detail for a particular project, you might be paid by the project or by the hour. Use the guidelines described in #9 in Chapter 1.

SALES CONTEST ORGANIZER

Description: Keeping salespeople motivated is an ongoing challenge; one method that works successfully is to run contests that offer great prizes they can win if their sales reach certain numbers. Designing and planning great contests can require more work and expertise than most sales managers can muster, so a sales contest organizer can be very helpful. Someone in this position works with the client's budget to create prizes and various other incentives that really will make salespeople work extra hard. The organizer has many resources available and can usually get discounts for travel and accommodations as well as gifts that businesses and individuals cannot get. Part of the job is to keep track of the salespeople's efforts and determine who wins. The organizer takes charge of most, if not all, of the written communication regarding the contests.

Time Schedule: Contest organizers almost always work as freelancers and, therefore, once again, can work whenever they want to. Heavy periods of work will occur right before the contest ends and awards are announced.

Requirements: You must be a good motivator and have an understanding of the client company's salesperson profile in order to select good prizes. Imagination helps, as does being detailed-oriented. Being able to get great value for your client's money will help ensure your success.

Compensation: Your pay will usually be a percentage of the total budget. Depending on how much work a specific contest entails, it can be anywhere from 10 percent to 25 percent. If you choose to sell the prizes to the client company, you can charge a few percentage points above the cost (if it is very reasonable) and then charge a lower "planning fee." All expenses, such as mailings and literature, should be paid for separately by the company.

SALES PROMOTER AND COUNSELOR

Description: Look at "giveaway" prizes on the back of cereal boxes or at coupons that allow you to send in enough proofs-of-purchase to buy a watch. These ideas are generated by sales promotion services who meet with clients—both large and small—and advise them on what giveaways will work best for their products or services.

Time Schedule: People who run a sales promotion business are usually self-employed and therefore in control of the hours that they work.

Requirements: You'll need a good imagination and an understanding of the business and the resources available .

Compensation: You can charge a counseling fee for giving advice, and you can also sell the prizes and make a markup from them. The prizes themselves may not be very expensive, and so any income you would make from selling them individually wouldn't be great. However, you will be selling in huge quantities, and that is where the money can be significant.

SALES TRAINER

Description: Works with client companies to determine what needs to be sold and why people should buy it—and then creates special training resources that will help the company's salespeople be more productive. This training might include new sales materials, ways to find customers, and presentations. The sales trainer usually writes manuals and also produces inspirational and instructional meetings.

Time Schedule: If you are a freelancer (and most sales trainers are), your time is your own. When working in the client's facility, you will usually put in long hours, but you can take whole weeks or months off if your business allows it. Refer to #2 in Chapter 1.

Requirements: Obviously, you should be an excellent salesperson with impressive credentials. You must also be a master communicator (through speech and the written word) and be able to quickly identify what the company's people need to do to succeed. Then you have to create the right program—all within the company's timetable and budget.

Compensation: Most sales trainers charge by the project and charge separately for all expenses. Refer to #2 and #9 in Chapter 1.

STORE DESIGNER AND PLANNER

Description: This kind of designer plans and designs the layouts of retail stores. The work includes the placement of fixtures, the color scheme, and any other visual effects.

Time Schedule: Because this is similar to a consultant's position, refer to #2 in Chapter 1.

Requirements: You will need a design education and background as well as experience working in retail stores so that you can bring actual working knowledge to your designs.

Compensation: Refer to #2 in Chapter 1.

SWAP MEET MERCHANT

Description: Sets up booths at swap meets and other fairs and sells all types of merchandise (usually goods that are available through stores) to the people who attend the swap meet. Often these swap meets advertise that prices will be much lower than in conventional stores.

Time Schedule: As an independent operator, your weekdays are generally your own, but since most swap meets occur on weekends (and this often includes holiday weekends), you must be willing to work then.

Requirements: You must be able to select merchandise that will attract customers and sell well in this type of setting—where people truly expect to get something wonderful for next to nothing. It is also important to take an assistant with you when you work these meets because theft is higher than usual in these settings.

Compensation: You make your money from the markup of your merchandise. If you can buy closeouts or find good things at garage sales (a resource many swap meet merchants use if they are selling used goods), you can make a great deal of money because your overhead is not large. This is an excellent business for someone who wants to work only part-time or is retired.

TEMPORARY BUSINESS WORKER

Description: Temporary service companies provide businesses with experienced people who want to work only temporarily. The jobs that can be filled cover both office workers and blue collar workers. If you are interested in working for a "temp service," there are excellent ones in almost every community.

Time Schedule: If you want to be a temp worker, you will usually have to put in a full day's work for a period of time. You can, however, determine what weeks or months you do not wish to work and take that time off.

Requirements: If you are going to work for a temp service, you need to have experience in your particular field so that they can place you. You must conduct yourself as a responsible worker while never forgetting that you are working for the service.

Compensation: As the worker, you will be paid an hourly wage that often is more than it would be for the same work if you were employed by one company. Many temporary service companies also offer benefits if you work for a certain number of weeks in a year. If you run a temporary service, your income is generated from what the company pays you for providing a worker, minus your business costs (including the salary you pay the worker).

TYPIST

Description: Types manuscripts, letters, memos, forms, and the like. Today typists normally use a word processor or computer rather than a typewriter.

Time Schedule: You can set your own hours, but this is a business where you must be reliable and meet deadlines. Refer to #9 in Chapter 1.

Requirements: The obvious requirement is being able to type accurately and rapidly. Having top-quality computers and word processors also helps as does being able to promote your business to those who would use it—professionals, writers, students, businesspeople.

Compensation: How much you earn for a particular job is usually determined by the page count of what you type, with number of copies also considered. Quantity is where your money is made.

Chapter 4

The World of Communications

Thanks to modern communications technology, this world of ours has shrunk to intimate proportions. With the use of fax machines, computer modems, cellular phones, electronic and voice mail, I can sit on my terrace in the little town of Big Bear Lake and interact with Wall Street giants or European financiers. And I'm not alone: millions of people all over the planet are communicating with one another by taking advantage of all the technology available to us.

The communications industry includes a wide variety of professions. Forty-four are profiled here.

ANSWERING SERVICE PROVIDER

Description: Answers telephones for businesses or professional people twenty-four hours a day, seven days a week (including holidays). Also included might be the ability to immediately page the client or to give callers information that they might require. For this reason, physicians usually use answering services instead of other types of telephone-answering devices.

Time Schedule: If you work for an answering service, you can frequently work part-time or have flexible hours. If you own the business, you will be able to hire employees to help you, as outlined in #7 in Chapter 1.

Requirements: A good telephone voice and personality are musts. Accurate reporting (of names and telephone numbers) is also very important.

Compensation: If you work for a service, you will usually be paid an hourly wage. If you own the business, you will be paid a monthly fee that takes into account the number of calls answered for each business.

AUDIOVISUAL CONSULTANT

Description: Advises businesses on the use of audiovisual communications to sell their product or service, to train employees, or send an important message about their business in an entertaining manner.

Time Schedule: Refer to #2 in Chapter 1.

Requirements: Besides those requirements outlined in #2 in Chapter 1, you will need an extensive background and expertise in this new and highly competitive field.Compensation: Refer to #2 in Chapter 1.

AUDIOVISUAL EQUIPMENT DEALER

Description: Sells audiovisual equipment, usually from a retail establishment.

Time Schedule: Refer to #7 in Chapter 1.

Requirements: You will need the finances to purchase inventory in audiovisual equipment and knowledge of how it can be used. Also refer to #7 in Chapter 1.

Compensation: Refer to #7 in Chapter 1.

AUDIOVISUAL EQUIPMENT INSTALLER AND REPAIRPERSON

Description: A person in this field installs and services audiovisual equipment, which includes overhead projectors, videocassette recorders, and the like. The job might include transferring home movies to videocassettes.

Time Schedule: If you are working out of a retail environment, refer to #7 in Chapter 1. If you are an independent service person, please refer to #9 in Chapter 1.

Requirements: You will need to know how to install and service this kind of equipment. You can gain the needed experience by working for the manufacturers of these products or for audiovisual installers or service shops.

Compensation: Refer to #9 in Chapter 1.

AUDIOVISUAL EQUIPMENT RENTAL AGENT

Description: Rents or leases audiovisual equipment to others. Although this can be done from a retail setting (and usually is), this business can also be run from home. You would find your customers through hotels (whose patrons would rent your equipment for meetings) and other organizations. A significant ad in the yellow pages of the telephone directory would help with the marketing of this home-based business.

Time Schedule: If you work out of a retail environment, refer to #7 in Chapter 1. If you work out of your home, you will be able to have significant flexibility in your schedule, except that you will have to arrange for delivery and pickup of your equipment.

Requirements: You will need the ability to market your business. You will have to network with companies and organizations that might use your equipment. You will also need working capital to purchase an inventory of audiovisual equipment adequate enough to cover rental demands.

Compensation: You will make your income from the rental of your equipment. Check the competition before establishing your fees. If you deliver the equipment, you can also charge a pickup and delivery fee.

AUTHOR OF BOOKS

Description: Writes books intended for publication. These can be fiction or nonfiction works.

Time Schedule: Refer to #11 in Chapter 1.

Requirements: Refer to #11 in Chapter 1.

Compensation: Refer to #11 in Chapter 1.

AUTHOR'S AGENT

Description: Represents the author to publishers and others who would produce the author's works. The agent does all the selling and negotiating of contracts.

Time Schedule: Most agents are in business for themselves, so they can set their own hours. However, the agent must be available for meetings with producers and publishers.

Requirements: It's important to know people in the book, film, or television industry and to know what projects they are interested in. Keeping in constant communication is vitally important. It's also essential to have a good sense of what is new or particularly good in the field. Agents are successful only if they have a successful stable of writers whom they can sell for large bucks.

Compensation: Agents make a percentage of everything they earn for their writers. The rate usually starts at 15 percent and can go higher for foreign and other subsidiary rights. Some agents charge a reading fee to potential new clients, but that does not generate much income, and many in the industry frown on it.

BOOKBINDER

Description: Binds new and used books. Bookbinding can be done either in a retail setting or as a home-based business.

Time Schedule: If you are working out of a retail store, refer to #7 in Chapter 1 for advice on getting help from your employees. If you are working as a service person from your home, please refer to #9 in Chapter 1.

Requirements: You must have the skill and equipment to bind books. You can learn what you need to know as an apprentice with another bookbinder.

Compensation: Refer to #9 in Chapter 1.

BOOK DEALER—RARE AND USED BOOKS

Description: Sells used and rare books from a retail store or catalogue.

Time Schedule: Refer to #7 in Chapter 1.

Requirements: In addition to those requirements outlined in #7 (Chapter 1), you should be particularly interested in old, used, and rare books and should know how to find these. You will probably have to go to garage sales and book sales to find your inventory; people who come to your store to sell their books to you will be one of your best sources for inventory.

Compensation: Your income will derive from the profit on the sales of your books. Because used books do not retail as high as new books do, your income will come from volume and from the occasional sale of a rare or much-in-demand book that you have managed to find. Refer to #7 in Chapter 1 for some additional information.

BOOK PUBLISHER

Description: Publishes books, usually from original manuscripts; sometimes books are reprinted. Your books can be aimed at the public or at a specific audience (such as legal books for lawyers).

Time Schedule: If you are a small publisher, you can work from your home office and contract out much of the work. Therefore, you can set your own schedule without difficulty.

Requirements: You will need a knowledge of publishing (best received through experience and education) and the ability to select books that people will buy. It is also critical that you know how to effectively market your books. You will need considerable capital to get started.

Compensation: Your income will be generated from the sale of your books. In the publishing industry, there are several ways of marketing books; one anomaly in this business is that books that are not sold by retail stores can be returned for credit to the publisher. This factor can seriously affect your net profit.

BOOKSELLER

Description: Sells books to the public, usually through a retail store but sometimes through mail order.

Time Schedule: Refer to #7 in Chapter 1. If you are selling through mail order, you can set your own schedule.

Requirements: Obviously, you should love books. If you are knowledgeable about publishing and local history, all the better.

Compensation: Your compensation works the same way as for any other retail business. However, you can return books you do not sell for credit, which helps considerably with your inventory costs. Refer to #7 in Chapter 1 for additional suggestions on this topic. A word of caution: Book superstores found in every heavily populated city are practically running "the little guy" out of business. Therefore, if you want to own a bookstore, specialize in a certain genre (such as mysteries or children's books) or open your store in a small town where the giants won't go.

CELLULAR PHONE REPAIRPERSON

Description: Repairs cellular telephones. This can be done either from a retail setting or at the clients' locations.

Time Schedule: Refer to #7 in Chapter 1 if you are working from a retail store or to #9 if you repair and service cellular phones at the clients' locations.

Requirements: You will need an ability to repair and service these telephones and a knowledge of how to market your service.

Compensation: Refer to #7 and #9 in Chapter 1.

CELLULAR PHONE SERVICE PROVIDER

Description: Sells cellular telephone services, either from a retail setting or as an outside salesperson.

Time Schedule: If you are working in a retail store, please refer to #7 in Chapter 1. If you are an outside salesperson, refer to #8.

Requirements: Refer to #7 and #8 in Chapter 1.

Compensation: Refer to #7 and #8 in Chapter 1.

COMIC BOOK DEALER

Description: Sells new and used comic books to the public from a retail store.

Time Schedule: Refer to #7 in Chapter 1.

Requirements: In addition to those requirements outlined in #7 (Chapter 1), you obviously have to truly enjoy your product and be able to pass this enthusiasm on to the public. While new comic books are acquired from publishers, there is great interest in "old" comics, and significant income can be made from their sale. The best ways to find them are to go to garage and estate sales, to attend comic book "clubs" and conventions, and to let your customers know you are willing to buy old books.

Compensation: Refer to #7 in Chapter 1.

COMMUNICATION CONSULTANT

Description: Advises individuals, either for personal or business reasons, on their written and verbal communication ability. Typical projects might include helping individual clients solve problems with communication skills, coaching, and holding workshops on verbal and written presentation skills.

Time Schedule: Please refer to #2 in Chapter 1.

Requirements: In addition to those requirements outlined in #2 (Chapter 1), you will need to be a professional writer and speaker.

Compensation: Refer to #2 in Chapter 1.

COMMUNICATIONS EQUIPMENT PROVIDER FOR HEARING-IMPAIRED AND DISABLED PEOPLE

Description: Provides communications equipment, such as special telephones, for hearing-impaired people and others who cannot use ordinary equipment. This service can be run from a home.

Time Schedule: You can schedule your own appointments, but you will have to work around your clients' needs.

Requirements: You will need an understanding of your special clients' challenges and the ability to provide them with excellent equipment; you will need sources for the equipment. Knowing how to market and advertise your service is also essential.

Compensation: Your income will be generated from your markup on the equipment you sell. Refer to #7 in Chapter 1 for an explanation of how this works.

COMPUTER CONSULTANT

Description: This type of consultant advises businesses and individuals on the types of computers and software they need for their specific operations. The job may also involve locating the equipment and computer professionals necessary to meet the client's needs.

Time Schedule: Refer to #2 in Chapter 1.

Requirements: In addition to those requirements outlined in #2 (Chapter 1), you will need education and experience in the computer industry and must have a network of computer professionals to work with.

Compensation: Refer to #2 in Chapter 1.

✪ COMPUTER INSTALLER AND REPAIRPERSON

Description: This job entails installing, servicing, and repairing computers, usually at a client's location; service occasionally is done in a retail setting, and in that case, clients drop their computers off. Some people in this field repair but do not install computers.

Time Schedule: Refer to #7 or #9 in Chapter 1.

Requirements: Besides those requirements outlined in #7 and #9 of Chapter 1, you will obviously need to know how to service many different kinds of computer systems.

Compensation: Refer to #9 in Chapter 1.

✪ COMPUTER PROGRAMMER

Description: Creates computer programs that fulfill the unique needs of clients.

Time Schedule: If you are working as a consultant, refer to #2 in Chapter 1; if you are working as a service person, refer to #9.

Requirements: You will need a college degree in programming, plus some business experience. The latter is particularly important when you deal with clients in the business world.

Compensation: Refer to #2 and #9 in Chapter 1.

✪ COMPUTER SALESPERSON

Description: Sells computers to the public, usually from a retail setting.

Time Schedule: Refer to #7 in Chapter 1.

Requirements: In addition to those requirements outlined in #7 (Chapter 1), you need a thorough knowledge of computers and the ability to explain their technicalities to the public in easy-to-understand language (not computer jargon).

Compensation: Refer to #7 in Chapter 1.

COMPUTER SOFTWARE TECHNICIAN

Description: This kind of business provides services to individuals and businesses who need help with computer software. The kinds of services provided include duplicating and formatting disks, CD-ROM duplication, package assembly, database creation, and so on. This business can be run from your home.

Time Schedule: Refer to #9 in Chapter 1.

Requirements: You will need education and experience in this particular branch of the computer industry.

Compensation: Refer to #9 in Chapter 1.

COMPUTER TEACHER

Description: Someone in this field teaches computer classes for beginners as well as advanced students. Classes can be held in corporate settings or computer schools.

Time Schedule: Refer to #5 in Chapter 1.

Requirements: Refer to #5 in Chapter 1.

Compensation: Refer to #5 in Chapter 1.

CONVERSATIONAL ENGLISH TEACHER

Description: Teaches conversational and written English as a second language in private schools, community colleges, and school districts in the United States as well as in foreign countries.

Time Schedule: This job can be full-time or part-time. Refer to Chapter 18 if you are an employee working full-time or to #5 in Chapter 1.

Requirements: You need a bachelor's degree, though not necessarily in English. You also must meet the requirements outlined in #5 (Chapter 1).

Compensation: If you are an employee, you will be paid a salary. If you are a freelancer, refer to #5 in Chapter 1.

DESKTOP PUBLISHING PROVIDER

Description: Provides desktop publishing services for individuals or businesses who cannot do the job themselves, because they lack either skill or equipment. Desktop publishing includes word processing, design, final printout—for one-page flyers to multi-page newsletters and even books. It can also involve art and photography. This job can be done from home.

Time Schedule: As a freelancer, you can control your own schedule; however, it is imperative that you meet deadlines.

Requirements: Besides having the necessary equipment and expertise, you must be creative and know how to market your service.

Compensation: Consult #9 in Chapter 1.

EDITOR

Description: Edits manuscripts for publishing houses and writers. This job can be done from an office or from home as a freelancer.

Time Schedule: If you are hired as an employee, refer to Chapter 18. If you are a freelancer working out of your home, you are able to set your own hours. You will have to meet deadlines set by whoever hires you.

Requirements: You will need an education in writing and an ability to work with writers. In most cases, a knowledge of all aspects of book publishing is helpful. Some publishers require that freelancers have had previous experience working with a publishing house, and many require that freelancers take and pass a test of editing skills.

Compensation: You will be paid a salary if you are an employee. If you are a freelancer, refer to #2 and #9 in Chapter 1.

ELECTRONIC MAIL SERVICE PROVIDER (E-MAIL)

Description: Someone who works in this field installs electronic mail programs into the computers of businesses so that they can handle mail faster than the postal service would. Service of these systems is also part of the job.

Time Schedule: As a freelancer, you can establish your own schedule, but you have to be available to serve your clients.

Requirements: You will need knowledge and expertise in this business. It's important to be sensitive to and respond to the special requirements of your clients.

Compensation: Refer to #9 in Chapter 1.

FAX MESSAGE PROVIDER

Description: Provides fax services for individuals and small businesses. In most cases, fax service is offered in conjunction with some other kind of service (such as a secretarial or mailing service).

Time Schedule: As long as your fax machine is turned on and loaded with paper, you don't need to worry about a schedule. But you do have to make the fax available to the customer, which is the reason that this business is best done in association with others. If you are in a retail setting, consult #7 in Chapter 1.

Requirements: You need to have a telephone line and a good fax machine. Broadcast machines that can send the same message to many numbers by pressing just one programmed button is the best machine for this business.

Compensation: You charge a fee for each page of incoming fax and a fee plus a charge for making the telephone call for outgoing faxes.

FOREIGN LANGUAGE INSTRUCTOR

Description: Teaches foreign languages to individuals or groups, either in a corporate setting or through a school.

Time Schedule: Refer to #5 in Chapter 1.

Requirements: You must be able to teach, read, and speak fluently the language you are teaching.

Compensation: Refer to #5 in Chapter 1.

GHOSTWRITER

Description: Writes books for someone else and allows that other person to claim authorship. Thus the name "ghostwriter"—because you are an invisible writer who gets no credit for the work.

Time Schedule: Your schedule can be set up as you'd like. Please refer to #11 in Chapter 1.

Requirements: You have to be able to write well enough for publication, and you have to be able to put aside your own ego because you will not be credited with the writing. Again, refer to #11 in Chapter 1.

Compensation: You will be paid a set sum for your writing. Rarely, if ever, will you share in the royalties. Be sure that the sum you are paid takes into account all the hours of interviewing the subject as well as time spent writing.

HISTORICAL AND FAMILY RESEARCHER

Description: A historical researcher verifies historical details for authors, film companies, and others who need to know how things were done or how they looked during a certain time in history. Similarly, a family researcher examines historical documents to trace the lineage of families through surnames, country of origin, and so on.

Time Schedule: You can work totally on your own but will have to meet deadlines.

Requirements: You'll need an education and love of history if you are planning on being a historical researcher. You also need to be interested in genealogical studies if you choose to be a family researcher. Attention to detail is especially important. Although the Internet has made such research much easier than it once was, travel might be necessary, especially for family research.

Compensation: You will be paid a fee. Refer to #2, #9, and #11 in Chapter 1 for advice on how to price your services.

MAGAZINE DEALER

Description: Sells magazines, usually from a retail setting, but sometimes over the telephone from home.

Time Schedule: If you work from a retail setting, refer to #7 in Chapter 1. If you work from home, you can set your own hours. Just be sure that if you're telephoning other states, you consider the time difference (9 a.m. on the East Coast is 6 a.m. on the West Coast).

Requirements: Besides those requirements outlined in #7 in Chapter 1, you will need to appreciate magazines and enjoy selling them.

Compensation: Your income will be generated from the markup on the magazines if you sell them from a retail store. Refer to #7 in Chapter 1 for an explanation of how that works. If you sell them by telephone, you will be paid a commission.

MAGAZINE PUBLISHER

Description: Most independent magazine publishers concentrate on special-interest publications that are targeted toward a particular market.

Time Schedule: Assuming you publish a small magazine, you might be able to do much of it by yourself or with a small group of helpers. If yours will be a larger undertaking, refer to #7 in Chapter 1 for suggestions on how to get employees to relieve you of long hours.

Requirements: You need an ability to recognize good writing so that you can buy the right articles from freelance writers, and you need the skill to put together a quality product that will attract enough subscribers and advertisers to keep you going. With so many magazines on the market today, if you can find a subject that hasn't already been done, you might have a better chance for success.

Compensation: Your income will be generated from subscriptions and advertising. Refer to #7 in Chapter 1 for advice on how markups generate profit.

NEWSLETTER PUBLISHER

Description: Publishes a newsletter on a particular topic of interest to a specific segment of the public. A newsletter can focus on almost any subject.

Time Schedule: Refer to #11 in Chapter 1.

Requirements: You need the ability to write, and you must also be an expert on the subject of your newsletter.

Compensation: The money you make will come from subscriptions to your newsletter. Refer to #7 in Chapter 1.

NEWSPAPER PUBLISHER

Description: Publishes a newspaper, either a daily, weekly, or monthly. Although your newspaper could be a large-city daily, for the purposes of this book, I will profile a small weekly or monthly paper.

Time Schedule: If you are publishing a weekly (or monthly), you will be able to enjoy more time flexibility, although right before you go to press, your days will be more hectic. Refer to #7 in Chapter 1 for suggestions on how to delegate some of the work to your employees.

Requirements: You'll need a newspaper background, gained through both experience and education. Marketing and sales abilities are also important as is the necessary networking to find freelance reporters to work with.

Compensation: Your income will be generated from advertising and subscriptions. Refer to #7 in Chapter 1 for suggestions on how to make money after pricing your product.

NEWSPAPER REPORTER

Description: Writes about news that is pertinent to the interests of the community the newspaper serves.

Time Schedule: If you work as an employee for the newspaper, refer to Chapter 18 for suggestions on turning a full-time job into a flexible one. If you are a freelancer—which is often the case—you have more control over your schedule.

Requirements: A degree in journalism is always helpful, although some reporters have degrees in other fields and learn news writing on the job. Experience on a newspaper will make it more likely that you'll get a freelance job. You need the ability to discover news stories that your paper will be interested in printing. (Those in the newspaper business call it having a "nose for news.")

Compensation: If you are an employee, you will be paid a salary. If you are a freelancer, you will be paid by the article.

SECRETARY

Description: Provides secretarial services for business people who need them. This includes typing, word processing, or data entry; taking shorthand; filing; and any and all tasks normally done by a secretary in a business setting.

Time Schedule: If you work out of your home, you can keep your own hours as long as you meet your clients' deadlines. You might contract to work for an individual for a day or week, or you might set up a regular part-time schedule in someone's office. In these instances, you can still, to a great extent, control your own schedule.

Requirements: You need secretarial skills. A good background with a large company would be a help in establishing your credentials for your own business.

Compensation: You are usually paid by the hour or by the project. If you are typing a large manuscript and you are fast, you will make the most money by charging by the page.

SIGN LANGUAGE TEACHER

Description: Teaches sign language to those who wish to communicate with hearing-impaired people and might also teach hearing-impaired people themselves to communicate, through "signing," with each other.

Time Schedule: If you are a teacher who is employed by a school, your hours might well be similar to those described in #5 in Chapter 1.

Requirements: You need to know sign language; you also need a sensitivity to hearing-impaired people as well as to the frustrations of those who can hear in their efforts to learn signing.

Compensation: Refer again to #5 in Chapter 1.

TELEMARKETER

Description: Sells products or sets appointments by telephone for companies and/or services.

Time Schedule: If you are hired as an employee, you will probably be hired as a part-time worker. If you are a freelancer or working from home (which is often the case), you can set your own schedule.

Requirements: You need a good personality and a pleasant voice over the telephone. You must also be able to take rejection when people hang up on you. It is not easy to speak convincingly over the telephone.

Compensation: You will be paid an hourly wage and, in many instances, a commission on what you sell or an additional bonus on appointments that you set. A good telemarketer can make a very good income.

TECHNICAL WRITER

Description: Writes about technical subjects for businesses. Projects might include a brochure on how to manufacture something, a description of how machines operate, an operating manual, or a product manual.

Time Schedule: As a freelancer, you can schedule your own hours, taking care to be available for the clients' schedules.

Requirements: You need to understand the language and technicalities of whatever you are writing about. Also essential is an ability to take the complicated and make it easy to understand and interesting. This can be very challenging.

Compensation: You will generally charge by the project. Be sure to charge enough to compensate you for the time it takes to do the job.

TELEPHONE CONSULTANT AND SALESPERSON

Description: Advises businesses on the type of telephone services that will be most effective for their needs. This job might include selling the service.

Time Schedule: Refer to #2 in Chapter 1.

Requirements: You will need a knowledge of telephone services and how they can aid users. You must be able to market your services, and you'll need an understanding of many different types of businesses and industries.

Compensation: Refer to #2 in Chapter 1 for information on how you can expect to be compensated for your consulting services. You will also make a markup or commission on the telephone service that you sell.

TELEPHONE INSTALLER AND REPAIRPERSON

Description: Repairs and installs telephones and telephone services. Now that the telephone companies charge large amounts for installing new services, there are excellent opportunities for freelancers to be very successful.

Time Schedule: As a freelancer, you can control your own schedule. Refer to #9 in Chapter 1 for additional advice.

Requirements: You need the skill and knowledge to install telephone services. This usually comes from working as a line person in a telephone company.

Compensation: Refer again to #9 in Chapter 1.

VIDEO PRODUCER

Description: Produces videos of all kinds (product introductions, tours of plants, training) for businesses and also occasionally produces business videos for individuals (giving speeches, making presentations, conducting meetings).

Time Schedule: As a freelancer, you can set your own schedule; however, you will have to be available to work with your clients at their location.

Requirements: You must have good equipment and know how to use it. You will need to be an expert at video photography if you will be taking the videos as well as producing them.

Compensation: Refer to #2 and #6 in Chapter 1.

VOICE MAIL SERVICE PROVIDER

Description: Provides a voice mail service for individuals and businesses. The service is provided through a computer system and telephone lines at your place of business—which can be your home office.

Time Schedule: Your time can be very flexible; however, you do have to set up the service and interact with the client. And if anything goes wrong, you have to be available to solve the problem.

Requirements: You must have the computer system and available telephone lines. Marketing and sales skills are also necessary.

Compensation: Your income is generated from set-up fees and markup from the phone calls. In most cases, you will set a flat fee based on the number of expected telephone calls. The more calls, the less is charged per call, but the higher the overall cost to the client—and the higher the income to you!

✪ WORD PROCESSOR

Description: Operates a word processor for companies or individuals whose needs are too sporadic to justify hiring a staff word processor.

Time Schedule: If you are a freelancer, your schedule is your own. You can also work at this job as a temporary or part-time employee.

Requirements: You will need to know how to operate a word processor; and if you are going to own the business, you will need to own a good one and know how to market your services.

Compensation: You will be paid either hourly or by the job. Refer to #9 in Chapter 1 for suggestions on how to charge for your services.

Chapter 5

The Creative World

You know who you are. You're the creative one who can't watch television without knitting, embroidering, or doing something with your hands. You look at another person's creation and figure out not only how to duplicate it but also how to make it better. You always give a handcrafted gift.

This chapter will kindle your imagination as you discover how to make money from that unique avocation of yours. And if you aren't clever but love to be surrounded by handcrafted items, you can earn a living supporting the craftspersons you admire.

ANIMATOR

Description: Creates drawings for animated motion pictures and television programs.

Time Schedule: If you are a freelancer, you can control your own schedule; however, you will have to attend meetings with your clients. You may be hired as an employee (for major studios like Disney or Hanna-Barbera). Consult

Chapter 18 for advice on how to turn a full-time job into a flexible one.

Requirements: You'll need a formal art education and training, plus as much experience as you can get by working for the major studios. You also need marketing and networking skills in order to get business from advertising agencies and others who might employ your animation services.

Compensation: You might be paid a flat rate or a rate plus royalties or residuals. Refer to #2 and also #11 in Chapter 1.

ARTIST

ANIMAL ARTIST

Description: Specializes in painting or drawing animals, frequently portraits of people's pets.

CARICATURE ARTIST

Description: Draws caricatures of people. Customers are often found at amusement parks or fairs.

FABRIC DESIGN ARTIST

Description: Creates designs that can be used on fabrics—for clothing, window coverings, bedding, and so on.

GRAPHIC ARTIST

Description: Designs anything visual—logos, symbols, environmental designs, billboards, truck sides, T-shirts, and the like.

HOME/LANDSCAPE/SCENERY ARTIST

Description: Draws and paints scenery, landscapes, houses and buildings, and seascapes.

PORTRAIT ARTIST

Description: Paints portraits of people.

Time Schedule for All Types of Artist: As a freelancer, you can set your own hours. If you have contracted to complete a job for someone, you will have to meet deadlines.

Requirements for All Types of Artist: Obviously, you need the ability to draw or paint or both. You should have a formal education in art; however, there are many gifted "natural" artists who are very successful without a degree. The degree gives you credibility. You must have an interest in and love of your subject. If you are painting people or animals, patience is a must.

Compensation for All Types of Artist: You generally charge by the project. Remember to consider how much time it will take you—from start to finish—for each project. It is also appropriate to charge your expenses to the client. Many artists, particularly those who paint scenery, sell their works through galleries. Refer to #1 in Chapter 1 for more advice on this subject.

CARTOONIST

Description: Draws cartoons for publication, often on the editorial or comics page of newspapers. You might have a syndicated cartoon that appears in several newspapers, or you can submit a single cartoon for publication in periodicals that feature them.

Time Schedule: As a freelancer, you can control your own time.

Requirements: You must be artistic, imaginative, and persevering. An education in cartoon art is helpful but not mandatory. The wide variety of cartoons and their popularity demonstrate that there is always room for another cartoon *if* it appeals to enough people, is well done, and looks at life in a new way.

Compensation: You will be paid in much the same way writers are. Please refer to #11 in Chapter 1.

CRAFTS FAIR PROMOTER

Description: Plans and puts on a fair or expo where craftspersons can sell their wares to the public.

Time Schedule: Refer to #4 in Chapter 1.

Requirements: Refer to #4 in Chapter 1.

Compensation: Refer to #4 in Chapter 1.

CRAFTS INSTRUCTOR

Description: Teaches people how to make a particular craft. There are thousands of crafts, and there are people interested in learning how to make all of them. Frequently you will be teaching in a crafts store.

Time Schedule: If you work as a freelancer, which is the way most crafts teachers operate, you will be able to set your own schedule. Usually you will work in a crafts store, and the store will "book" students for you when you say you will hold the class. Refer to #5 in Chapter 1 for additional information.

Requirements: You will need expertise in the craft you are teaching and more than average patience for slow learners.

Compensation: You will usually earn a flat rate per class. See #5 in Chapter 1.

CRAFTSPERSON

Description: Makes crafts to sell—either on his or her own or through others.

Time Schedule: Refer to #1 in Chapter 1.

Requirements: You must do a better-than-average job of making your particular craft. People who buy your wares will do so because they cannot make them as well. You should also make things that people will want to buy and that are in some way unusual.

Compensation: Refer to #1 in Chapter 1.

CRAFTS RETAILER

Description: Sells handcrafted items through mail order, at fairs, or from a retail store or boutique.

Time Schedule: If you are selling your crafts from a store, refer to #7 in Chapter 1. If you are selling via mail order, you can control your own schedule as long as you fulfill your orders on a timely basis. Selling at fairs also offers flexibility because you can choose to attend fairs that fit your schedule.

Requirements: You must be able to locate well-made and unusual items and know how to merchandise and price them. You must sell these where there will be sufficient traffic to make it profitable.

Compensation: Refer to #7 in Chapter 1. You can also sell on consignment, which means that you do not buy the merchandise but make a commission on it when it sells.

CRAFTS SUPPLIES SALESPERSON

Description: Sells crafts supplies to crafts stores (as an outside salesperson) and to craftspersons (usually from a retail store).

Time Schedule: If you work in a retail store, refer to #7 in Chapter 1. If you are out in the field, refer to #8 in Chapter 1.

Requirements: You need knowledge of the crafts made from the supplies you sell so that you can advise your customers.

Compensation: If you work in a retail store, you will usually be paid by the hour; however, if you own the store, refer to #7 in Chapter 1. If you are an outside salesperson, refer to #8 in Chapter 1.

DESIGNER

BADGE DESIGNER AND SALESPERSON

Description: Designs badges for individuals and businesses. These badges, which are large metal pins, are used in many ways. Companies have their logos or messages printed on them and give them away in advertising campaigns for their products or services. Individuals, such as politicians or candidates for public office, give them to the public. Organizations also use badges to identify their members or advertise a special event.

DOLL DESIGNER

Description: Designs and makes dolls, in porcelain, vinyl, cloth, or some other medium. These dolls can be sold to individuals or can be sold wholesale to stores.

DOLLHOUSE/FURNITURE DESIGNER

Description: Designs and makes dollhouses and the furniture that goes into them. The job is similar to that of doll designer.

GREETING CARD DESIGNER/WRITER

Description: Designs and writes greeting cards, usually for greeting card companies.

PACKAGE/GIFT-WRAPPING DESIGNER

Description: Designs packages and gift wrapping—usually for companies that manufacture these items.

PARTY GOODS DESIGNER

Description: Designs party goods, including paper plates, napkins, and tablecloths, for manufacturers of these items.

SIGN DESIGNER

Description: Designs signs for businesses and individuals.

TOY/GAME DESIGNER

Description: Designs toys and games, to sell individually to the end user or to toy manufacturers.

Time Schedule for All Types of Designer: In most cases, you will be working as a freelancer and will be in control of your schedule.

Requirements for All Types of Designer: You need the skill to design the product, and you should probably understand its manufacturing process. You should have a good idea of what the public wants. Understanding marketing is an additional plus.

Compensation for All Types of Designer: If you are selling your product yourself, you will make your money from what you charge. If you have sold your design to a manufacturer, you will usually get a fee for the design and, ideally, a royalty on every one that is sold. Be sure that you contract for royalties before allowing a manufacturer to purchase any rights to your product.

✪ EMBROIDERER

Description: Embroiders uniforms, jackets, caps, shirts, and patches for individuals, companies, and clothing manufacturers. Monograms are also usually included in this business, and now much of it is done by computer. Many embroiderers also sell garments for monogramming.

Time Schedule: If you run this business from a retail store (and most people do), refer to #7 in Chapter 1. As a freelancer, however, you can control your schedule as long as you have the work done when you have promised.

Requirements: You must have the necessary equipment and be able to perform the job extremely well and rapidly. Knowing how to market your business is also very helpful.

Compensation: Refer to both #1 and #7 in Chapter 1.

✪ ENGRAVER IN GLASS, METAL, PHOTO, WOOD, PLASTIC

Description: Makes custom signs and nameplates for desks, walls or doors, award plaques, labels, tags, gifts, and trophies. This job can be done from a retail setting or from a home shop environment.

Time Schedule: If you work from your home, you can control your own work hours; if you are running your business from a retail store, refer to #7 in Chapter 1.

Requirements: You will need the necessary tools and the ability to use them to turn out exceptional work (so that you will get return business). It will also help if you know how to market your business to your community.

Compensation: Refer to #1 and #7 in Chapter 1 for suggestions on how you can make money in this business.

GIFT BASKET CREATOR

Description: Designs gift baskets for all occasions and sells them either individually or through retail outlets.

Time Schedule: You set your own hours. If you do have to adhere to someone else's schedule, it will be while selling at fairs or expos.

Requirements: You need to be imaginative in putting interesting, attractive baskets together. You also need sources for a wide variety of items to put in the baskets.

Compensation: You will be paid a markup on what you create. See #1 in Chapter 1.

ILLUSTRATOR

Description: Illustrates books through drawings and paintings. Often, illustrators work on picture books for children.

Time Schedule: You have control of your schedule, but you have to meet deadlines.

Requirements: You need drawing and painting ability, which is a matter of talent, education, and experience.

Compensation: You might be paid by the job, but if you are illustrating a children's book or any book where the art is as important as the text, you will get royalties, just like an author does. Refer to #11 in the Appendix.

Chapter 6

The Fashion World

Adam and Eve wore the first garments, and ever since then, men and women have been busy improving upon them. Today, opportunities have never been greater for entering this field, which can make use of many different talents and abilities—from salespeople to fashion designers. Check out these forty-two possibilities and you'll surely find your niche.

ALTERATIONS PROVIDER

Description: Alters ready-made clothes. An alterations provider, often a freelancer, is likely to work through a retail clothing store or dry-cleaning business.

Time Schedule: Most establishments that would hire you will work around your schedule. If you do alterations from your home, then obviously the schedule is up to you.

Requirements: Being an expert at sewing is a must, but it's also important to enjoy fixing clothes that have already been sewn by someone else. Many people who are great tailors or dressmakers *hate* doing alterations.

Compensation: Most people who have this job charge by the piece, taking care to compensate for the time it takes to alter the garment. If you work for a retail store where you have to put in so much floor time, you should be paid an hourly wage plus a commission or fee for the garments altered. Refer to #1 in Chapter 1 for more advice concerning pricing your services.

BRIDAL GOWN DESIGNER

Description: Designs bridal gowns, either for a company or independently.

Time Schedule: You will usually work as a freelancer and will be able to set your own time schedule.

Requirements: You will need education in fashion design. A "love affair" with weddings and brides will contribute to your success and enjoyment. Of necessity, you must be aware of young people's preferences in fashion.

Compensation: How you are paid depends on who you work for. If a company employs you, you will probably make a salary and earn royalties. If you work strictly for yourself (and many designers do), then you will charge a flat fee for the gown design. How much depends on whether you are selling an exclusive design or whether you will use it again. Refer to #1 in Chapter 1 for additional advice.

BRIDAL GOWN RETAILER

Description: Sells bridal gowns through a retail store.

Time Schedule: Refer to #7 in Chapter 1.

Requirements: You will need a love of weddings and all things bridal; it's important to be interested in young people (because so many of them will be your customers). The better established you are in your community, the more successful you will be because much of your business will be generated by satisfied customers.

Compensation: Your income derives from the markup of your merchandise. Unlike other forms of fashion retailing, you need only have samples of gowns (which you can later sell) for brides to see. When they make their selections, they give you a deposit of at least your cost for the gown; and you then order the gown from the manufacturer. The rest (your markup) is paid when the bride takes delivery of her gown. And if she should not need the gown after all, she loses her deposit and you have a gown to sell. Refer to #7 in Chapter 1 for additional advice.

BUTTON AND TRIM WHOLESALE SALESPERSON

Description: Sells buttons and trims, primarily to yardage retailers, but sometimes also to designers or clothing manufacturers. This is an outside sales position.

Time Schedule: Refer to #8 in Chapter 1.

Requirements: You need a knowledge of and interest in buttons and trims. If you aren't excited about your product, you can't expect to sell it. (See also #8 in Chapter 1.)

Compensation: Refer again to #8 in Chapter 1.

BUTTON DESIGNER

Description: Designs buttons and other trims for notions companies; some button designers work for clothing manufacturers and their designers.

Time Schedule: As a freelancer, you will be able to establish your own schedule.

Requirements: You need an understanding of how buttons will be used on the finished garment and how they are made.

Compensation: Refer to #1 and #2 in Chapter 1.

CHILDREN'S CLOTHING DESIGNER

Description: Designs children's clothing for manufacturers or privately for select patrons.

Time Schedule: As a freelancer, you can establish your own schedule; however, you will have to make time to meet with your customers and attend trade shows.

Requirements: Besides having the obvious education in fashion design, you must love and understand children. It helps to know about the latest toys and entertainment fads.

Compensation: You may be paid by a manufacturer for the design (you might make a royalty on every garment sold). If you design for an individual and make the garment, refer to #1 in Chapter 1.

CHILDREN'S CLOTHING RETAILER

Description: Sells children's clothing from a retail store. This can be new clothing or, increasingly popular, used children's wear.

Time Schedule: Refer to #7 in Chapter 1.

Requirements: You'll need a love of children and, as is true of all clothing retailers, an ability to spot trends.

Compensation: Please again consult #7 in Chapter 1.

COLOR CONSULTANT

Description: Counsels people on what colors they should wear based on which are most becoming to them. "Colors" include not just clothing but also makeup. This job fits the work-at-home situation perfectly, or it can be done in conjunction with another business (such as a retail clothing store or beauty shop).

Time Schedule: Refer to #2 in Chapter 1.

Requirements: There are many companies that can train you to do this job; these companies also sell franchises.

Compensation: Refer to #2 in Chapter 1.

COSTUME RENTAL STORE—OWNER

Description: Rents costumes to the general adult public (rarely to children) and also to theater and movie companies. Most costume-rental businesses operate from retail stores.

Time Schedule: Because this is a retail operation, regular hours are necessary. Refer to #7 in Chapter 1. At certain times of the year, such as right before Halloween, you will put in long hours to accommodate the public.

Requirements: You'll need a fascination with costumes and a knowledge of what's "hot" with the public. It's also important to know how to care for and clean garments so that they can be fresh with each wearing.

Compensation: Your income is generated by how much you charge for each costume. Because your great expense is in purchasing the costume, you will need to rent it several times in order to recoup your cost. Only then will you start making money from it. What you can charge for your costumes depends on how elaborate they are. The fancier, the more costly. The least ornate adult costumes start at about $25; more elaborate costumes can cost several thousand dollars to rent. Where your shop is located will also have a bearing on how much you can charge.

✪ DRESSMAKER

Description: Makes clothes for women, usually from home.

Time Schedule: Your schedule is your own.

Requirements: You'll need to be an excellent seamstress and know how to make garments to fit. Your creations are in competition with ready-made clothes in stores: if you expect people to buy from you instead, you must be able to give them something they can't find in a store. You should be able to offer them the perfect fit they won't get from off-the-rack clothes.

Compensation: Please refer to #1 in Chapter 1.

✪ FABRIC RETAILER

Description: Sells fabrics to the general public, usually from a retail store.

Time Schedule: Refer to #7 in Chapter 1.

Requirements: You need to know about fabrics and which are most appropriate for a particular project, how a fabric wears, how to launder a fabric, and so on, but it's also important to know about sewing so that you can advise your customers.

Compensation: Refer to #7 in Chapter 1 to learn how your primary income will be generated. You can add to your income by giving sewing classes and charging for the class. If you cannot teach sewing yourself, you can find someone who can and split the fee.

✪ FABRIC SALESPERSON

Description: Sells fabrics to the retail fabric stores and clothing manufacturers. This is an outside sales position.

Time Schedule: See #8 in Chapter 1.

Requirements: You need to know about the various types of fabrics and how they should be used.

Compensation: Refer to #8 in Chapter 1.

✪ FASHION ACCESSORIES DESIGNER

Description: Designs accessories such as belts, scarves, purses, shoes—anything and everything that adds to one's outfit.

Time Schedule: As a freelance designer, you will be able to control your own schedule.

Requirements: Besides formal education in designing whatever accessory you choose, you must keep pace with society and fashion in general and know how accessories can enhance an outfit.

Compensation: You can sell your designs outright to a manufacturer for a fee and a royalty (which is always preferable). If you plan on selling your designs directly to the public, refer to #1 in Chapter 1.

✪ FASHION ACCESSORIES RETAILER

Description: Sells fashion accessories from a retail store. There don't seem to be as many of these as there used to be, perhaps because of the well-stocked department stores. If you are going to have such a store, be sure that it includes all accessories and offers unique merchandise.

Time Schedule: Refer to #7 in Chapter 1.

Requirements: You should have a passion for fashion accessories. Also refer to #7 in Chapter 1 for general requirements for retailers.

Compensation: Refer to #7 in Chapter 1.

✪ FASHION ACCESSORIES WHOLESALE SALESPERSON

Description: Sells fashion accessories to retailers. This is an outside sales position.

Time Schedule: Refer to #8 in Chapter 1.

Requirements: In addition to the general abilities required of all outside salespeople (see #8 in Chapter 1), you must have an interest in and passion for fashion accessories.

Compensation: Refer to #8 in Chapter 1.

✪ FASHION BUYER

Description: Buys fashions for specialty and department stores. The best way to have flexible hours with this career is to work as a freelancer or within a "buying company" that works for various client stores.

Time Schedule: As a freelancer, you will control your own hours, with the exception of market weeks when all the manufacturers are showing their new lines. Then you will have to work nonstop like everyone else.

Requirements: You need to know what the public will buy. A good way to start your buying career is by working in a department store where you can learn your profession and make contacts with various manufacturers. Because you will be buying for other retailers who, for whatever reason, cannot make their own contacts, you will need to understand their particular clientele and you will have to work within their budgets.

Compensation: You might be compensated with a flat fee or a retainer, or you might be paid on an hourly basis. Your pay might also be a percentage of the client's budget. Refer to #2 in Chapter 1.

FASHION CRITIC

Description: Reviews and gives personal opinion of current new fashion trends. Critiques might be written for a trade newspaper, magazine, or radio or television station.

Time Schedule: Refer to #3 in Chapter 1.

Requirements: You'll need an understanding of the fashion world and how its trends change. It also helps to have developed a reputation in the fashion industry, either as a designer, manufacturer, performer, or model. Otherwise, why would anyone take you seriously?

Compensation: Refer to #3 in Chapter 1.

FASHION DESIGNER

Description: Designs fashions for clothing manufacturers or for individuals. A fashion designer usually specializes in a particular kind of fashion, such as swimwear, suits, leisure wear, and the like.

Time Schedule: If you work for an employer, refer to Chapter 18 for suggestions on how to make a full-time job flexible. If you are a freelancer (which is how designers most frequently work), you can schedule your own time, but you will have to be available to consult with your clients and attend trade events.

Requirements: You'll need education and experience in fashion design. Having a fresh look and new ideas also helps.

Compensation: You can sell your designs directly to manufacturers for a flat fee or a royalty on every garment sold. Refer to #1 in Chapter 1 for some suggestions on how to price your work. In addition to those details, keep in mind that it helps to have a name and a following. To get that you have to be socially active and good at networking.

FASHION DESIGN TEACHER

Description: Teaches fashion design at schools or universities specializing in this type of study.

Time Schedule: Refer to #5 in Chapter 1.

Requirements: You need experience in your field, usually as a successful fashion designer. Again refer to #5 in Chapter 1.

Compensation: Refer to #5 in Chapter 1.

FASHION MODEL

Description: Models garments at fashion shows or for print advertising or television commercials. Clients for your service are clothing manufacturers, designers, or retail stores.

Time Schedule: As a freelancer, you will have some control of your own schedule; but you will have to work whatever hours your assignments require once you have accepted them.

Requirements: You must have an attractive face and also be exceptionally thin so that the clothes will hang well on you. You need to be registered with a modeling agency and have training in fashion modeling (which is often given by the agencies). Acting ability is important if you aspire to being in television commercials.

Compensation: You will generally be paid a flat or hourly rate, plus expenses. Usually the agency will pay you.

FASHION MODEL AGENT

Description: Schedules models to display fashions at fashion shows for clothing manufacturers or retail stores selling the merchandise. You can either specialize in a certain type of model (women, men, or children) or handle all of them. Some agencies also provide models for commercials or magazine ads.

Time Schedule: You will probably need to keep certain hours in an office. Refer to #7 in Chapter 1 for suggestions on how to delegate your work among employees.

Requirements: You'll need to have experience in the fashion world, either as a former model, designer, or manufacturer. You will also need excellent marketing skills and must be able to network successfully with people in the trade.

Compensation: You will be paid a sum for each model you provide, and out of this you will have to pay your model. The quality of your models and clients will greatly affect your income. This is not an easy business to break into, but it is often very lucrative.

✪ FASHION MODEL PHOTOGRAPHER

Description: Takes photographs of fashion models, usually for the print media.

Time Schedule: You will usually be able to determine your own schedule. Refer to #6 in Chapter 1.

Requirements: Besides those requirements outlined in #6 (Chapter 1), you will need to like and understand fashion and be creative so that your photographs show off the clothes to the best advantage. Before going off on your own, spend time working with a fashion photographer to gain experience and, perhaps, a name.

Compensation: Refer again to #6 in Chapter 1.

✪ FASHION NEWSLETTER PUBLISHER

Description: Publishes and writes a newsletter about fashion for people in the industry and others who care about it.

Topics can include anything about fashion and can be very specialized (you might focus only on men's fashions or on accessories, for instance).

Time Schedule: Other than needing to fit trade shows into your schedule, you can control your time.

Requirements: In addition to those requirements outlined in #11 (Chapter 1), you need to be aware of the hot trends in fashion and be privy to what is happening before it happens. Being respected in the industry will add greatly to your credibility and success.

Compensation: Your income will be generated from subscriptions to your newsletter. Refer to #1 in Chapter 1 for some suggestions on how to price your product.

FASHION SHOW PRODUCER

Description: Produces fashion shows for the public. These shows may be fund-raisers for clubs or may be sponsored by retail stores within the community.

Time Schedule: You'll have a great deal of control over your time. Refer to #4 in Chapter 1.

Requirements: In addition to those requirements outlined in #4 (Chapter 1), you must have a good knowledge of fashion.

Compensation: Your income depends on the purpose of the fashion show. If you are producing the show as a fund-raiser, you will be paid a percentage of the earnings. If you are promoting certain stores, you should charge a flat rate, plus a percentage of sales. Refer to #4 in Chapter 1 for additional recommendations.

FOOTWEAR DESIGNER

Description: Designs footwear (for men, women, or children). Footwear designers usually work for a manufacturer.

Time Schedule: If you are employed in-house by the manufacturer, you will have to arrange flexible hours as described in Chapter 18. Many companies, however, employ freelancers, and then your schedule can be more flexible.

Requirements: This job may be more complicated than it seems; footwear design requires a knowledge of the anatomy of the foot and an understanding of how shoes or boots affect the foot. This knowledge is obtained through a scientific or medical education (though you don't need to be a doctor).

Compensation: If you work as an employee of a manufacturer, you will be paid a salary and possibly a royalty. If you are an independent contractor, you may be paid outright for the design or you may receive a royalty.

FOOTWEAR RETAILER

Description: Sells footwear to the public.

Time Schedule: Refer to #7 in Chapter 1.

Requirements: You'll need to understand the importance of good-fitting footwear to one's well-being; you'll also need to be aware of the importance of footwear as a fashion item. Also refer to #7 in Chapter 1.

Compensation: Refer to #7 in Chapter 1.

FOOTWEAR SALESPERSON

Description: Sells footwear to retailers as an outside salesperson or sells to the public as a retail salesperson.

Time Schedule: Refer to #7 in Chapter 1 if you are working from a retail store and to #8 if you are an outside salesperson.

Requirements: You have to know your product and have the qualities any good salesperson would need.

Compensation: Whether you sell wholesale or retail, you should have at least part of your compensation tied into the sales you make. Refer to #7 and #8 in Chapter 1.

HISTORICAL CLOTHING CONSULTANT

Description: Gives advice on historical clothing. Clients for this service include fashion designers for historical motion picture and television productions, authors of historical works, and anyone else who has an interest in historical clothing.

Time Schedule: Refer to #2 in Chapter 1.

Requirements: You'll need an interest and education in history and fashion, and you must be able to handle extensive research and present it effectively. Refer to #2 in Chapter 1 for additional requirements.

Compensation: Refer to #2 in Chapter 1.

MEN'S ACCESSORIES DESIGNER

Description: Designs men's accessories, such as ties, suspenders, handkerchiefs, and so on. This work is usually done for a manufacturer.

Time Schedule: If you are a freelancer, you can schedule your own working hours; if you are an employee, you will have to negotiate with your employer. Chapter 18 offers suggestions to help you.

Requirements: A background in design and an understanding of fashion trends.

Compensation: You can sell your designs to a manufacturer for a flat fee or for a fee and royalties on the number of items sold. Whenever possible, try to negotiate the latter.

MENSWEAR DESIGNER

Description: Designs menswear—usually for manufacturers but occasionally for individuals.

Time Schedule: You can set your own schedule as a freelancer.

Requirements: An education in fashion design and an understanding of men's fashions. Although men's fashions don't change as fast or often as women's, it is still very important to keep abreast of women's fashions and of trends that could affect men's roles and thus their clothing needs and desires.

Compensation: You can sell your designs to a manufacturer for a fee or for a fee and a royalty. If you are selling your designs to individuals, refer to #1 in Chapter 1 for advice on how to price your work.

MENSWEAR RETAILER

Description: Sells menswear to the public.

Time Schedule: Please refer to #7 in Chapter 1.

Requirements: Besides the knowledge of how to run a store (outlined in #7 of Chapter 1), you need an interest in menswear.

Compensation: Your income is generated from your markup. See #7 in Chapter 1.

MENSWEAR SALESPERSON

Description: Sells menswear in a retail store or sells to retail stores in an outside sales position.

Time Schedule: If you sell wholesale, refer to #8 in Chapter 1. If you are working in a retail store you can probably arrange to have flexible hours.

Requirements: Besides the qualities all salespeople should have, you need to have an interest in and understanding of menswear.

Compensation: Your pay should be generated at least in part from commissions on your sales whether you are a retail or outside salesperson.

MODERN CLOTHING CONSULTANT

Description: Counsels businesses, motion picture fashion designers, clothing buyers, and individuals on modern clothing trends; suggests fashions to execute the particular look desired by the client's unique needs.

Time Schedule: Refer to #2 in Chapter 1.

Requirements: You'll need an education in and knowledge of fashion and how it can be used to enhance a person's appearance as well as the ability to communicate effectively. Refer to #2 in Chapter 1 for general requirements for a consultant.

Compensation: Refer to #2 in Chapter 1.

PATTERN DESIGNER

Description: Designs paper patterns that can be used to make garments. This service can be provided for fashion designers, pattern companies, or clothing manufacturers.

Time Schedule: If you work for a company, such as a clothing manufacturer, you might be a full-time employee. Consult Chapter 18 for suggestions on how to turn that job into a flexible one. As a freelancer (which is often the case), you can have better control of your schedule.

Requirements: You'll need an education in apparel design and manufacture; and experience is a must. The ability to solve problems is also necessary.

Compensation: As an employee, you will receive a salary and probably benefits. As a freelancer, you might receive a flat rate for your work. Refer to #2 in Chapter 1 for suggestions on how to price your service.

PERSONAL CLOTHING SHOPPER

Description: Shops for clothing for individuals who usually have neither the time nor the knowledge to do it themselves. This business can be run from home or in conjunction with another similar business.

Time Schedule: Refer to #10 in Chapter 1.

Requirements: You'll need a knowledge of fashion and how it can enhance all kinds of figures and lifestyles. You have to like to shop and must be good at marketing your services. Refer to #10 in Chapter 1 for additional requirements.

Compensation: Refer to #10 in Chapter 1.

SEWING INSTRUCTOR

Description: Teaches sewing, either in a school, through a retail store, or individually.

Time Schedule: As a freelancer, you can control your own hours. See #5 in Chapter 1.

Requirements: Being a good teacher and knowing how to sew are obvious requirements. Refer to #5 in Chapter 1 for additional requirements.

Compensation: Refer to #5 in Chapter 1.

TAILOR

Description: Either sews garments or alters garments for men; the counterpart to a dressmaker for women. This job can be done in a retail setting or from one's home.

Time Schedule: As a freelancer, you can control your own schedule. If you are working in a retail store, you can usually request certain hours. Consult Chapter 18 for advice on how to have flexible hours in a full-time job.

Requirements: You must sew extremely well; you must know about men's garments.

Compensation: You might be paid a salary or hourly wage if you are an employee. If you are working as an independent contractor, refer to #1 in Chapter 1 for ideas on how to price your service.

TRIM DESIGNER

Description: Designs trims to go on clothes or to be sold to fabric stores. These trims include ribbon, braid, jewel designs, and so on.

Time Schedule: As a freelancer, you can determine your own schedule.

Requirements: You need to know how to design various trims and how they will complement the design of the finished garment.

Compensation: You can sell your designs directly to a manufacturer for a fee or for a fee and royalty on what is sold. If you are making the trims to sell yourself, refer to #1 in Chapter 1 for suggestions on how to price your works.

TUXEDO RENTAL SHOP—OWNER

Description: Rents tuxedos and other formal apparel to the public from a retail store.

Time Schedule: You'll have to keep the same kind of hours as other retail stores do, except that weekends, from Fridays through Sunday, are usually busiest because that's when most weddings and proms occur. Refer to #7 in Chapter 1 for some advice on getting employees to help with the responsibilities so that you can have a more flexible schedule.

Requirements: You'll need an understanding of the formalwear business; patience is a necessity because you will be dealing with nervous grooms and teenage boys. You will also need significant capital at the beginning in order to purchase and maintain a large inventory with many different sizes.

Compensation: You will make your money from the rental of your merchandise. Generally, it will take several rentals before the items are paid for. At that time you will start generating profit from them.

USED CLOTHING RETAILER

Description: Sells used clothing to the public from a retail setting.

Time Schedule: Refer to #7 in Chapter 1.

Requirements: You need to appreciate the value of used garments and the people who buy them. It will also help to know how to "glamorize" previously worn apparel.

Compensation: This is an interesting business because you can start it up for little or nothing. You acquire your merchandise by getting people to give you their "used, but still good" (still wearable) clothes on consignment. This means that you will pay them a percentage of what you sell the garments for—and you mark the price. Usually storekeepers get 60 to 70 percent of the sale because they incur all the costs of selling the garments. The people who bring in these clothes are getting some money for them, whereas if they threw them out or gave them to charity, they would get nothing. These stores, especially those dealing in children's apparel, are gaining in popularity and are a great way to go into business without a lot of up-front cost.

VINTAGE CLOTHING PROVIDER

Description: Provides clothes from earlier eras to production companies or individuals on a rental basis; sometimes the clothes are sold.

Time Schedule: If you work out of your home (and this is a possibility), you can set your own schedule. If you do business from a retail store, see #7 in Chapter 1.

Requirements: You'll need an understanding and appreciation of vintage clothing and contacts for getting it. You'll need to attend estate sales and garage sales of retired people; you'll have to get the word out to everyone in your community (and those surrounding it) that you are interested in acquiring such items.

Compensation: If you are renting your garments, your income will be generated from their rental. If you are selling, your markup will contribute to your income. Refer to #7 in Chapter 1 for a full explanation of how this works.

✪ WHOLESALE APPAREL SALESPERSON

Description: Sells apparel to the public at close to wholesale prices. This can be done through party plans, at swap meets or flea markets, or from your home. Rarely is it done through a retail store because of the high cost of running a retail store.

Time Schedule: You control your own hours if you sell through a party plan (although most of your parties will be at night because that's when most women are able to shop) or at home. If you sell at a flea market, you will have to work when it is open.

Requirements: You need to be interested in clothing and also should have sources for buying at really low wholesale prices so that you can make a good markup and still offer attractive deals to the public.

Compensation: Your compensation will be based on your markup for the garments you sell. Because your overhead will be low, you will net more than most retailers. Refer to #7 in Chapter 1.

CHAPTER 7

The World of Foods: Gourmet and Simple

My grandfather was a butcher, and I can remember sitting with him and his cronies on the front porch of his Iowa home. Though I was only five I can still recall what he said about his job in a small grocery store.

"Work with food," Grandpa said, "and you'll never go hungry."

My grandfather was right about food: nothing else is as necessary to life or has as much universal appeal. So if you earn your livelihood from a food-related profession, you might feel an above-average sense of security. Out of these thirty-six possibilities, one might be perfect for you.

BAKER

Description: Bakes food products of all kinds (pastries, cakes, pies, breads, and the like) for food manufacturers, bakeries, or caterers.

Time Schedule: If you are employed by a bakery or food manufacturer on a full-time basis, refer to Chapter 18 for suggestions on how to turn it into a flexible job. If you work as a freelancer, you will have more control of your time.

Requirements: You'll need experience in professional baking and the skill that goes with it.

Compensation: As an employee you will be paid a salary and possible benefits. If you are a freelancer, refer to #1 in Chapter 1 for suggestions on how to price your products.

BAKER'S EQUIPMENT SALESPERSON

Description: Sells baker's equipment to bakeries, restaurants, and stores that have bakeries. This is an outside sales position.

Time Schedule: Refer to #8 in Chapter 1.

Requirements: Besides the requirements outlined in #8 (Chapter 1), you will need to be able to demonstrate how your equipment can fill a baker's needs.

Compensation: Refer to #8 in Chapter 1.

BARTENDER

Description: Mixes alcoholic drinks at bars, cocktail lounges, restaurants, and public parties.

Time Schedule: You can generally request some flexibility in your work schedule. See Chapter 18 for some suggestions on how to convince your employer to work with you.

Requirements: You need to know how to mix drinks. You can learn at a bartender training school or by working in an establishment that is willing to take the time to train you. If you have a lot of contact with the public, you will also need a good personality and a willingness to listen.

Compensation: Although you will be paid an hourly wage, your greatest remuneration will come from tips. You can get good ones if you make excellent drinks and are personable so that people like you and come back often.

BARTENDER INSTRUCTOR

Description: Instructs and prepares people to become bartenders; usually works for bartender schools.

Time Schedule: Refer to #5 in Chapter 1.

Requirements: You must have experience in bartending and the patience to teach.

Compensation: Refer to #5 in Chapter 1.

CAKE DECORATOR

Description: Decorates cakes for special occasions (such as weddings, birthdays, and so on) for bakeries, food stores, or individuals.

Time Schedule: In most instances, you can probably set your own hours; however, you will have to deliver the cakes according to the customers' deadlines.

Requirements: You'll need training in decorating cakes and a good reputation. It also helps to know how to market your service, and the best way to do so is through recommendations and repeat business from happy customers.

Compensation: Please refer to #1 in Chapter 1 for suggestions on how to price your product and service.

CANDY MAKER

Description: Makes candy for caterers, manufacturers, gift stores, or gourmet food shops.

Time Schedule: If you work as a freelancer, you have the most control of your schedule. If you work for a manufacturer, you will be treated as an employee. Refer to Chapter 18 for help in turning a traditional job into a flexible one.

Requirements: As a freelancer, you'll need experience in candy making and a reputation for producing an exceptional product. If you are hired as a worker in a candy factory, the biggest requirement is a willingness to work and put up with a certain amount of repetition.

Compensation: A salary and possible benefits are yours as an employee. If you choose to be a freelancer, refer to #1 in Chapter 1 for suggestions on how to price your product.

CATERER

Description: Prepares and serves food for events held by businesses and individuals. Your clients might require full meals or perhaps just desserts or appetizers for such occasions as weddings, holiday parties, grand openings, conferences, or celebrations of any kind; they might want you to set up picnics or barbecues.

Time Schedule: Although you can choose weeks or days you do not wish to work, you will have to be available around holiday times and popular wedding seasons. And once you have accepted the booking, you do have to put in whatever time is necessary to meet your commitment. If you employ people to help you, delegate as much work as you can to your employees.

Requirements: You need the knowledge and ability to prepare foods and serve them attractively. You'll learn best through experience in a restaurant or with another caterer. You will also need the necessary local licenses and the ability to market your service.

Compensation: Refer to #1 and #9 in Chapter 1 for suggestions on pricing your services to make the most profit.

COFFEE SERVICE SALESPERSON

Description: An outside sales position selling coffeemakers and supplies to businesses. This might also include bottled water and dispensers for it.

Time Schedule: Refer to #8 in Chapter 1.

Requirements: Besides those outlined in #8 in Chapter 1, you need to believe in your product and be particularly sensitive to the needs of businesses in their desire to give their employees and visitors good refreshments at a nominal cost.

Compensation: Again please refer to #8 in Chapter 1.

COOK

Description: Prepares food either in an eating establishment or in a private residence.

Time Schedule: If you work in a restaurant, you will usually cook during certain shifts (breakfast, lunch, dinner). Therefore, you can select which shift you choose to work. In a private residence, you will generally have to work all day but will have certain days off. Your wishes will be considered in some cases, but you most likely will be expected to be available on special occasions.

Requirements: You need professional cooking skills, which are usually gained from studying at a cooking school.

Compensation: How much you make depends on the restaurant where you work and the shift you work. A dinner chef will generally earn more than a breakfast chef. Usually you will be paid a salary, but some chefs make a percentage of what the restaurant makes because the quality of the food is what builds a restaurant's reputation and success. If you work in a private residence, you will generally be given a salary, although room and board might be part of the compensation too.

COOKBOOK WRITER

Description: Writes cookbooks for publication, both general cookbooks and specialty books.

Time Schedule: Your schedule is your own; however, you will have to meet deadlines. See #11 in Chapter 1.

Requirements: Although you don't have to be a cook to write a cookbook, it will contribute greatly to your success and credibility. You need to be able to write clearly, and you'll have to test the recipes (or have someone else do it).

Compensation: Refer to #11 in Chapter 1 for an explanation of how authors are generally paid.

COOKING SCHOOL INSTRUCTOR

Description: Teaches people how to become chefs for restaurants or private residences. This teaching usually takes place in a culinary school.

Time Schedule: Refer to #5 in Chapter 1.

Requirements: An education and a successful career as a chef.

Compensation: Refer to #5 in Chapter 1.

DECORATIVE FOOD CREATOR

Description: Prepares decorative food items such as ice and pastry sculptures, decorative breads and cakes, hors d'oeuvres, and the like. Clients purchase these for parties, cruise ships, hotels, and so on.

Time Schedule: Although you can schedule blocks of time when you do not want to work, once you accept an assignment you will have to deliver; much of your work will be over holiday periods.

Requirements: You'll need training and experience in this type of food preparation—which can best be gained by working with other food creators. You will also need the necessary licenses for your state and community.

Compensation: Refer to #1 in Chapter 1 for suggestions on how best to price your service and products.

FOOD BASKETS SALESPERSON/CREATOR

Description: Creates and sells gift food baskets—from a retail store, from home, or through mail order.

Time Schedule: If you are running this business from a retail store, refer to #7 in Chapter 1. If you work from your home or through mail order, you will have more flexibility.

Requirements: You'll need a knowledge of gourmet foods and skill in creating clever baskets. Marketing ability is also very important.

Compensation: You will be paid by the basket if you are the creator and salesperson. If you work in a retail store you will be paid an hourly wage. Refer to #7 in Chapter 1 if you run a retail store, and refer to #1 if you work out of your home as a craftsperson.

FOOD BROKER

Description: Represents food manufacturers to the retail food establishment. This usually includes supermarkets, drug stores, mass merchandisers, and convenience stores as well as restaurants and military bases.

Time Schedule: Since much of your work will involve making outside sales calls, you will have some time flexibility. However, you will have to be available for meetings with clients and your colleagues and, to some extent, you'll need to work around your customers' schedules.

Requirements: You'll need the ability to sell and an understanding of your particular marketplace. In this business, building relationships with your customers and other members of your industry is of the greatest importance. See #8 in Chapter 1 for more requirements.

Compensation: If you head the brokerage, you will be paid a commission on all that you sell. This can be anywhere from 1.5 percent to 8 percent—depending on the product and the volume it generates. If you work for a food broker company, you will generally be paid a salary plus such benefits as a company car.

FOOD DEMONSTRATOR

Description: Helps sell food products by giving people samples in retail food outlets, usually grocery stores or mass merchandisers.

Time Schedule: Usually this is weekend work. If you do not want to work Fridays, Saturdays, and sometimes Sundays, this job is not for you. However, it does offer the chance to have weekdays off.

Requirements: You need the ability to talk to strangers and the physical strength to stand in one place for a long period of time. You also will need to know how to cook and serve food.

Compensation: You will be paid an hourly rate. How much depends on whom you work for (there are many agencies), your experience, and other factors. This job will not make you rich; but if you are looking for a little extra money, it is an excellent choice.

FOOD EDITOR

Description: Writes about foods for magazines and periodicals. The job usually includes creating recipes around the featured foods.

Time-Schedule: You can usually set your own schedule. Refer to #11 in Chapter 1.

Requirements: You'll need to know about foods, food preparation, consumer trends, and so on; you also have to be able to write for your particular medium.

Compensation: Refer to #11 in Chapter 1.

FOOD INSPECTOR

Description: Inspects restaurants and food manufacturers on behalf of government agencies.

Time Schedule: Although this is usually a full-time position, it is an outside job; consequently, you will have a bit more flexibility than would someone who is inside all day. Refer to Chapter 18 for some suggestions on making your employer more receptive to flexible hours.

Requirements: Training in this field is usually provided by the agency hiring you. Experience in the food industry would be a help.

Compensation: You will be paid a salary and benefits, which would include travel expenses.

FOOD MANUFACTURER'S REPRESENTATIVE

Description: Manages the marketing of a food product in a specific geographic market. This involves managing the food broker and interacting with the product's customers.

Time Schedule: People in these positions usually work out of their homes and are generally able to set their own schedules. However, travel is a big part of this job, making it somewhat less flexible.

Requirements: You'll need a marketing or sales education and experience in and an understanding of management; also needed is the ability to motivate people to sell and buy your product.

Compensation: You are generally paid an excellent salary and given a company car, plus other standard benefits and bonuses based on the sales your market produces.

FOOD PHOTOGRAPHER

Description: Photographs foods for magazines, cookbooks, menus, and the like.

Time Schedule: Refer to #6 in Chapter 1.

Requirements: You need the knowledge and ability to photograph all kinds of foods so that they will look their most appetizing.

Compensation: Refer to #6 in Chapter 1.

FOOD PRODUCT INVENTOR

Description: Invents different foods for a particular food manufacturer. For example, you would invent a new cereal for a cereal manufacturer, a new frozen dinner for a frozen foods manufacturer, and so on.

Time Schedule: If you work in the company's research center, you will have to keep specific hours. See Chapter 18 for pointers on how to make that situation more flexible. If you work from your home, you will have a great deal more flexibility.

Requirements: You need an education and background in food preparation and all the scientific aspects of it.

Compensation: You will receive either a salary or royalties on the product.

FOOD PRODUCT PACKAGE DESIGNER

Description: Designs food product packages for food manufacturers. You might work directly for the manufacturer as an employee or a freelancer, or you could work for an advertising agency.

Time Schedule: If you are an employee, refer to Chapter 18 to learn how to convince your employer to allow you flexibility. As a freelancer, you will have more control of your own schedule.

Requirements: You will need a graphic arts background and training plus experience with food products. You must understand what will entice someone to pick up the package and then buy the product.

Compensation: If you are an employee, you will be paid a salary. If you are a freelancer, you will be paid for the design. Refer to #1 in Chapter 1 for suggestions on how to price yourself and your product.

✪ FOOD SERVICE SALESPERSON

Description: Sells foods in their unprepared form to restaurants. Foods can include beverages such as teas, coffees, and liquor as well as other food products. This is an outside sales position.

Time Schedule: Refer to #8 in Chapter 1.

Requirements: Besides those detailed in #8 (Chapter 1), you must have an understanding of the restaurant business.

Compensation: Refer to #8.

✪ FOOD VENDOR AT SPECIAL EVENTS

Description: Prepares and sells food (such as hot dogs, hamburgers, ice cream, and soft drinks) at events like ball games, circuses, and conventions. You may either own the vending company or work for it.

Time Schedule: If you own the vending company, you will still be able to have some flexibility because special events generally are not weeklong in duration. If you work for the vending company, you can usually request days off.

Requirements: As an owner, you will need insurance and the appropriate licenses for your community. You will need to know how to prepare the food. Workers simply need to be available and healthy. In some communities workers will need to be licensed as food handlers; the employer will know whether this is necessary.

Compensation: If you are the vendor, refer to #7 in Chapter 1. If you work for the vendor, you will be paid an hourly wage—probably the minimum wage.

GOURMET FOOD RETAILER

Description: Owns, manages, or works in a retail store that specializes in gourmet foods.

Time Schedule: Refer to #7 in Chapter 1.

Requirements: A love of and interest in gourmet foods and the customers who buy them. You'll need exceptional marketing skills if you are the owner of the shop.

Compensation: Refer to #7 in Chapter 1.

KITCHEN GADGET RETAILER

Description: Sells cooking and kitchen gadgets (from the basics, like spatulas, to the more exotic, like candy dippers) from a retail outlet.

Time Schedule: The same as for any retail store. See #7 in Chapter 1 for details.

Requirements: You'll need to know about cooking and how to use all the different gadgets. The love of cooking is a must.

Compensation: Refer to #7 in Chapter 1.

NUTRITION CONSULTANT

Description: Counsels individuals on nutrition so that they can reach their health goals (lower blood pressure, weight loss, and so on).

Time Schedule: Refer to #2 in Chapter 1.

Requirements: A degree in nutrition and experience in this field is very helpful. Some states require special licensing and education. You also need to have empathy for your clients' problems and be truly interested in helping them. Also refer to #2 in Chapter 1 for additional requirements.

Compensation: Refer to #2 in Chapter 1. You can also generate money from selling vitamins and food supplements. Refer to #7 for an explanation on how markup works.

PERSONAL FOOD SHOPPER

Description: Shops for food products for individuals who haven't the time or are unable to do their own shopping. Usually you will be given a list of the items needed.

Time Schedule: You are your own boss, so you set your own hours around your clients' needs. Refer to #10 in Chapter 1.

Requirements: You'll need a good car, patience to fight the crowds in grocery stores (although your flexible hours mean you can shop when it's less crowded), and marketing ability. You must also be very reliable.

Compensation: See #10 in Chapter 1.

POPCORN AND SNACK RETAILER

Description: Sells popcorn and other snacks from a retail setting.

Time Schedule: Refer to #7 in Chapter 1.

Requirements: Refer to #7 in Chapter 1.

Compensation: Refer to #7 in Chapter 1.

RESTAURANT CRITIC

Description: Critiques restaurants for magazines, newspapers, television, or radio.

Time Schedule: Please refer to #3 in Chapter 1.

Requirements: The ability to be fair in analyzing a restaurant's service, food, and ambiance.

Compensation: Refer to #3 in Chapter 1.

✪ RESTAURANT INTERIOR DESIGNER

Description: Decorates the interiors of restaurants.

Time Schedule: As a freelancer, you can set your own hours.

Requirements: You'll need a background and education in interior design, particularly as it applies to dining establishments.

Compensation: Please refer to #2 in Chapter 1. You can also make money by charging a markup on furniture that you sell. Refer to #7 in Chapter 1 for an explanation on how that works.

✪ RESTAURANT MENU PLANNER

Description: Develops new food products, menus, and recipes for restaurants and even major food manufacturers; also creates promotional concepts.

Time Schedule: Some weeks will be very busy, others not so full. It depends on how much interaction with the clients you do. This job requires travel.

Requirements: You need education, such as study at a professional cooking school, and experience in hotels and restaurants.

Compensation: Refer to #2 in Chapter 1.

✪ RESTAURATEUR

Description: Runs a restaurant that might be open only during certain hours (such as dinner) or on certain days. Only a restaurant with limited hours will allow you the flexibility you are interested in.

Time Schedule: If you limit your serving times to a few each day, you will have more flexibility. However, refer to #7 in Chapter 1 for suggestions on how to get help from employees.

Requirements: You'll need knowledge of and experience in the restaurant business. This type of business has a high failure rate, so be sure you know what you are doing. Although it's essential that the food be good in any restaurant, a restaurant with limited hours had better offer *exceptional* service and food in order to build a loyal clientele.

Compensation: Your compensation will be similar to that outlined for retail storekeepers; see #7 in Chapter 1.

WAITRESS/WAITER

Description: Serves food and drinks to the general public in a restaurant.

Time Schedule: These jobs are not normally full-time but are worked during shifts (breakfast, lunch, dinner). Therefore, you will probably be able to request a certain shift and possibly days or blocks of days that you wish not to work.

Requirements: You must be personable and physically strong enough to carry heavy trays.

Compensation: You will be paid an hourly wage, which is usually no more than minimum wage. Much of your compensation will come from tips. Good waiters or waitresses working during a busy shift (dinner and possibly lunch) can triple their salary without too much difficulty.

WINE CONSULTANT

Description: Counsels restaurants, businesses, and wine collectors on the best wines to serve and collect.

Time Schedule: Refer to #2 in Chapter 1.

Requirements: Besides those outlined in #2 (Chapter 1), you must have a great understanding of and passion for wines. Having experience in the manufacture of wine will help.

Compensation: Refer to #2 in Chapter 1.

WINE SALESPERSON

Description: Sells wines to retail stores and eating establishments. This is an outside sales position.

Time Schedule: Refer to #8 in Chapter 1.

Requirements: In addition to those requirements outlined in #8 (Chapter 1), you'll need an understanding of wine and the ability to explain it to your customers.

Compensation: Refer to #8 in Chapter 1.

Chapter 8

The World of Houses and Homes

Next to food, every living thing needs shelter, and for us humans that means some kind of house. There are many careers that support the building and upkeep of homes. If being part of this industry appeals to you, check out these seventy-one options.

ACCESSORIES DECORATOR/SALESPERSON

Description: Plans accessories (paintings, statuary, plants, flowers, and the like) to enhance the furnishings in homes and offices. The job includes selling the accessories, and it is usually an outside sales position.

Time Schedule: Refer to #8 in Chapter 1 for a description of how outside salespeople can have a flexible schedule. If you are working solely as a decorator, refer to #9.

Requirements: You must understand how accessories add character and style to a room. Training and education in interior design is usually required.

Compensation: Refer to #8 and #9 in Chapter 1. If you sell the pieces to your customers, you can also earn money from the markup you charge.

AIR CONDITIONING & HEATING SALESPERSON/INSTALLER

Description: Sells and installs air conditioning and heating equipment for homes and commercial buildings. You might be hired by the end user (the homeowner) or by contractors.

Time Schedule: If you are in the sales end of this business, refer to #8 in Chapter 1. If you are an installer, refer to #9.

Requirements: Refer to #8 and #9 in Chapter 1. In addition, you must understand every facet of the air conditioning and heating business—especially the kind of equipment needed by the customer in terms of the building's structure, the cost-effectiveness, and so on. Both salesperson and installer must be professionals in the field.

Compensation: Refer to #8 and #9 in Chapter 1. If you own the business, you will generate your income from the markup on the units. Refer to #7 in Chapter 1 for further details.

ALARM SYSTEMS INSTALLER/SALESPERSON

Description: Sells and installs all kinds of alarms—fire, gas, burglar—to homes and commercial buildings.

Time Schedule: If you are selling the alarms, refer to #8 in Chapter 1. If you install them, refer to #9.

Requirements: Besides those requirements listed in #8 and #9 in Chapter 1, you will need a professional knowledge of what you are selling and installing.

Compensation: Refer to #8 and #9 in Chapter 1. If you own the business, you will make the majority of your income from the markup of the products.

APARTMENT MANAGER

Description: Manages an apartment building for the company or person who owns the property. Duties include showing and renting the apartments, taking care of apartment and grounds maintenance, collecting the rents, and keeping peace among the tenants.

Time Schedule: Most apartment managers live on the site and keep regular hours; however, some flexibility is possible if the apartment building is large enough to afford an assistant manager or clerical helper. If you are a one-person manager of a small (under twenty-five units) building, your office may be attached to your apartment. This means that you can work out of your home.

Requirements: You must be very well organized in order to keep track of work orders and completions, tenants' names, tenants' reliability in paying rents, and so on. An apartment manager should be able to communicate well and should be personable and adept at managing conflicts.

Compensation: Although your apartment and its paid utilities form a significant part of your compensation, you will also receive a salary and possibly benefits. Some apartment managers also receive bonuses or commissions based on the percentage of units rented.

APARTMENT RENTAL AGENT

Description: Helps people locate apartments to rent or lease. This business is usually operated from a commercial site that is accessible to the public.

Time Schedule: Refer to #7 in Chapter 1 for recommendations on delegating work to employees.

Requirements: You will need any necessary community licenses and the ability to market your business. You will also need the highest integrity. This profession has the reputation of attracting operators who do not always handle clients' monies as honestly as they should. Thus it has a stigma to overcome.

Compensation: You will usually be paid a commission (generally a percentage of the rent) by the apartment owners when you find them a tenant. Occasionally tenants may also pay a fee for your services. Check your competition before establishing your prices.

APPLIANCE SALESPERSON AND SERVICE PERSON

Description: Sells or services large appliances, such as stoves, refrigerators, washing machines, and dryers. The sales are generally made from a retail setting.

Time Schedule: Refer to #7 in Chapter 1 for retailers, to #8 for salespeople, and #9 for service people.

Requirements: Refer to #7, #8, and #9 in Chapter 1. For this job, you'll also need to know about the many different types of appliances and the manufacturers who make them.

Compensation: Refer to #7, #8, and #9 in Chapter 1.

ARCHITECT

Description: Draws up plans that a builder will follow in constructing a house or building.

Time Schedule: Your time will be your own except that you will have to be available for consultations with your client and the builder.

Requirements: A degree in architecture is absolutely necessary; architecture involves engineering as well as artistry. You must also know about the zoning laws in your community.

Compensation: Refer to #2 in Chapter 1.

✪ BABY AND CHILDREN'S FURNITURE RETAILER

Description: Sells furniture for babies and children, usually from a retail store.

Time Schedule: Refer to #7 in Chapter 1.

Requirements: Although the sale of children's furniture takes place in a retail setting, this job has the same requirements that an outside salesperson's job does; refer to #8 in Chapter 1. Also refer to #7 in Chapter 1 for retail storekeeper. It's a big help if you like children.

Compensation: Refer to #8 and #7 in Chapter 1.

✪ BATHROOM SPECIALIST

Description: Designs bathrooms for the end user, bathroom-fixture manufacturers, architects, or interior designers.

Time Schedule: Refer to #2 in Chapter 1.

Requirements: Training in design, particularly as it pertains to bathrooms. Refer also to #2.

Compensation: Refer to #2 in Chapter 1. If you sell bathroom fixtures to individuals, you can also charge a markup.

✪ BUILDING CONTRACTOR

Description: Contracts with individuals to build houses or commercial buildings on a plot of land. You may do all the work yourself or you may subcontract out much of it. You will still have to oversee any work you subcontract.

Time Schedule: To some degree you can block out months when you choose not to work; if you live in a northern climate you will not work during the snowy season. However, once a project is undertaken, you have to spend much time working or overseeing the workers at the site.

Requirements: You will need any licenses required by your state and community. You'll get the training you need by working in the industry.

Compensation: Generally you are paid a fee and compensated for any materials. Refer to #9 in Chapter 1 for suggestions on pricing your services. Be sure to check out your competition before establishing your rates.

BUILDING SUPPLIER

Description: Supplies lumber, nails, cement, and all the other things needed to build a house or commercial structure. A building supplier usually works from a retail store.

Time Schedule: See #7 in Chapter 1.

Requirements: You must know what supplies builders need and must have many resources so that you can find everything at the right price and during the required time frame. You also must know a lot about building in order to give advice and make good buying decisions. Refer to #7 in Chapter 1 for additional requirements.

Compensation: Refer to #7 in Chapter 1.

BUTLER

Description: Works for an individual or family as an overseer of most, if not all, of the house staff. Also takes over the care of guests.

Time Schedule: You will work full-time and live in the home of your employers; however, you will have days off, and you might have some choice in these. You will have more freedom when your employers are not in residence.

Requirements: You'll need training, probably from one of the schools that specialize in training people for this job and placing them in a position. This profession is gaining in popularity.

Compensation: You'll receive a salary plus room and board and possibly a bonus at the end of the year. This job can be very rewarding, but it is demanding.

CABINETMAKER

Description: Builds cabinets in homes and commercial buildings. Either the end user or a building contractor hires a cabinetmaker.

Time Schedule: Although you can block out certain months or weeks when you wish not to work, you will have to meet deadlines once you have contracted to do a job.

Requirements: You must know how to do the work, which is ordinarily learned by being an apprentice cabinetmaker. You may have to belong to a union and have state or local licenses.

Compensation: Your fee will be based on the hours that a project will take and the cost of the materials used.

Obviously, the more expensive the wood and fixtures, the more money you will make based on your markup. Refer to #9 in Chapter 1.

CARPET CLEANER

Description: Cleans carpets in commercial and residential properties.

Time Schedule: Refer to #9 in Chapter 1.

Requirements: You must have not only the necessary equipment but also any licenses required by your state or city. Good service is vital in this business because you are dependent on repeat customers and referrals to make your business successful. Refer to #9 in Chapter 1 for further requirements.

Compensation: Refer to #9 in Chapter 1.

CARPET DESIGNER

Description: Designs carpets for manufacturers and possibly end users. This includes every facet of carpeting, from color, texture, thickness of the fibers to elaborate designs and borders. Area rugs and their patterns are part of this as well. A carpet designer works with carpet manufacturers and interior designers.

Time Schedule: As a freelancer, you can control your own schedule.

Requirements: You'll need an education in design and experience in carpeting. Refer to #9 in Chapter 1.

Compensation: Refer to #9 in Chapter 1. If you also sell the carpeting, you can charge a markup.

CARPET REPAIRPERSON

Description: Repairs carpets that have been burned, water-stained, torn, or damaged in some other way. You are usually hired by the end user or insurance companies.

Time Schedule: Your schedule is that of a service person; refer to #9 in Chapter 1.

Requirements: You need expertise and the correct tools. Refer to #9 in Chapter 1 for additional information.

Compensation: Refer to #1 in Chapter 9.

CARPET RETAILER

Description: Sells carpeting from a retail store or at the customer's location.

Time Schedule: If you own the store, see #7 in Chapter 1. If you are an outside salesperson showing carpet samples in people's homes or offices, refer to #8 in Chapter 2.

Requirements: In addition to the requirements listed in #7 and #8 in Chapter 1, you also need to know how to decorate with carpeting. This includes a good understanding of how color affects a home.

Compensation: Refer to #7 and #8 in Chapter 1.

CHIMNEY SWEEP

Description: Cleans out chimneys, usually in residences.

Time Schedule: Although this may be seasonal work, you can generally set your own schedule.

Requirements: You'll need the knowledge and tools to do the job, plus any licenses that might be required by your community or state. Excellent physical condition is also vital.

Compensation: Refer to #9 in Chapter 1.

CLEANING PERSON

Description: Provides cleaning service to residences and commercial establishments. You can either own the service or work for it. This business can be run from home.

Time Schedule: If you own the business, you have to be available to handle calls and dispatch workers. This is perfect for a housebound individual (such as a mother with children at home). Refer to #7 in Chapter 1 for ideas on delegating some of the work to trusted employees. If you work for a cleaning service, you can generally establish your own availability.

Requirements: As the owner, you must be able to attract and keep good workers. You also must have high standards that will earn you repeat customers. Marketing ability is very important. Check with your local government regarding any licensing you'll need. You and your employees will also have to be bonded.

Compensation: Your income will be generated from what you charge for your service. If you own the business, you will have to pay your employees and cover your overhead. Refer to #7 in Chapter 1 for an explanation of how retailers make money because their situation is very similar to yours. If you are a worker, you will be paid an hourly salary plus expenses. Some cleaning services also offer benefits and bonuses to good employees who have been with them for a long time.

CONCRETE CONTRACTOR

Description: Works for general contractors and is responsible for pouring foundations for all types of buildings. The job includes selecting the right concrete for the job, excavating and moving dirt, and building basements.

Time Schedule: In many parts of the country this work is seasonal, with the winter months being dead. When you can work, you need to work as much as possible to build a good financial cushion. This job is wonderful for someone who wants to take time off during the winter months.

Requirements: You will need a mastery of all the technical aspects of this job, which can be learned by working for a concrete contractor. You will also need the necessary equipment and any bonding that might be required. Be sure to check with your local government to determine whether or not you will need any state or local licenses.

Compensation: Your fee should take into account the cost of your materials, labor, and overhead. Refer to #7 in Chapter 1 for advice on how to figure this kind of profit.

DESIGNER OF CLOSETS AND ACCESSORIES

Description: Designs and sells the necessary accessories to maximize the efficiency of closets. This is usually done at the customer's location.

Time Schedule: Refer to #8 in Chapter 1 if you are going to sell and to #9 if you are going to design and install the closet accessories. Frequently both are done by the same person.

Requirements: In addition to the requirements outlined in #8 and #9 (Chapter 1), you will have to be well trained in this business and have some mechanical ability. You should also know how to market your services.

Compensation: Refer to #8 and #9 in Chapter 1.

DESIGNER OF FURNITURE FOR CHILDREN AND BABIES

Description: Designs furniture that will be used for children and babies. This job is generally done for manufacturers of this furniture.

Time Schedule: As a freelancer, you have control of your own schedule.

Requirements: You need formal education in furniture design and safety; you also need an understanding of children and should keep up with the latest fads that excite them.

Compensation: You will generally sell your design to a manufacturer for a fee and possibly royalties on the sales of the items. Always try to negotiate the latter.

DRAPERY DESIGNER

Description: Designs draperies and other window treatments for individuals and possibly retail stores that sell them. Drapery manufacturers might also use a drapery designer. You might even design the fabric to be used for draperies.

Time Schedule: Refer to #2 in Chapter 1.

Requirements: You'll need education and experience in this field. The ability to market yourself and your service is also critical as is sales ability. Refer to #2 and #8 in Chapter 1.

Compensation: If you sell the designs for draperies or fabrics outright to drapery manufacturers, you will be paid a fee and possibly royalties for your designs. If you design drapery treatments for the end user, you can charge a markup on the drapery plus labor for your time.

DRAPERY MAKER

Description: Sews draperies, either for the end user (custom made) or for a drapery manufacturer (to be sold ready-made).

Time Schedule: If you work as an employee for a manufacturer, refer to Chapter 18 for suggestions on how to arrange some flexible scheduling. As a freelancer, you can dictate your own hours; however, you will have to meet deadlines.

Requirements: You'll need experience and knowledge in drapery making; if you are working on your own, you'll need good equipment and a large place to work. You'll need to know how to market your services if you are self-employed.

Compensation: Refer to #1 in Chapter 1 for suggestions on how to price your service.

DRAPERY REPAIRPERSON

Description: Repairs draperies that have been damaged by tearing, fire, smoke, water, or any other disaster. This business ties in well with drapery making or carpet repairing.

Time Schedule: Refer to #9 in Chapter 1.

Requirements: Obviously you need the expertise to repair draperies, and you can acquire this by sewing them. You also need to know how to repair fabric itself and that can be learned with experience working for fabric manufacturers, dry cleaners, and the like. It also helps to know how to market yourself and your services to anyone who might need them, including insurance companies.

Compensation: Refer to #9 in Chapter 1.

DRAPERY SALESPERSON

Description: Sells custom-made draperies to the end users, usually people who need window treatments for their homes or offices. This is usually an outside sales job.

Time Schedule: See #8 in Chapter 1.

Requirements: In addition to those requirements outlined in #8 in Chapter 1, you must also have a flair for decorating and should understand how draperies and other window coverings enhance an interior environment.

Compensation: Refer to #8 in Chapter 1.

ELECTRICAL CONTRACTOR

Description: Installs the electricity in new homes and buildings, usually working through a building contractor.

Time Schedule: Although you have to work during certain phases of the building, you can establish blocks of days or weeks when you will not be available. Because building is frequently seasonal, you may have the winter months free to do other things.

Requirements: Besides the licensing and bonding required by your state and community, you must have training and experience in electrical installation.

Compensation: Refer to #9 in Chapter 1.

EVICTION SERVER

Description: Aids landlords in evicting tenants. This job includes helping landlords fill out the legal paperwork and also serving the tenants with the eviction notice.

Time Schedule: Refer to #2 and #9 in Chapter 1.

Requirements: You need to understand the laws pertaining to evictions and should be able to fill out the legal paperwork.

Compensation: You will usually be paid a flat rate. Refer to #2 and #9 in Chapter 1.

FENCE DESIGNERS/CONTRACTOR

Description: Installs fences for residences and commercial properties. The job might include designing decorative fences.

Time Schedule: To some extent you can control your own schedule, but once you start a project you must finish it within the time established.

Requirements: You need expertise and the necessary licenses—and also the appropriate tools. Knowing how to market yourself and your services is very important.

Compensation: Refer to #9 in Chapter 1.

FLOOR CLEANER AND WAXER

Description: Provides a floor-cleaning and waxing service for homes and commercial establishments. This is much more extensive than what a mere housecleaning does to floors.

Time Schedule: Refer to #9 in Chapter 1.

Requirements: You'll need the right equipment and must know how to clean many different types of floors (the wrong kind of cleaner can permanently ruin some finishes). You will need to be bonded and possibly licensed. Check with your city about the latter.

Compensation: Refer to #9 in Chapter 1.

FLOORING CONTRACTOR

Description: Installs floors in new buildings, both commercial and residential, usually through a building contractor.

Time Schedule: Although you have some control over your schedule, especially in blocking out times when you are not available, you will have to do whatever work you contract for within the established time. Because building is seasonal in some parts of the country, you may have the winter months free.

Requirements: In addition to any licenses and bonding required by your state and city, you need to know how to install floors and should be able to purchase the supplies at a good price.

Compensation: Refer to #9 in Chapter 1. If you supply the materials, you can make money from your markup on those as well.

FLOOR REFINISHER

Description: Refinishes floors in residences and commercial buildings. You might work directly for the end user or for real estate brokers or contractors who are fixing up houses for resale. You might also work for insurance companies who will hire you to repair damages from fire or water. This business ties in well with a similar one and can be run from home.

Time Schedule: Refer to #9 in Chapter 1.

Requirements: You'll need to know how to refinish floors and have the necessary bonds and licenses. Knowing how to market your services is also vital.

Compensation: Refer again to #9 in Chapter 1.

FURNITURE REPAIRPERSON/REFINISHER

Description: Repairs and refinishes wood furniture, usually for those who own the pieces. This is an excellent business to run out of your home workshop.

Time Schedule: Refer to #9 in Chapter 1.

Requirements: Besides having the ability and necessary tools to repair and refinish furniture, you will need to check with your local government regarding any licensing or bonding requirements.

Compensation: Refer to #9 in Chapter 1.

FURNITURE RETAILER

Description: Sells furniture of all kinds from a retail store.

Time Schedule: You will have to work when the store is open, but you usually can request certain times and days off. Most people purchase furniture on weekends, however, so you will want to work then to maximize your income.

Requirements: You'll need the ability to relate well to people; it's very important to have an understanding of how furniture is made, its design, and how it can be used to make a home or office efficient and attractive. You will also need all the usual selling skills. (Refer to #8 in Chapter 1.)

Compensation: You will be paid a salary or "draw" against a commission. Refer again to #8 in Chapter 1.

HANDYMAN

Description: Fixes things for people around their houses or businesses. As the name implies, you should be "handy" with tools and should be able to do many different tasks, from assembling furniture to installing chandeliers to nailing down loose shingles on a roof. Anything and everything that needs to be fixed around a home is worked on by a handyman service.

Time Schedule: As an independent contractor, you can set your own schedule, but you do have to be available pretty consistently in order to stay in business.

Requirements: You have to be able to fix almost anything, and you need to be able to work with tools. The ability to improvise is helpful.

Compensation: See #9 in Chapter 1.

HOMEBUILDER

Description: Builds homes, either under contract to individuals or for future resale.

Time Schedule: You can establish your own schedule but will have to work around client needs and the weather in your locale.

Requirements: You need to know how to build houses and how to find good subcontractors (electricians, plumbers, and so forth) to do the work you cannot; you also need to be bonded and licensed.

Compensation: If you are working for an individual, refer to #9 in Chapter 1. If you are working for yourself, your income will come from the difference between your costs and the selling price of the houses you build.

HOME DECORATING WRITER

Description: Writes about home decorating for magazines and books.

Time Schedule: Refer to #11 in Chapter 1.

Requirements: In addition to those requirements outlined in #11 in Chapter 1, you must understand and like home decorating.

Compensation: Refer to #11 in Chapter 1.

✪ HOME DESIGNER AND PLANNER

Description: Offers a home designing and planning service for people who might want to build their house themselves or act as their own contractor. This service helps clients find a design (building blueprints) as well as subcontractors and resources.

Time Schedule: Refer to #2 in Chapter 1.

Requirements: You need to know about home design and building, either from education or experience or both.

Compensation: Refer to #2 in Chapter 1.

✪ HOME OFFICE DESIGNER

Description: Designs an office in the home.

Time Schedule: Refer to #2 and #9 in Chapter 1.

Requirements: You must know how to design an efficient office that is aesthetically attractive and in keeping with the ambiance of the home. This isn't as easy as it sounds.

Compensation: See #2 and #9 in Chapter 1.

✪ HOME PHOTOGRAPHER

Description: Photographs houses for their owners, for magazines, and for real estate agents to use in multiple listing books and advertisements.

Time Schedule: Refer to #6 in Chapter 1.

Requirements: You must have the abilities outlined in #6 (Chapter 1), plus specialized ability to photograph houses to their advantage.

Compensation: Refer to #6 in Chapter 1.

HOT TUB AND WHIRLPOOL CONTRACTOR

Description: Installs hot tubs and whirlpools either for the end user or for builders.

Time Schedule: Refer to #9 in Chapter 1.

Requirements: You will need expertise in this field in addition to all the necessary bonding and licensing required by your community.

Compensation: Refer to #9 in Chapter 1. You can also earn a markup on the hot tubs and whirlpools if you sell them.

HOUSEKEEPER

Description: Keeps house for individuals, which includes all facets of running a household, from shopping to cleaning to possibly even cooking. In a hotel, the position of housekeeper is limited to cleaning rooms.

Time Schedule: If you work for an individual, you will have a full-time position, and it might even be a live-in position. However, you might be able to arrange your own days off and some flexible time. If you work for a hotel, you may work part-time. Check Chapter 18 if you are expected to work full-time.

Requirements: If you clean rooms in a hotel, you will need a willingness to do the work well. If you are a housekeeper for an individual family, you will probably need experience and references.

Compensation: You will be paid an hourly rate at a hotel and a salary and board and room if you work for individuals.

HOUSE PAINTER

Description: Paints the inside and outside of houses for individuals or builders.

Time Schedule: As an independent contractor, your time is your own, although you will have to work around your customers' needs.

Requirements: You'll need the ability to paint neatly and frugally; you'll need to be punctual about getting the work done on time. In your area, you may need special licenses, bonding, and membership in a union.

Compensation: See #9 in Chapter 1.

HOUSE-SITTER

Description: Stays in people's homes and takes care of pets, plants, and the house while the owners are away on a trip. This service is designed to protect the house and its contents from robbery and any other mischief.

Time Schedule: You can choose weeks or months when you do not wish to work; but when you do, you may be on an assignment for days or weeks at a time. Generally, however, you are free to leave the premises during the day or a part of it. Most people who employ house-sitters want them there during the night.

Requirements: Honesty and integrity are paramount for the obvious reason that you have access to people's valuables. Being neat and clean is also important. You need to know how to take care of pets and plants. For your own protection, you may wish to be bonded.

Compensation: You are usually paid a flat fee for the period of time you are watching the house. Be certain that it is enough to compensate you for your trouble.

INTERIOR DESIGNER

Description: Designs the interiors of homes and offices as well as commercial buildings. These designs include everything, from floor, wall, and window coverings to furniture and accessories.

Time Schedule: As an independent businessperson, your schedule is up to you, but you do have to work around your clients' needs.

Requirements: You'll need education and training in designing interiors, plus the selling ability to convince people to consider your professional opinion even when they have decided opinions of their own—perhaps quite different from yours. Some states require special licensing, so check with yours. If you have the necessary education and experience to become a certified member of the National Council for Interior Design, you will be more likely to attract clients.

Compensation: You will get a fee for doing the job, which can be based on an hourly rate. You can also charge a markup on items that you sell to your clients, and if you do so, most of your income will come from the markup. Refer to #2 and #7 in Chapter 1.

JANITOR

Description: Cleans halls, basements, patios, and the grounds of apartment and office buildings.

Time Schedule: You will probably have to keep specific hours; however, you may be able to negotiate your days off. Also see Chapter 18 for ideas on how to get your employer to let you have some flexibility.

Requirements: You need to know how to clean efficiently; you must be conscientious. And because you may be "on call" to answer tenants' sudden demands, you will need patience, a sense of humor, and a general liking for people.

Compensation: You will probably be paid a salary, which can be set by the week or hour. At Christmas time, however, hard-working janitors are usually given sizable tips from grateful tenants.

KITCHEN SPECIALIST

Description: Specializes in designing and setting up efficient and attractive kitchens. You might work for the end user or for a builder or architect.

Time Schedule: Refer to #2 in Chapter 1.

Requirements: You'll need education, training, and experience in design—especially of kitchens. You'll also need the ability to market yourself and your service.

Compensation: Refer to #2 in Chapter 1.

LAMP/LIGHTING DESIGNER

Description: Designs lighting and lamps, possibly for lighting manufacturers as well as for builders.

Time Schedule: As a freelancer, you can pretty much control your own schedule.

Requirements: Education and experience in design and some knowledge of the principles of lighting.

Compensation: If you sell your designs to manufacturers, you will be paid a flat rate for the design and perhaps royalties on the sales. If you are designing lighting for the interior of a builder's project, refer to #2 in Chapter 1.

LAMP/LIGHTING REPAIRPERSON AND INSTALLER

Description: Repairs and installs lighting and lamps.

Time Schedule: See #9 in Chapter 1.

Requirements: You must understand—from education as well as experience—how to repair and install many different kinds of lighting fixtures and lamps.

Compensation: Refer to #9 in Chapter 1.

LAMP/LIGHTING RETAILER

Description: Sells lamps and lighting fixtures from a retail store.

Time Schedule: See #7 in Chapter 1.

Requirements: Besides those requirements outlined in #7, you must be interested in lighting and should know how it can be used to decorate as well as to illuminate.

Compensation: Refer to #7 in Chapter 1.

LANDLORD LEGAL SPECIALIST

Description: Helps landlords with all legal services pertaining to renting property. This includes creating leases, checking credit, and helping with evictions.

Time Schedule: Refer to #2 in Chapter 1.

Requirements: You'll need to understand all the laws that pertain to managing properties. You can acquire this knowledge by working in law firms or the real estate industry. You need skill in marketing your own service; refer also to #2 in Chapter 1.

Compensation: Refer to #2 in Chapter 1.

✪ LOCKSMITH

Description: Installs and repairs locks in homes, commercial buildings, automobiles, and so on. This job also includes unlocking doors for people who find themselves without their keys. This business can be run from home, using a van supplied with all the necessary materials and tools.

Time Schedule: Refer to #9 in Chapter 1.

Requirements: You'll need expertise in locks and the ability to market your services as outlined in #9 (Chapter 1).

Compensation: Refer to #9 in Chapter 1.

✪ MOBILE HOME DESIGNER

Description: Designs mobile homes for mobile home manufacturers.

Time Schedule: As a freelancer, you will usually be able to schedule your own hours.

Requirements: You'll need knowledge and training in design, especially mobile home design. You'll also need the ability to market yourself, as outlined in #2 in Chapter 1.

Compensation: You will usually sell your design to the manufacturer for a fee, but you can also try to negotiate royalties on the sales. Refer to #1 in Chapter 1 for suggestions on how to price yourself and your product correctly.

✪ MOBILE HOME MOVER AIDES

Description: Drives the lead automobile, equipped with flags and signs calling attention to a "wide load," as the mobile home is being moved.

Time Schedule: You can choose the days you wish to work.

Requirements: A good, low-mileage car and the desire to do the job, which can be obtained through mobile home dealers and movers. Reliability is necessary.

Compensation: You'll usually be paid by the hour plus mileage.

MOBILE HOME SALESPERSON

Description: Sells mobile homes from mobile home dealerships.

Time Schedule: Although you will be working for an employer, you should be able to negotiate for the days you want to work.

Requirements: You'll need sales ability. Refer to #8 in Chapter 1. You should also understand and enjoy the mobile home industry and those who choose this form of living.

Compensation: Your income will come mostly from commissions; however, you may get an advance or small base salary. Refer to #8 in Chapter 1.

PAPERHANGER

Description: Hangs wallpaper in homes or buildings.

Time Schedule: See #9 in Chapter 1.

Requirements: You must know how to hang all kinds of wallcoverings neatly and quickly. Check with your local government regarding any necessary licenses, bonds, and union membership.

Compensation: Refer to #9 in Chapter 1. Many paperhangers charge by the roll instead of by the hour. Much depends on the job. Charge by the hour if it is a large job, by the roll if small.

PATIO BUILDER

Description: Builds patios for homeowners or contractors.

Time Schedule: If building is seasonal where you live, you will have the winter months off. As a freelancer, you should have some control of your schedule.

Requirements: Besides knowing how to build a patio, you will also need to be bonded and licensed. Also refer to #9 in Chapter 1.

Compensation: Refer to #9 in Chapter 1.

PERSONAL SERVANT

Description: Cares for an individual, sometimes by taking care of personal needs and sometimes by also overseeing the running of the household. This job might even include light housecleaning and cooking.

Time Schedule: If you work full-time, you might even have to live in. However, you should be able to request definite days off as well as specific working hours.

Requirements: Knowledge and experience or training in the specific duties that will be required of you. There are now domestic help agencies that train people and place them in these positions.

Compensation: You will probably be paid a salary and benefits.

PLUMBER

Description: Repairs and replaces broken plumbing; might also install plumbing for an end user or plumbing contractor.

Time Schedule: Refer to #9 in Chapter 1.

Requirements: You'll need training and experience in plumbing, plus necessary local licenses, bonds, and possible union membership.

Compensation: Refer to #9 in Chapter 1.

PLUMBING CONTRACTOR

Description: Installs plumbing for building contractors.

Time Schedule: Refer to #9 in Chapter 1.

Requirements: You'll need training and experience in plumbing. You'll also need the bonds and licenses required by your community. Refer to #9 in Chapter 1 for additional requirements.

Compensation: Refer to #9 in Chapter 1.

REAL ESTATE APPRAISER

Description: Appraises real estate for individuals, banks and lending institutions, and government agencies (such as the Veterans Administration).

Time Schedule: Refer to #9 in Chapter 1.

Requirements: Training and licensing in real estate appraisal.

Compensation: Refer to #9 in Chapter 1.

REAL ESTATE SALESPERSON

Description: Sells real estate.

Time Schedule: Although you can control your own time schedule, success in this business requires that you be available most weekends and during the summer seasons when more people are buying houses and moving.

Requirements: In addition to those requirements outlined in #8 in Chapter 1, you will need the appropriate licenses required in your state. Patience is especially important in this field because most people take a long time to decide on a house.

Compensation: You will make a commission on what you sell; you will also make commissions when houses you list for sale are sold, even if another salesperson is responsible for the sale. Houses are expensive, so your commissions will be very high; but remember that you may go for several months without a sale.

SEWING MACHINE REPAIRPERSON

Description: Repairs and services sewing machines.

Time Schedule: Refer to #9 in Chapter 1.

Requirements: You must have a knowledge of sewing machines—all brands—and how to repair and service them.

Compensation: Refer to #9 in Chapter 1.

SEWING MACHINE SALESPERSON

Description: Sells sewing machines, usually from a retail store.

Time Schedule: Refer to #7 and #8 in Chapter 1.

Requirements: In addition to those requirements listed in #7 and #8 in Chapter 1, you must know how to sew on a machine well enough to give demonstrations and understand the importance of the various machine features.

Compensation: Refer to #7 and #8 in Chapter 1.

SMALL APPLIANCE REPAIRPERSON

Description: Repairs and services many different small appliances, such as coffeemakers, toasters, blenders, irons, and the like from a store or a mobile van or both. Sometimes new small appliances or rebuilt ones are offered for sale to customers whose appliances cannot be fixed.

Time Schedule: Refer to #6 and #9 in Chapter 1.

Requirements: You will need to know how to fix a diversity of small appliances and must be resourceful in helping people save money.

Compensation: Refer to #9 in Chapter 1. If you sell small appliances, you can also increase your income by the markup that you charge.

SUN ROOM, GREENHOUSE, AND SOLARIUM BUILDER

Description: Builds sunrooms, greenhouses, and solariums for end users or for builders.

Time Schedule: Refer to #9 in Chapter 1.

Requirements: You'll need to know how to build these home additions as well as have the necessary bonding and licensing. Refer to #9 in Chapter 1 for additional requirements.

Compensation: Refer to #9 in Chapter 1.

SWIMMING POOL CONTRACTOR

Description: Builds swimming pools either for the end user or for a builder.

Time Schedule: Refer to #9 in Chapter 1. Of course, you will have to work around the builder's or customer's schedule.

Requirements: Expertise in and licensing to build a swimming pool. Also refer to #9 in Chapter 1.

Compensation: Refer to #9 in Chapter 1.

UPHOLSTERER

Description: Upholsters furniture. This could also include making custom upholstered furniture.

Time Schedule: Refer to #9 in Chapter 1.

Requirements: Experience and training in upholstering furniture. This can best be gained from working for upholstered furniture manufacturers or upholsterers. You will also need a bond and possibly state and city licenses.

Compensation: Refer to #9 in Chapter 1.

WALLPAPER DESIGNER

Description: Designs wallpaper for wallpaper manufacturers.

Time Schedule: As a freelance designer, you should be able to control your own schedule.

Requirements: You'll need an art background, especially in design.

Compensation: If you sell your designs to a manufacturer, you will probably receive a fee. You might also be able to receive royalties from the sales.

WINDOW SUPPLIER

Description: Sells windows to contractors and end users, usually from a retail store.

Time Schedule: Refer to #7 in Chapter 1.

Requirements: Refer to #7 in Chapter 1. You'll also need to know about the different kinds of windows, how they should be used in homes and buildings; you should be familiar with the various manufacturers.

Compensation: Refer to #7 in Chapter 1.

WINDOW TINTER

Description: Tints windows of residences and commercial buildings.

Time Schedule: Refer to #9 in Chapter 1.

Requirements: You'll need a bond and the proper licenses as well as expertise in window tinting. Refer to #9 in Chapter 1.

Compensation: Refer to #9 in Chapter 1.

WINDOW WASHER

Description: Washes windows of residences and commercial buildings.

Time Schedule: Refer to #9 in Chapter 1.

Requirements: You'll need the know-how and patience to do a really good job of cleaning windows. Otherwise, all you need is a pail, rags, cleaning supplies, a tall ladder, and the ability to market yourself.

Compensation: Refer to #9 in Chapter 1. This can be a much more lucrative business than most people realize because almost no one washes windows anymore.

Chapter 9

The Legal World

Say the word *law*, and lawyers, courtrooms, and law enforcement come to mind. There are many positions related to the law that allow you to work when you want and still make money—and you will love your job as well. Make your selection from the seventeen that follow.

ATTORNEY

Description: Handles legal affairs for individuals, businesses, and corporations. A lawyer may handle criminal cases, divorces, adoptions, personal injury cases, wills, contracts, and so on. Most attorneys specialize in one category (for example, criminal law) because the laws change frequently and are so complex that it's difficult to keep up with them all.

Time Schedule: Although most attorneys work full-time, some are cutting back on hours in order to "have a life." One that I spoke with works five hours a day and uses a part-time secretary. He limits the cases he handles and works with other lawyers. Refer to #7 in Chapter 1.

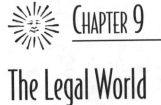

Requirements: You need to graduate from law school, pass the bar exam, and be licensed in your state. It's best to be an experienced attorney before you cut back on your hours; you will have a roster of clients to serve and a network of other lawyers to work with—to give cases to and to get cases from, as your schedule and wishes allow.

Compensation: Lawyers are paid by the hour and also, in personal injury cases, by a percentage of the settlement. Refer to #7 in Chapter 1.

ATTORNEY REFERRAL SERVICE—OWNER

Description: Provides attorney referrals to people seeking a lawyer for a specific legal problem. Attorneys pay to be listed with the service and provide essential background information.

Time Schedule: You or an employee will need to cover the phones during weekday business hours. Refer to #7 in Chapter 1 for suggestions on delegating work to employees.

Requirements: You'll need the ability to market your business and knowledge of the legal profession; it's very important to have a friendly, confidence-building telephone presence.

Compensation: You receive a monthly fee from attorneys. The amount depends on how much business you send their way.

ATTORNEY SUPPORT SERVICE PROVIDER

Description: Provides support services, such as investigators, process servers, and so on for lawyers.

Time Schedule: Although this business can be run from a home office, someone has to cover the telephone during business hours. If you use employees to help you, refer to #7 in Chapter 1 for suggestions on delegating some of the work to them.

Requirements: You must have a vast network of legal professionals available to go to work; you must know how to market your services to attorneys.

Compensation: Your income is generated from what you charge the attorneys for the people you provide, minus your costs of doing business (which includes paying the people who do the work).

COURT REPORTER

Description: Records every word spoken in court on a special machine and then transposes it into a written report that can be used by the attorneys and judge involved in the case.

Time Schedule: Depending on your community's court system, this can be a full-time position or a freelance one. If the former, refer to Chapter 18 for suggestions on making the job more flexible. If you work as a freelancer, you will be able to better control your schedule.

Requirements: Special training, which is gained by attending special court reporter schools as well as vocational schools. You learn at a much more accelerated pace in a court reporter school.

Compensation: A full-time employee will be paid a salary, plus time and a half for overtime. Freelancers will be paid by the hour.

JURY CONSULTANT

Description: Counsels lawyers and district attorneys on the selection of specific people to serve on a jury for a particular trial.

Time Schedule: Refer to #2 in Chapter 1.

Requirements: You'll need a law degree; you must have passed the state bar examination and must hold your state's license. You'll also need experience in studying juror profiles and selecting juries so that you can predict how a prospective juror would be likely to vote on a case. Psychological training is also helpful.

Compensation: Refer to #2 in Chapter 1.

LAW SCHOOL INSTRUCTOR

Description: Teaches law in universities or in schools that train paralegals and legal secretaries.

Time Schedule: Refer to #5 in Chapter 1.

Requirements: You'll need legal expertise and possibly a law license; refer also to #5 in Chapter 1.

Compensation: Refer to #5 in Chapter 1.

LEGAL CONSULTANT

Description: Gives legal counsel to other lawyers or to individuals. This counsel usually pertains to a very specialized area of the law.

Time Schedule: Refer to #2 in Chapter 1.

Requirements: In addition to having a legal background and being licensed by your state, you must be an acknowledged expert in the area you plan to counsel in.

Compensation: Refer to #2 in Chapter 1.

LEGAL RESEARCHER

Description: Researches all points of law, which include past verdicts on similar cases, common law, legislation, and the like. The work is done for attorneys.

Time Schedule: If you work full-time for a law office, refer to Chapter 18 on ways to gain flexibility. You may also work part-time or be on call (you work when they need you and if you are available). If you have the latter arrangement, you can control your own time schedule.

Requirements: You will need a legal background, preferably as a paralegal.

Compensation: If you are a full-time employee, you will be paid a salary and benefits. If you work part-time or on call, you will be paid an hourly rate dependent on your background.

LEGAL SECRETARY

Description: Works in a law office; duties usually include typing all kinds of legal documents and perhaps handling billing for the attorney.

Time Schedule: Most law offices require a secretary to be there during office hours. However, you might be able to convince your employer to let you have some flexibility by using the techniques in Chapter 18. Some legal secretaries do freelance work from their homes as well.

Requirements: You need to know how to type; you need some familiarity with legal terms and formats for legal documents; you'll also have to be able to take dictation or use a dictating machine. Good organizational skills are also very important.

Compensation: Legal secretaries are usually at the top of the income scale for secretaries. If you work from home, charge by the hour based on the going rate for full-time legal secretaries in your area.

LEGAL SEMINAR SPEAKER

Description: Gives seminars to groups of laypeople who have an interest in the particular legal subject presented. Common subjects include wills and trusts, bankruptcy, family law, and information that would be of interest to writers.

Time Schedule: You can set your own hours and schedule as outlined in #2 in Chapter 1.

Requirements: You need to be an acknowledged expert in the fields you speak about; in most cases, that will require a law degree and experience as an attorney. You also must have excellent public speaking ability and be entertaining.

Compensation: You'll be paid a fee if you're speaking at a seminar marketed by someone else. If you're marketing the seminar yourself, then your income will come from what you charge for attendance minus your costs (such as rental of the facility you use).

LEGAL WRITER

Description: Writes legal textbooks, articles for trade periodicals, and articles read by the general public.

Time Schedule: Refer to #11 in Chapter 1.

Requirements: In addition to the requirements outlined in #11 that pertain to writing, you will also need a legal background.

Compensation: Refer to #11 in Chapter 1.

PATENT ATTORNEY

Description: Specializes in handling all the legalities pertaining to patents. This work is usually done for a person or corporation securing a patent.

Time Schedule: This practice can be limited to part-time. (See "Attorney" in this chapter.)

Requirements: You'll need to be a licensed attorney in your state, and you'll need expertise in the legalities of patents.

Compensation: This type of attorney is generally paid by the hour.

PATENT CONSULTANT

Description: Gives counsel to people who are interested in getting a patent on an invention.

Time Schedule: Refer to #2 in Chapter 1.

Requirements: You'll need to be an acknowledged expert in patent law. It would help to have experience as a patent attorney. You should also know about marketing, because you will be advising people on whether they have invented something that is marketable.

Compensation: Refer to #2 in Chapter 1.

POLYGRAPH TECHNICIAN

Description: Provides polygraph testing for clients, who are usually attorneys and law enforcement professionals. The polygraph technician records people's responses to questions by using a specially designed machine (polygraph) that records subtle changes in the subjects' heart rate, blood pressure, breathing rhythm, and body moisture as they respond to the questions. This is commonly called a lie detector test.

Time Schedule: You can set your own schedule to some degree; however, you will have to be available to accommodate your clients and their subjects.

Requirements: You need to know how to administer the test and read its results. Depending on where you live, you may need a psychologist's degree and special licensing.

Compensation: You will be paid a fee. Refer to #2 in Chapter 1.

PRIVATE INVESTIGATOR

Description: Investigates individuals with the intent of finding certain evidence. People who hire investigators can be spouses, attorneys trying a case where the individual being investigated plays a pertinent role, businesses interested in how their employees or potential employees live, and so on.

Time Schedule: You can set your own hours and your own pace, but once you accept an assignment, the hours might be long.

Requirements: You must be licensed in all the states that you intend to work in. A background in law enforcement (such as experience as a police officer) is also necessary. In order to get business, you also need to get on your city's court-approved investigator list and network with attorneys.

Compensation: You will be paid an hourly fee plus expenses. How much you make depends on your reputation and how difficult the assignment is.

PROCESS SERVER

Description: Serves court summonses or notifications of court actions to individuals, usually at their homes or in public places.

Time Schedule: Because you work as a freelancer, you can arrange your own schedule; but when you have papers to serve, you may have to wait for several hours until the person you are serving is available.

Requirements: There are no specific requirements other than the willingness to do the work efficiently. You will need reliable transportation. Visit lawyers' offices and introduce yourself in order to get business.

Compensation: You will be paid by the hour, plus expenses.

SECURITY GUARD

Description: Works for security companies guarding commercial buildings, apartment buildings, hotels, gated communities, hospitals, and so on.

Time Schedule: Security guards usually work certain shifts. However, you can generally request the shift you wish to work and the days.

Requirements: In most states, security guards need licenses. If you carry a gun, you will need a license for that as well. Every company has basic training that employees have to undergo before they can do the job, but the training usually is not difficult. Students, retired persons, and off-duty police officers usually enjoy this job.

Compensation: You will be paid an hourly rate depending on your experience and length of time on the job. Occasionally you might get paid vacations and holidays. This is not a high-paying job but offers a good supplemental income.

Chapter 10

The World of Money Matters

Take a dollar bill out of your pocket and look at it. In this chapter, I identify twenty-three job possibilities related to that dollar. One of these opportunities might well interest you.

BANKRUPTCY CONSULTANT

Description: Counsels individuals and companies on whether to declare bankruptcy or to consider other alternatives.

Time Schedule: Refer to #2 in Chapter 1.

Requirements: You'll need expertise in the legal aspects of declaring bankruptcy and its alternatives. Experience in this field, as a bill collector, bankruptcy attorney, or paralegal, would be very helpful.

Compensation: Refer to #2 in Chapter 1.

BANK TELLER

Description: Waits on the bank's customers, helping them make deposits, cash checks, buy traveler's checks, and make payments on loans. The teller also answers questions about their accounts.

Time Schedule: Many banks today are hiring part-time tellers or offering flexible hours. Refer to Chapter 18 for suggestions on turning a full-time job into a flexible one.

Requirements: The better your education, the better chance you have of getting a job with a bank (and the more likely you are to get promoted); however, a college degree is not necessary. A professional appearance and pleasing personality, mathematical skills, and honesty are all necessary. You may be given a polygraph test before being hired.

Compensation: If you are a full-time employee, you will be paid a salary, plus possible benefits. If you work part-time, you will receive an hourly wage.

CHECK CASHING SERVICE PROVIDER

Description: Cashes payroll and personal checks from a retail location, usually in a place where banks are not easily accessible. Additional financial services, such as wiring money through Western Union, might also be offered.

Time Schedule: You will have to keep regular hours to accommodate the public; and if you are located in a shopping center, you will have to be open during the times outlined in your lease. Refer to #7 in Chapter 1 for suggestions on delegating work to employees.

Requirements: You will need any necessary local licenses, plus a sufficient inventory of currency to use for cashing checks. A security-sensitive environment (bulletproof windows over teller cages) is also critical.

Compensation: You will charge a fee—a percentage of the amount of the check.

COIN DEALER

Description: Sells rare coins, usually from a retail setting.

Time-Schedule: Refer to #7 in Chapter 1.

Requirements: In addition to those requirements listed in #7 of Chapter 1, you will need to know about coin collecting and the value of coins.

Compensation: Refer to #7 in Chapter 1.

COLLECTION AGENCY OWNER

Description: Collects past-due and generally hard-to-collect bills for professionals (such as doctors) and businesses. This can be done from a home-based office.

Time Schedule: You will have to be available daily (including weekends) to call the debtors to try to elicit payment and also to send out the necessary notices. If you use employees to help you, refer to #7 in Chapter 1.

Requirements: Before you go into business for yourself, you'll need a background in collection, preferably for lending institutions or department stores. You'll also need to know how to market your business, and you'll need to check with your local government regarding any necessary licenses and ordinances concerning this business. Be sure to know what you can legally say and write to the debtors.

Compensation: You receive a percentage, which is usually quite high, of what you collect.

CREDIT COUNSELOR

Description: Counsels individuals in the correct handling of their credit. This can include putting them on budgets and even taking their money and paying their bills so that they can get out of debt and restore their credit rating. Other services usually offered are debt and credit negotiations, debt consolidation, out-of-court settlements, and working out payments with creditors.

Time Schedule: Refer to #2 in Chapter 1.

Requirements: A background in credit, possibly as a credit manager for a lending institution. You also need the ability to communicate and empathize with people because most people are very sensitive about their financial problems.

Compensation: You will receive a fee based on the individual's income and number of creditors. If you are dealing with debt consolidation, you will be paid an administrative fee to pay the creditors.

CREDIT DEPARTMENT CLERK

Description: Works in department stores and lending institutions as a clerk in the credit department. Duties include approving credit applications, approving charges, taking payments, arranging a payment program for those who cannot pay their total bills, and dealing with everything concerning credit. This is a wonderful entry-level position if you want a career in credit services.

Time Schedule: Though you might be hired to be a full-time employee (in which case, check out the advice in Chapter 18), you also can be hired part-time.

Requirements: Check with the companies in your area to find out how much education they require. Because this is an entry-level job very closely monitored by a supervisor, you may need nothing more than the desire and ability to be trained.

Compensation: If you work full-time, you will be paid a salary plus benefits. If you work part-time, you'll be paid an hourly wage.

FINANCIAL WRITER

Description: Writes newsletters, books, and newspaper and magazine articles for both the public and the financial industry.

Time Schedule: Refer to #11 in Chapter 1.

Requirements: In addition to those requirements outlined in #11 (Chapter 1), you must have an extensive background in the financial world, perhaps as a broker of stocks and bonds.

Compensation: Refer to #11 in Chapter 1. If you are writing a newsletter, your income will come from subscriptions; so refer to #1 in Chapter 1 to be sure that you are pricing your product correctly.

FINANCING CONSULTANT

Description: Counsels people and businesses on the best type of financing for a specific need. This might include helping to fill out the necessary applications and meeting with lending institutions as well as getting credit ratings and other necessary information.

Time Schedule: Please refer to #2 in Chapter 1.

Requirements: You'll need a background in the lending business. This may be as a credit manager for a lending institution or for the credit department of a store. Refer to #2 in Chapter 1 for additional requirements.

Compensation: Refer to #2 in Chapter 1.

FORECLOSURE ASSISTANCE PROVIDER

Description: Assists lending institutions in the foreclosure of properties. This includes filling out and filing the necessary legal paperwork, serving the registered owners of the properties, and possibly going to court. You might also assist property owners who are facing foreclosure.

Time Schedule: Refer to #2 in Chapter 1.

Requirements: You'll need a background in foreclosure, which is usually gained by working for lending institutions where foreclosures are initiated. It also helps to have legal training. Check with your city to determine any special licenses you may need.

Compensation: Refer to #2 in Chapter 1.

FUND-RAISING CONSULTANT

Description: Works with nonprofit organizations on fund-raising. Sometimes a consultant does no more than give ideas to committees, who do all the work, but more often the consultant handles every phase of the fund-raising effort.

Time Schedule: You can set your own hours; refer to #2 in Chapter 1. During the time of the fund-raising event, you will have to devote many long hours to it.

Requirements: Knowledge of and experience in putting on events that make significant money. You will also need the ability to motivate volunteers to help you, and you'll have to be experienced in marketing so that you can get free advertisement and media exposure.

Compensation: In addition to a flat fee or a retainer as described in #2 (Chapter 1), you will make a percentage of the funds raised (after expenses). This is where the good income in fund-raising is found.

INCOME TAX ACCOUNTANT/PREPARER

Description: Prepares income tax returns, both federal and state, for individuals and businesses.

Time Schedule: From January to the middle of April, you will probably work very long hours. After that you can set very flexible hours.

Requirements: You'll need to be familiar with most recent tax laws, plus any that pertain to legal deductions for particular clients. If you are going to handle complicated projects, you will need to be a certified public accountant. Some national income tax services train people to work part-time for them in preparing income taxes.

Compensation: You will be paid a flat fee based on how many hours the tax return takes to prepare.

INSURANCE CONSULTANT

Description: Counsels people and companies on the types of insurance that will best serve their purposes.

Time Schedule: Refer to #2 in Chapter 1.

Requirements: You need knowledge about the insurance business, which would come from education and experience in this field, and you'll need the appropriate state licensing. It is also very important to understand different businesses and how insurance can help them.

Compensation: Refer to #2 in Chapter 1.

INSURANCE INSPECTOR AND AUDITOR

Description: Audits businesses for workers' compensation and liability insurance premiums. This is done by evaluating payroll records, general ledgers, cash receipts, cash disbursement journals, and profit-and-loss statements. Loss control inspections consist of interviewing the business owners about their business, the number of employees, and estimated annual payroll and gross sales.

This job also includes physical examination of the business site to determine liability hazards, such as fire, theft, and accident. Then recommendations regarding these hazards are given and later an inspection is made to see if the corrective actions have been taken. All types of business sites, from retail shops, offices, factories, churches, parking lots, shopping centers, restaurants, and even brothels are audited and inspected for insurance companies.

Time Schedule: Although this job can take up a full work week, as an independent operator, you can still set your own hours. The large amounts of paperwork can be done at any time from your home office.

Requirements: You need to be perceptive and detail-oriented. You should understand how businesses work and should understand their financial operations. Working in the financial department of a large company will give you good experience.

Compensation: You will be paid an hourly fee. As an independent contractor, you probably will not be paid expenses, so make sure that what you charge covers your time and expenses. Refer to #1 and #9 in Chapter 1 for suggestions on how to price yourself.

INSURANCE INVESTIGATOR

Description: Investigates accidents, thefts, and anything that requires insurance companies to pay claims. Insurance companies are the clients for this service.

Time Schedule: You can set your own schedule; however, an accident site must be investigated immediately while the evidence is fresh.

Requirements: You'll need a background in investigation, which might include experience in law enforcement. State and local licenses might be necessary. You should know how to market your services to insurance companies.

Compensation: Your fee will be generated by the number of hours it takes to complete the investigation. Refer to #2 and #9 in Chapter 1 for some suggestions on pricing yourself.

INSURANCE SALESPERSON (AGENT)

Description: Sells life, disability, health, automobile, fire, and other forms of insurance to businesses and individuals. This is an outside sales job.

Time Schedule: Refer to #8 in Chapter 1.

Requirements: In addition to those requirements outlined in #8, you will need to know how insurance can help the client and which kind and how much to sell. Most states also require licensing of agents.

Compensation: Most income is earned from commissions at the time of the original sale plus residuals or royalties, which are a percentage of the premiums clients continue to pay year after year. It is from these residuals that the bulk of an agent's income is generated because, after several years in the business, an agent will have developed hundreds of clients who are regularly paying premiums.

INVESTMENT ADVISOR

Description: Gives advice to individuals and companies on investment programs that will best meet their needs and financial objectives. This type of consultant usually does not sell investments.

Time Schedule: Refer to #2 in Chapter 1.

Requirements: You'll need expertise in investments and any necessary licenses. Also refer to #2 in Chapter 1.

Compensation: Refer to #2 in Chapter 1; you could charge a percentage of the investment budget.

LIVING TRUST ADVISOR

Description: Assists people in creating living trusts.

Time Schedule: Refer to #2 in Chapter 1.

Requirements: You need expertise in creating living trusts. You might gain this by working with attorneys who handle them. Check your community's laws to determine whether you need any special licensing.

Compensation: Refer to #2 in Chapter 1.

LOAN BROKER

Description: Arranges loans for people. Although any type of loan might be involved, most frequently they are real estate or business loans of significant size. Loan brokers have access to many different lenders, not just one.

Time Schedule: Refer to #2 in Chapter 1.

Requirements: Experience with a lending institution would be helpful; you'll need any specific state or city licenses for your area. You also should be able to communicate well with people because you will be "selling" them on a loan.

Compensation: You will be paid through commissions—a percentage of the loan in the form of points.

MUTUAL FUND AND ANNUITY SALESPERSON

Description: Sells mutual funds and annuities to individuals.

Time-Schedule: Refer to #8 in Chapter 1; however, due to the nature of these products, much of your selling might be done at night in the clients' homes. If you work for a company where routine office hours are kept, you will have to be available for some, if not all, of those. See Chapter 18 for pointers on getting your employer to allow you flex time.

Requirements: In addition to all the sales abilities outlined in #8 (Chapter 1), you will need to understand mutual funds and annuities and have the appropriate licenses.

Compensation: You will be paid primarily by commission. Depending on whom you work for, you might receive a small salary or advance, but the bulk of your income will come from your commissions.

PAWN SHOP OWNER

Description: Buys good merchandise (such as jewelry, electronics, musical instruments) from individuals who need money and cannot get loans from the normal resources, such as banks. Once the money for the item has been given to the owner (and it is a small percentage of its actual worth), the owner has a certain length of time to buy the merchandise back by repaying not only the amount of the loan but interest as well. This business is handled from a retail setting.

Time Schedule: Refer to #7 in Chapter 1.

Requirements: You have to be able to determine whether the merchandise has resale appeal because, if the owner doesn't come back, you will want to sell it to get your money back. Pawn shops are strictly regulated in most cities and states, so get good legal advice before going into this business.

Compensation: Your income will be generated from the interest you receive when people come back to repay the loan and collect their goods. If they do not repay the loan, then you can sell the items, usually for a great deal more than you paid for them.

RETIREMENT INVESTMENT COUNSELOR

Description: Counsels individuals as to the best investments that they can make with their retirement incomes. This type of counselor also advises people on what types of investments they need to make to maximize their future retirement incomes. A counselor probably will not sell any investments.

Time Schedule: Refer to #2 in Chapter 1.

Requirements: You'll need expertise in investments. This may include previous experience with investment companies, perhaps in a sales capacity.

Compensation: Refer to #2 in Chapter 1; however, your fee could be based on a percentage of the investment budget.

STOCKS AND BONDS SALESPERSON

Description: Sells stocks and bonds to individuals and companies, usually from an office.

Time Schedule: You will generally have to keep some daytime hours, but because you will be working primarily from appointments, you should be able to have some control of your schedule.

Requirements: You'll need to know about stocks and bonds and have the federal license allowing you to sell them. Sales ability is also necessary as is an understanding of the business. This business demands complete integrity.

Compensation: Depending on whom you work for, you might receive an advance or small salary, but most of your income will come from commissions.

Chapter 11

The Nature Lover's World

There's nothing more effective than time spent in a natural setting to refresh our souls. Many people have found that working in the world of nature is especially satisfying. There's room for you too; look through these jobs and see what interests you.

ANIMAL ACCESSORIES DESIGNER

Description: Designs collars, leashes, dog and cat coats, toys, beds, and all other accessories that are carried in pet stores. The designers are usually freelancers, who sell their designs to animal accessory manufacturers.

Time Schedule: You can usually control your own schedule.

Requirements: Besides a background in design, you must know about and understand the animals you are designing accessories for. When it comes to prints and colors for coats, however, whatever fashion colors are "hot" for humans are usually popular for animals too—because it is people who purchase them.

Compensation: You will be paid a fee for selling your designs to the manufacturer. Try to negotiate a royalty or residual on all that are sold.

✪ ANIMAL ACCESSORY SALESPERSON

Description: Sells accessories for animals (collars, coats, care products, and the like) from a retail establishment or as an outside salesperson calling on pet stores and animal supply stores.

Time Schedule: If you run a retail store, refer to #7 in Chapter 1. If you are an outside salesperson working for a manufacturer of animal supplies, refer to #8 in Chapter 1.

Requirements: In addition to those requirements listed in #7 and #8 (Chapter 1), you should understand and like not only animals but also the people who deal with them; "animal people" are usually so involved with their animals that if you do not speak their language, you will not be successful in this business.

Compensation: Refer to #7 and #8 in Chapter 1.

✪ ANIMAL ADOPTION SERVICE PROVIDER

Description: Takes in animals for adoption and finds homes for them among the general public. Although most of these services are run by volunteers, some facilities, especially large ones, do have paid managers.

Time Schedule: Assuming that you are the manager, you will have volunteers to help you and make your time a little more flexible. However, you will have to take the bulk of the responsibility.

Requirements: You'll need the ability to motivate people to volunteer to help you; you should understand public relations and media development. A love of and commitment to animals is a necessity.

Compensation: You will generally be paid a salary. You won't get wealthy from this job, but it can be very fulfilling.

ANIMAL CRUELTY INVESTIGATOR

Description: Investigates reports of animals being mistreated or abused. You can work for one of the many animal advocate groups (such as PETA) or the community's humane department.

Time Schedule: If you work for the community, you might be expected to work full-time. Check out the advice in Chapter 18 for suggestions on how to make a full-time job more flexible. Working for a private agency will probably give you more flexibility.

Requirements: A degree in animal husbandry would be helpful, although it probably is not an absolute necessity (particularly for the private groups). You will have to know investigative techniques and be totally committed to animals. You have to be emotionally strong enough to deal with the animal-abuse situations you will encounter.

Compensation: As a full-time employee, you will be paid a salary and benefits. As a freelancer for a private organization, you will probably be paid by the hour. Refer to #9 in Chapter 1 to be sure that you are getting the money you need.

ANIMAL FIGURINE AND GIFT SALESPERSON

Description: Sells figurines and other gift items featuring animals out of a retail outlet, at swap meets, or as an outside salesperson calling on stores that sell these kinds of items.

Time Schedule: Refer to #7 and #8 in Chapter 1.

Requirements: In addition to those requirements identified in #7 and #8 in Chapter 1, you must love animal decor and gift items. Whenever you contemplate selling anything—and this is particularly true of these items—ask yourself, "Would I buy it or use it myself?" If the answer is "no," then don't try to sell it.

Compensation: Refer to #7 and #8 in Chapter 1.

ANIMAL GROOMER

Description: Bathes and cuts the hair and fur of dogs and cats (as required by a particular breed's criteria); other species, such as horses, are also groomed occasionally. Grooming is usually done from a retail establishment, a kennel, or a vet's office; however, some groomers drive vans and go to their clients' homes.

Time Schedule: If you work from a retail establishment, you may have to be open during the hours that the mall is open. Be sure to check this out before taking on a lease. If that is the case, refer to #7 in Chapter 1 for advice on finding help in a retail environment. If you work for such a place (such as a pet store or veterinarian's office), you should be able to establish your own days and hours—as you should if you run your grooming business from a van.

Requirements: You can get specialized training by working for a groomer or by attending schools; you'll also need an inordinate amount of patience and love of animals. Your state or city might require you to have a license.

Compensation: Your income is generated from what you charge for your work. Refer to #1 in Chapter 1.

ANIMAL PHOTOGRAPHER

Description: Photographs animals for periodicals, books, and calendars; also takes pictures for individuals who want pictures of their pets.

Time Schedule: Refer to #6 in Chapter 1.

Requirements: In addition to those requirements outlined in #6 in Chapter 1, you must also know how to handle the animals in order to get the best photographs. Extraordinary patience is also required.

Compensation: Refer to #6 in Chapter 1 for advice on how to make money photographing animals.

ANIMAL-SHOW HANDLER

Description: Shows pedigreed dogs at American Kennel Club shows so that they can earn their "points." A good handler can show the dog to its best advantage and make it perform in the ring to impress the judge. Very frequently the handler can enable the animal to take first, second, or third place—all of which enhance its value. This job also requires the handler to take care of basic grooming so the dog will look its best. Much of this job involves traveling with the dogs.

Time Schedule: You have a great deal of flexibility; however, you work very hard when you participate in shows—of which there are many. Then, depending on the number of dogs you show, you might work very long hours.

Requirements: You'll need education and expertise in handling dogs as a professional handler. You start by learning how to show your own dog in the ring. Then, as you get better, others will ask you to show their dogs. If you can work as an assistant to a well-respected handler, it will be worth it for your career.

Compensation: You will be paid a fee per dog. The size of that depends on where the show is going to be held and its importance. If the dog you show wins, you usually get a bonus.

ANIMAL-SHOW JUDGE

Description: The judge selects the dogs that win first, second, and third place in the ring as they are being shown by handlers. The shows are usually sponsored by the American Kennel Club.

Time Schedule: You can control most of your everyday life, but during show times you will be very busy.

Requirements: The AKC has very specific requirements for judges. Contact the organization for its guidelines. Most judges start out as handlers and, after many years of experience, move up to judge. Because there are so many breeds and classes of dogs, judges usually specialize in only a few. As a judge, you must know what all the standards are for all the breeds in your particular class.

Compensation: You will be paid a fee and usually expenses. The amount you are paid depends on the prestige of the show.

ANIMAL-SHOW PROMOTER

Description: Puts on animal shows, usually for the general public to observe. This includes dog, cat, and horse (all-breed plus specific breed) shows. Often these shows are put on by individual animal clubs (such as the American Kennel Club of Beverly Hills) and may be run totally by volunteers; but there is always the opportunity to work for one of these clubs.

Time Schedule: Refer to #4 in Chapter 1 to see how show producers can have flexible time.

Requirements: In addition to those requirements outlined in #4 (Chapter 1), you must love and have an understanding of animals.

Compensation: Refer again to #4 in Chapter 1.

ANIMAL TRAINER

Description: Deals with all kinds of situations where special training is required, usually with dogs. This could include breaking bad habits, such as excessive barking, biting, and destroying furniture. Animal trainers also prepare show dogs to behave appropriately in the show ring. This kind of trainer does not work with performing animals.

Time Schedule: You can block out certain weeks or months when you might not wish to work, but once you have accepted an assignment, you will have to fulfill it.

Requirements: You'll need education and experience in animal behavior, which can be gained through veterinarian's training and working with animal trainers. It also helps to know how to market your services. Finally, extraordinary patience is an absolute necessity.

Compensation: Your fee will be determined by how much time it will take to train the animal. Refer to #1 and #2 in Chapter 1 for further advice.

AQUARIUM SPECIALIST

Description: Designs and sells aquariums to individuals and businesses, generally from a retail setting.

Time Schedule: Refer to #7 in Chapter 1.

Requirements: You'll need an understanding of the different species of fish, how they interact with one another, and what they contribute to the interest and beauty of the aquarium. Refer to #7 in Chapter 1 for requirements that pertain to retailers in general.

Compensation: Refer to #7 in Chapter 1.

BIRD EQUIPMENT SUPPLIER

Description: Sells bird food, feeders, baths, and all other equipment needed for birds—usually for those found in the wild. You could work out of a retail store or as an outside salesperson calling on such a retail store.

Time Schedule: Refer to #7 and #8 in Chapter 1.

Requirements: In addition to those requirements listed in #7 and #8 (Chapter 1), you must be interested in and know about wild birds. You need to be able to communicate what you know to your customers through newsletters, seminars, and the like.

Compensation: Refer to #7 and #8 in Chapter 1.

BOARDING KENNEL OWNER

Description: Takes in cats and dogs and boards them for their absent owners. This job can be done from your own residence if you have the necessary facility (and the zoning laws allow it) or from a public building such as a retail establishment.

Time Schedule: Hours are those of any retail establishment, but responsible boarding facilities have someone on the premises even during the night. Refer to #7 in Chapter 1 to help you find employees who will give you some flexibility in your scheduling. It will be easier for you if you maintain this business from your home.

Requirements: You need to know about caring for animals; you must be able to give first aid. You'll need patience and a love of animals. Your city will also ask you to be licensed.

Compensation: You charge a set fee for each day an animal is boarded; the fee includes food. You can make additional money by selling animal supplies and providing grooming. Refer to #1 in Chapter 1 for advice on how to set fees that will enable you to have a profitable business.

✪ BREEDER

Description: Breeds pedigreed animals (dogs, cats, horses, cattle, and the like) in order to sell them to other breeders and members of the general public.

Time Schedule: You have control of your schedule because this business is generally run from home. However, you do have to care for the animals, so you will need to hire someone to help you if you can't be available. You have to be available when your females give birth.

Requirements: You need to know about and love the particular animals you are breeding; you need the integrity to refrain from making a fast buck at the expense of the breed or your animals.

Compensation: Your income is generated by the sale of your animals, minus any expenses (including the stud fee for the use of the male). The quality of your animals and their lineage all contribute to a higher price. To do well in this business, you must take your parent animals to the animal shows so that they can earn ribbons to make them more valuable. Most breeders are in this field not for the money but to contribute to their breed and for the fun of it. You won't make a lot of money in this job, but you'll have a supplemental income, which can offset the costs of maintaining your own animals.

✪ CAMPING EQUIPMENT SALESPERSON

Description: Sells camping equipment and the supplies used by campers from a retail outlet or as an outside salesperson representing camping equipment manufacturers to retailers.

Time Schedule: Refer to #7 in Chapter 1 if you are going to have a retail store; refer to #8 in Chapter 1 if you are going to sell these items to retail stores as an outside salesperson.

Requirements: In addition to requirements listed in #7 and #8 (Chapter 1), you need an expert knowledge of camping; such expertise could come only from personal participation.

Compensation: Refer to #7 and #8 in Chapter 1. You could earn extra money from giving seminars at travel shows about camping, the proper equipment, and so on. You could also work as a backpacking guide.

CAMPGROUND HOST

Description: Works in state or federal campgrounds as a host. This job includes finding camping spots for campers, helping them to hook up their equipment and deal with any problems pertaining to it, keeping the public latrines clean and stocked with toilet paper. You will be living at the campground in your own camper or motor home.

Time Schedule: This is a seasonal job, worked during the summer months. During the season, you will be on the job all the time (but the work is not hard).

Requirements: You'll need to know about camping and basic first aid. You'll need some mechanical ability so that you can help campers make small repairs. Being personable is definitely important as is being an outdoors person (so that you can tell campers where the fish bite, where the good bike and hiking trails are, and so forth). This is a great job for senior citizens who have been ardent campers for a long time.

Compensation: Your camp site will be given to you free of charge. You may also receive a small salary. This job is done as much for fun as for the money.

DOG OBEDIENCE INSTRUCTOR

Description: Teaches the basics of obedience (sitting, staying, heeling, not jumping up) to dogs through classes in which the dog's owners do most of the work. Your classes can be arranged through pet stores, community parks and recreation services, or independent marketing.

Time Schedule: You can set your own schedule and can block out weeks or even months when you are not available. But once you've started a class—and most of them are once a week for six to eight weeks—you must be available to teach the class. Occasionally you can give private lessons for those who do not want to be part of a large group.

Requirements: You need to know about and have experience in training dogs. You usually learn this job by working with established trainers. Tremendous patience is also very important as is a love and understanding of all breeds of dogs.

Compensation: You will be paid a flat fee for the course. Take into account the amount of time you will be spending and charge accordingly. Refer to #1 and #5 in Chapter 1 for suggestions on pricing yourself. Also check out what your competition is charging.

EXOTIC BIRD SALESPERSON

Description: Sells exotic birds to the public, usually from a retail store. The birds to be sold include parrots, parakeets, and canaries.

Time Schedule: Refer to #7 in Chapter 1.

Requirements: In addition to those listed in #7 in Chapter 1, you need to know about and like birds. You have to know how to care for these birds.

Compensation: Refer to #7 in Chapter 1.

FARMER/RANCHER

Description: This job allows you to make an income from the land you live on. As a farmer, you will plant crops to sell. As a rancher, you will raise livestock for sale.

Time Schedule: You live your work. Some parts of the year, depending on the season, you won't work very hard at all. At other times, during planting and harvesting seasons, you'll be very busy.

Requirements: Today it takes great skill to be a successful farmer or rancher. Major universities offer formal education in this field. You should also have some experience because it's difficult to be successful in this business without some hands-on involvement.

Compensation: Your income is generated from the sale of your crops or livestock. Some people barely break even, while others make excellent livings. It all depends on where you are located, the quality of your product, the weather, and your expertise.

FISHING BOAT GUIDE

Description: Takes people on fishing trips. Most fishing guides know where the fish are biting in a particular lake or ocean; people hire them for this knowledge.

Time Schedule: This is a seasonal job, usually performed in the spring, summer, and very early fall. You work a lot during the season, but in the off-season you are free to do what you wish when you wish.

Requirements: You must have the necessary equipment, including a large boat with the basic amenities (like bathroom) and plenty of fishing rods and tackle. Having a fish finder, which is attached to the boat and records where fish are located, is very helpful also. It is equally important that you like people and have a great deal of patience—not so much to enable you to wait for the fish as to aid you in dealing with impatient people, many of whom have never fished before.

Compensation: You will be paid a flat fee for a definite number of hours spent fishing and on the water. Refer to #1 and #9 in Chapter 1 for suggestions on pricing your service. It is also wise to check what your competition is charging.

✪ FLORIST

Description: Sells flowers and flower arrangements, usually from a retail store but also, if only pre-ordered flower arrangements are sold, from home.

Time Schedule: Refer to #7 in Chapter 1 if you are going to have a retail establishment. If you are going to run your business from home, your schedule is your own except when you have to deliver the arrangements (such as for a wedding). Then you must meet deadlines.

Requirements: You need to know how to create beautiful floral arrangements. You'll need any license required by your city. Refer to #7 for additional requirements for retailers.

Compensation: Refer to #7 and also #1 (especially if you are going to be working from home) in Chapter 1.

✪ GARDEN DESIGNER

Description: Designs gardens for individuals or businesses. This can be either a vegetable or flower garden. Generally someone with this job designs the garden but does not put it in.

Time Schedule: You can set your own schedule.

Requirements: Education and experience in landscape design and specifically gardens. You can learn what you need to know from working with a successful garden designer or from working in a nursery that specializes in vegetables as well as flowers.

Compensation: You will be paid a flat fee. Refer to #2 in Chapter 1.

GARDENER

Description: Takes care of yards and gardens for individual homes and commercial buildings.

Time Schedule: You will usually have a set schedule or route that must be worked on a regular basis. The flexible hours come in when you can hire people to do the work for you, thus giving you some time off. Another way that you can have a flexible lifestyle is to select only certain days to work (for example, Monday through Thursday) so that you can have more days off.

Requirements: You'll need the basic tools of the trade, such as lawn mowers, weed pullers, hoses, and so forth. You need to know how to maintain lawns and gardens, and you also need to know how to treat plant diseases.

Compensation: You will be paid by the job. In setting your fees, you should take into consideration the costs of travel to the job and the costs of any people you hire to help you. Refer to #1 in Chapter 1 for ideas on how to price your product.

HUNTING GUIDE

Description: Takes people on trips to hunt game (within season and within the limits established by state). Novices are usually the ones who hire a hunting guide to help them find and hunt the animals.

Time Schedule: Your time is basically your own as far as setting your own schedule, but you will have to be available during the hunting season. You will have to work around your clients' needs, but if you want to take a certain period of time off—you can!

Requirements: Obviously you will have to be proficient in tracking animals and using weapons to hunt them. It also helps to be patient because you will be dealing with inexperienced people. You might also need to be licensed.

Compensation: You probably will be paid by the job and number of people in your party. Refer to #1, #2, and #9 in Chapter 1 for ideas on how to charge.

LANDSCAPE DESIGNER

Description: Designs landscapes for individual residences as well as commercial locations. Landscapes include all types of plants, trees, and flowers as well as walkways. Generally, a landscape designer simply draws up plans showing where specific plants are to be placed and does not do any of the work.

Time Schedule: As a freelancer, you can control your own hours.

Requirements: You'll need education and experience in landscape design, which is taught in many colleges. Experience is best gained by working in nurseries and for landscape designers.

Compensation: You will charge a flat fee. Refer to #1 and #2 in Chapter 1 for suggestions on pricing yourself and your service.

NATURE WRITER

Description: Writes about animals, the environment, ecological problems, forestry, camping and backpacking, canoeing, boating, and so forth. You could write books, magazine articles, newspaper columns, newsletters, and many other things.

Time Schedule: Refer to #11 in Chapter 1.

Requirements: Besides those outlined in #11 (Chapter 1), you will need expertise in the particular topic you are writing about.

Compensation: Refer to #11 in Chapter 1.

PET CARETAKER

Description: Goes into individuals' homes to care for their pets. The types of animals include dogs, cats, birds, fish, and possibly horses.

Time Schedule: You can set your own schedule; however, you will have to visit the animals during the time of the day that you have contracted for. This job is a good choice if you want to work part-time because it does not take the entire day. You can also block out whole months or weeks when you won't be available; however, you will not be able to block out specific days because people who go away for a week or more expect their pets to be taken care of every day of the week.

Requirements: You'll need to know about animals and have the patience to deal with a lonesome animal who misses its owner. You should be able to recognize sick animals and know how to deal with them (this subject should be discussed in advance with the owner).

Compensation: You will charge by the number of animals you take care of and the number of visits you make to them. Refer to #1, #2, and #9 in Chapter 1 for ideas on how to price your service.

PET FOOD MANUFACTURER'S REPRESENTATIVE

Description: Sells pet food to retail outlets, veterinarians, kennels, and breeders. You would usually work for the manufacturer or a distributor who sells to these outlets. This is an outside sales job.

Time Schedule: Refer to #8 in Chapter 1.

Requirements: In addition to those requirements listed in #8 in Chapter 1, you need to know about pet nutrition and those people who are interested in it (such as your customers).

Compensation: Refer to #8 in Chapter 1.

PET RETAILER

Description: Sells pets (such as cats and dogs) and pet supplies from a retail store.

Time Schedule: Refer to #7 in Chapter 1.

Requirements: In addition to those requirements listed in #7 in Chapter 1, you will need to know about and love animals.

Compensation: Refer to #7 in Chapter 1.

PET SUPPLY SALESPERSON

Description: Sells pet supplies to pet stores and others who use them. This is an outside sales job.

Time Schedule: Refer to #8 in Chapter 1.

Requirements: In addition to those requirements outlined in #8, you will need to know about and like animals and the people who deal with them.

Compensation: Refer to #8 in Chapter 1.

PLANT CARETAKER

Description: Takes care of plants in the homes of people who are going away on vacation. This service can also be provided to businesses that like to have plants as part of their interior design but that don't have anyone on staff to take care of them.

Time Schedule: You can block out periods of time and certain days. This is an excellent business to tie in with pet caretaking (outlined earlier in this chapter) or as a part-time job.

Requirements: You need to know about plants and their care, especially about how to deal with diseases.

Compensation: You will charge by the trip and the approximate amount of time it will take you to care for the clients' plants. Refer to #1, #2, and #9 in Chapter 1 for suggestions on how to establish your rates.

PLANT LEASING AND SALES AGENT

Description: Leases or sells plants to businesses and residences. This business is frequently tied in with plant caretaking or maintenance. This business is usually conducted at the site where the plants will be used.

Time Schedule: You should be able to block out periods of free time, especially if you are not doing plant caretaking.

Requirements: You'll need to know how to use plants to enhance the ambiance of a room. You will also need to have several reliable suppliers of plants because the bulk of your business will be in selling them to the end user.

Compensation: You will make your income from the sale of your plants. Refer to #7 in Chapter 1 for suggestions on how to maximize your income.

PRODUCER OF NATURE VIDEOS

Description: Produces videos about a special aspect of nature, such as scenery, animals, mountains, oceans, lakes, and so on. With the public's renewed interest in all things natural and the outdoors, this is an excellent business to pursue. And it can be done from home because the producer does not usually need to go on location to do the videotaping.

Time Schedule: You can set your own schedule.

Requirements: You need to know how to produce videos; this knowledge can be gained from both education and experience. You also need to know how to market your product. It takes a great deal of money to produce one of these; and the producer is the person who puts up the money, hires all the staff, and covers the expenses.

Compensation: Your income is generated from the sale of your product, minus all production and marketing costs. If you produce an excellent video and market it well, you make a great deal of money even with the great costs of the project.

TREE REMOVER

Description: Removes trees from landscapes. Homeowners as well as commercial buildings and malls use this service.

Time Schedule: You can choose which days you won't work, but it is difficult to take blocks of days, weeks, or months off. However, if you live in a part of the country where there are harsh winters, you will usually not have much work then.

Requirements: Besides having the necessary equipment, you need experience in this business; you will need all necessary local licenses, and you will need to be bonded.

Compensation: You will charge a fee that depends on the size of the tree and the amount of time it will take you to remove it. Refer to #9 in Chapter 1 for additional suggestions on how to price your services.

TREE TRIMMER

Description: Trims trees for landscapers, homeowners, or property managers.

Time Schedule: You can determine what days you are available to work, but it's hard to take long periods of time off because you might lose your business. During winter seasons, however, you may get a lot of free time because not many trees are trimmed then.

Requirements: You need experience, which includes knowing how each species of tree should be trimmed to retain its unique beauty. You also need the proper tools and the ability to market your service.

Compensation: Refer to #9 in Chapter 1 for suggestions on pricing your service.

TOUR GUIDE

Description: Takes people on tours of natural settings (such as mountain roads, large federal parks, ocean harbors of large cities).

Time Schedule: This is generally seasonal work, done most often in spring, summer, and early fall. You work very hard during your season so that you can relax during late fall and winter.

Requirements: You might need a four-wheel drive vehicle or boat to transport your clients. Obviously your means of transportation has to be in top condition. It's also important to be very personable and know a great deal about your subject. You should know how to market your services.

Compensation: You will charge a flat fee based on the number of hours of your tour. Refer to #1 and #2 in Chapter 1.

VETERINARIAN

Description: Gives medical care, which includes performing surgery, on domestic animals—most frequently cats, dogs, birds, and horses. Occasionally other animals, including snakes, lizards, iguanas, ferrets, and exotic wild animals are also treated, as are cattle, sheep, goats, and pigs. The kind of veterinarian imagined here specializes in cats and dogs, the most popular pets.

Time Schedule: Although this profession often demands a forty-hour work week or more, it's possible to gain some flexibility. You can be an "emergency vet," which means that you have office hours at night and during the weekends when most other veterinary offices are closed. This gives you weekdays free. You can also work for other vets, assisting them when they get overloaded or relieving them during vacation times. Or you can follow the lead of so many professional people today and simply cut back on hours so that you can have more free time. This might also include permanently hiring another vet to help you.

Requirements: You'll need a degree in veterinary medicine (which is an advanced degree, like an M.D. degree) and the appropriate licensing for your state and town. You also need patience (with both the animals and their owners) and a commitment to the animals you treat. Knowing how to market your practice is also important.

Compensation: This profession pays well. You will charge a fee just to examine the animal. There will be additional charges for any shots, medication, or x-rays. Refer to #1 and #9 in Chapter 1 for further recommendations. Also compare the fees charged by other vets in your area.

VETERINARIAN'S ASSISTANT

Description: Assists veterinarians with the treatment of animals. This includes giving shots, taking temperatures and histories of the animal, and maintaining records in the office. It might also include caring for boarded animals and cleaning up after them as well as assisting in the euthanasia of pets.

Time Schedule: Frequently this job is full-time. Refer to Chapter 18 for suggestions on how to make it more flexible.

Requirements: Some training is possible through community colleges; if you have a medical background (such as being a nurse's aide), you can probably get a job with a veterinarian. This job is also good for those studying to be vets because it can serve as an internship. Very often veterinarians will train their assistants.

Compensation: You will probably be paid a salary and benefits.

✪ VETERINARIAN'S TEMPORARY SERVICE PROVIDER

Description: Provides veterinarians, veterinarian assistants, front-office people, and kennel workers for veterinarians who need help on a temporary basis, perhaps because members of their staff are on vacation or ill.

Time Schedule: You will probably run this business from an office; therefore, you will have to keep set hours. Refer to #7 in Chapter 1 for suggestions on delegating some of your responsibilities to employees.

Requirements: In addition to understanding the various positions in a veterinarian's practice, you will need to know how to market your business.

Compensation: You will be paid a percentage of the worker's pay. In fact, you are paid by the vet and you then pay your worker.

✪ VETERINARY MEDICINE AND EQUIPMENT SALESPERSON

Description: Sells veterinary medicines and equipment to veterinarians and animal hospitals. This is an outside sales position.

Time Schedule: Refer to #8 in Chapter 1.

Requirements: In addition to those requirements outlined in #8 (Chapter 1), you will need an understanding of veterinary medicine and how the equipment can be used. Frequently these jobs are held by people who attended veterinary school and then decided not to become a vet.

Compensation: Refer to #8 in Chapter 1.

ZOO WORKER

Description: Works at a zoo; there are many interesting jobs that people without zoological education can get. These jobs include doing office work, working as a clerk in gift shops, covering the information booth, lecturing on the animals, driving the shuttles (if the zoo has them), and serving in the restaurants and snack stands.

Time Schedule: Many of these jobs are part-time or offer flexible hours. Refer to Chapter 18 for suggestions on turning full-time positions into those where you have more control over your schedule.

Requirements: Requirements depend on the particular job; you should be willing to work around animals.

Compensation: You will be paid a salary or hourly wage.

CHAPTER 12

The World of Entertainment

Careers in the entertainment field have always appealed to people because of the excitement and glamour they suggest. If you want to get into entertainment, you can—even if you are not a talented singer, dancer, or actor. There are many support jobs in the entertainment industry; this chapter introduces you to nearly forty. If you do have talents in the performing arts, I list careers for you to consider as well.

ACQUISITIONS CONSULTANT

Description: Reads novels and follows up on news stories with the idea of possibly using them for a motion picture or television production. This professional usually works for a producer or studio as a freelancer.

Time Schedule: Refer to #2 in Chapter 1.

Requirements: Experience in the industry, as a script consultant or writer, is helpful. The key requirement, however, is to have a sense of what will make a good movie. This means keeping abreast of the fickle tastes of the public and knowing what is going to be "hot" tomorrow.

Compensation: You might be paid as a consultant (see #2 in Chapter 1), or you might be paid a percentage of the production's earnings.

ACTOR

Description: Performs in television, motion pictures, and on the stage—even in television commercials. Although big stars usually come to mind whenever we think of actors, thousands of people make good incomes by playing secondary roles and bit parts. For the purposes of this book, it is those jobs that I shall explore.

Time Schedule: You can control your own schedule to a point, but when you have the chance to work, you should take it. This job lends itself best to blocking out whole months when you don't wish to work. Then you simply are not available for auditions.

Requirements: You'll need acting ability, generally gained from education and experience. It's important to have a marketable presence, though you don't necessarily have to be a striking beauty. You might want to concentrate on being a character actor. You will need an agent, whom you can find listed through the Screen Actors Guild in Hollywood.

Compensation: You'll generally be paid by the job in the form of a flat fee; however, if you perform in commercials, movies, or television, you will also get residuals each time the production is shown. This could mean a great deal of money. Your pay will depend on your role. You will also need to join the union. Your agent and producer can help you do this once you have a part.

AEROBIC DANCE INSTRUCTOR

Description: Instructs people, usually in a gymnasium setting, in aerobic dance. The dancing is usually part of an exercise program.

Time Schedule: Refer to #5 in Chapter 1.

Requirements: In addition to those responsibilities outlined in #5 (Chapter 1), you'll need to be able to perform all the aerobic dance movements yourself and teach them to others. You might want to specialize in cardiovascular and aerobic exercises for senior citizens or overweight people, because these segments of our society are often overlooked.

Compensation: Refer to #5 in Chapter 1.

BALLOON NOVELTY & TOYS CREATOR

Description: Blows up balloons and forms them into animals as part of the entertainment at children's events, such as birthday parties. You could also work at fairs and as a street vendor when weather permits.

Time Schedule: You can set your own schedule as to the days, weeks, and months when you will be available to perform. However, once you have booked your act, you must honor the commitment.

Requirements: You must know how to make toys and novelties out of balloons, and you should have an entertaining personality. Having the marketing skills to promote yourself will also help.

Compensation: You will generally charge by the hour, with a minimum number of hours. Refer to #1 in Chapter 1 for pointers. If you're selling at a fair or on the street, you'll charge a hefty markup on the balloons.

BAND LEADER

Description: Forms and leads a band to play at celebratory events put on by individuals or businesses. These events include bar mitzvahs, weddings, proms, anniversaries, grand openings, and holiday parties. The type of band you'll form depends on who you are, your area of expertise, and the kinds of people you wish to attract. Most bands used for this purpose can play a variety of different music but have a specialized look. Middle-aged musicians would appeal more to people of the baby-boomer generation, while prom-goers would prefer to have a band whose musicians are young and play the music they like.

Time Schedule: As a freelancer, you will be able to set your own schedule; but there are some times of the year (around Christmas, for instance) when bands are most in demand, and you will need to work then in order to make the most income.

Requirements: You'll need musical ability, which includes being able to play a musical instrument yourself and arrange music; you'll need the organizational abilities to form and lead a band as well as market it.

Compensation: You will be paid a lump sum for the entire band for the whole performance. This amount is determined by the number of people you have in your band and the number of hours you will be expected to perform. Therefore, you need to determine the hourly amount needed by the band before determining the fee. Because you have additional responsibilities, such as booking the engagements, you generally will make more than your musicians. Check your community to determine if you need to belong to a union. If you do, that affects the amount you charge.

BANQUET CONSULTANT

Description: Counsels people who want to put on banquets and other parties, usually in hotels.

Time Schedule: If you work for a hotel that provides banquet facilities, you will probably have to work set hours. However, refer to Chapter 18 for suggestions on how to convince your boss to let you have some flexible time.

Requirements: You need to like people and have extraordinary organizational skills. Clients will appreciate it if you can give them creative ideas.

Compensation: You will probably be paid a salary. Sometimes you are also given a commission or bonus based on the business you generate. This would be a perk well worth trying to get.

BEAUTY CONTEST PROMOTER

Description: Puts on beauty contests for the community or a specific group of people (such as the airline industry). Participants could include children, babies, or senior citizens, as well as the traditional young, unmarried women. These contests are usually held in convention centers, shopping malls, and so on.

Time Schedule: Refer to #4 in Chapter 1.

Requirements: In addition to those requirements listed in #4 (Chapter 1), you should have an interest in the group the contestants come from and be very active in your community because the contestants will most likely come from and be supported by the community.

Compensation: Refer to #4 in Chapter 1.

BODYGUARD

Description: Protects individuals (frequently celebrity entertainers) from being physically touched, jostled, or pounced upon by the public. You may or may not carry a gun. Your employer can be either the individual whom you are guarding or a security company.

Time Schedule: You will have to work whenever your client needs you if you are hired by an individual. If you work for a security company, you are better able to control your own hours.

Requirements: You will have to be physically fit and know how to defend your charge. There may be special state licenses required; if you carry a gun, you will need a permit.

Compensation: You will probably be paid a salary if you are an employee of the individual being protected. If you work for a company, you will usually be paid an hourly rate.

BOOKING AGENT

Description: Represents entertainers with the idea of securing them jobs in their particular field. These professionals are also known as agents.

Time Schedule: Because you are usually in business for yourself, you can set your own schedule.

Requirements: You must know the business well and network extensively in it. You also must be a very good negotiator and understand contracts and entertainment law.

Compensation: You will earn a percentage of what the people you represent earn. This can be anywhere from 10 percent to 20 percent. Obviously, the more "big names" you handle, the more income you will generate.

CELEBRITY BIOGRAPHER

Description: Writes the biographies of movie stars and other celebrity entertainers. You might work as a ghostwriter, allowing the celebrity to take credit for the writing, you might be listed as a co-author, or you might write an unauthorized biography, without the permission or cooperation of the celebrity.

Time Schedule: Refer to #11 in Chapter 1.

Requirements: In addition to those requirements outlined in #11 (Chapter 1), you will need interviewing skills in order to get a story out of your subject. It's also important to have a network of people who can put you in contact with celebrities who might use your services. This can best be done by working through an agent or "book packager" after you have published some of your own work.

Compensation: Refer to #11 in Chapter 1.

CELEBRITY IMPERSONATOR

Description: Impersonates a celebrity effectively enough to be employed to do so. Most of these impersonations are done for private parties and commercials.

Time Schedule: As a freelancer, you can set your own schedule; however, you won't be successful unless you are available when people want your services.

Requirements: You have to look physically like and be able to talk like and imitate the body language of the celebrity. Marketing skills will also help.

Compensation: You will generally be paid by the job, with a minimum number of hours. Please refer to #1 in Chapter 1 for some ideas on how to price yourself successfully.

CHOREOGRAPHER

Description: Designs dance performances for any kind of production that requires dance scenes. Choreography involves types of dance steps used, number of dancers, and the steps each one takes. The choreographer is part of the creative team that is responsible for the success of the production. Works with the costume designer on costumes that will "dance" well.

Time Schedule: As a freelancer, you will have a lot of flexibility in your schedule; however, you will be very busy when putting on a production.

Requirements: You'll need knowledge and experience in dancing as well as the ability to design dance scenes for others. Very frequently, successful dancers move into the role of choreographer.

Compensation: You will be paid a fee and possibly a part of the production's revenue. Refer to #2 in Chapter 1 for suggestions on pricing yourself.

CITY FILM COMMISSIONER

Description: Represents a city or specific location to the entertainment industry with the goal of getting producers to film in that location. The duties include attending various trade shows.

Time Schedule: If you work full-time for the city, refer to Chapter 18. You could also work as a freelancer and have total control of your time.

Requirements: You need to know what producers want in locations, what properties have been purchased, and so on. This comes from having experience in the film industry, particularly as a set locator for a studio. You also need to know how to market your town as a set.

Compensation: You may get a salary, or you may get a fee, depending on the size (number of days and locations) of the shoot.

CLOWN

Description: Dresses up and performs like a clown for special events, such as children's parties, grand openings, community events. Might also appear in parades.

Time Schedule: As a freelancer, you can set your own schedule.

Requirements: You need to be funny; and if you can do gymnastics, all the better. Although it helps to have professional clown training, this is a field where a good amateur can be successful.

Compensation: You will be paid by the job, usually for a set number of hours. Refer to #1 for some suggestions on pricing yourself properly.

DANCE EVENT PROMOTER

Description: Sponsors dances for specific groups of people or the community. These are usually held in hotel ballrooms or convention centers.

Time Schedule: Refer to #4 in Chapter 1.

Requirements: Refer to #4 in Chapter 1. It helps to be well known in your community.

Compensation: Refer to #4 in Chapter 1.

DANCE INSTRUCTOR

Description: Teaches dancing to the general public. This is usually done in a dancing school or through the public school system.

Time Schedule: Refer #5 in Chapter 1.

Requirements: In addition to those requirements listed in #5, you must be a professional dancer. If you're working through the public school district, you may need a special license.

Compensation: Refer to #5 in Chapter 1.

DIRECTOR

Description: Directs performances, usually of a dramatic nature, for stage, screen, and radio. This can also include directing commercials and community theater.

Time Schedule: As a freelancer, you will have control over what times of the year you don't want to work. But once you've started work on a production, you'll be very busy no matter what you are directing.

Requirements: You'll need drama training and experience, particularly as a director. However, people who have had successful careers as actors often become directors. It is absolutely essential for directors to understand the acting roles, but they also need to be able to visualize the performance as a whole so that they can direct it to that end. The success of a production falls squarely on the shoulders of the director.

Compensation: You will be paid a fee for the job and, usually, a residual or percentage of the production's revenue.

DISC JOCKEY

Description: Through the use of sound equipment and compact discs, supplies dance music and entertainment for events such as weddings, bar mitzvahs, and so on. Some people (particularly young people) prefer disc jockeys over live bands because disc jockeys are able to provide more diverse music, often of a better quality.

Time Schedule: As a one-person operation, you have total control of your schedule.

Requirements: You'll need a wide variety of music and the best portable sound equipment you can find. These requirements are critical and, without them, you won't be successful. You need to feel comfortable and be good at speaking before a group, because you will be acting as the emcee for the event. A pleasing personality that invites people to have fun is also important.

Compensation: You will be paid a fee, which is determined by the number of hours you perform. Refer to #1 and #9 in Chapter 1 for advice on pricing yourself and your service. Also check what your competition is charging before setting your rates.

DRAMA TEACHER

Description: Teaches dramatic acting and speaking. This can be done in a school or on an individual basis from one's home.

Time Schedule: Refer to #5 in Chapter 1.

Requirements: You'll need to be an accomplished actor—who understands all the techniques that make an actor great. Knowing how to teach and how to bring out the best in students is also critical, as is having many producer friends who can give your students a chance.

Compensation: The better known you are and the more successful your students, the more you are worth. Also refer to #5 in Chapter 1.

ENTERTAINERS' AGENT

Description: Books actors and other entertainers to appear in radio, television, film, and theater productions.

Time Schedule: You can set your own schedule to some extent; however, you must be available for conferences with clients, producers, and others.

Requirements: You must know about all aspects of the entertainment business and be a good negotiator. It's important to be able to network extensively with people in the business.

Compensation: Your income will be a percentage of what you earn for your clients. This percentage can range from 10 percent to 25 percent, depending on what all you do for your clients. Obviously the more bankable your clients, the more money you make.

EVENT AND CONFERENCE PLANNER

Description: Plans entertainment for events and conferences. This is usually done for businesses, clubs, and organizations (such as a political party planning an inauguration celebration), but occasionally individuals may require your services.

Time Schedule: Refer to #2 and #4 in Chapter 1 for suggestions on how to plan your time.

Requirements: In addition to those requirements outlined in #2 and #4 (Chapter 1), you will need many contacts and networking ability.

Compensation: Refer to #2 and #4 in Chapter 1.

EVENT ENTERTAINMENT CONSULTANT

Description: Counsels individuals and businesses on the type of entertainment to have at events such as holiday parties, weddings, grand openings, anniversaries, and class reunions. This type of consultant can also serve as a booking agent.

Time Schedule: Refer to #2 in Chapter 1.

Requirements: You'll need the imagination to design unusual and dynamic entertainment, and you'll need to know a wide variety of performers. Patience and the ability to work within a budget are also important, as is knowing how to market your service.

Compensation: Refer to #2 in Chapter 1. If you also serve as a booking agent, you will make a commission from the fees paid to the entertainers you book.

LITTLE THEATER PRODUCER

Description: Produces musical and dramatic productions for little theaters (such as are found on college campuses or in small communities). The job entails getting the appropriate performers, the director, and all others involved in the production, down to the people who move the sets and sell the tickets.

Time Schedule: As a freelancer, you will have control of your own schedule; but once you start the production, you will be busy all the time.

Requirements: You'll need a background in the arts, specifically in producing or directing. An imagination and good business acumen are also important. You will also need to be well known in the community and know all the talented people that live in it because these people will make up your performers and audience.

Compensation: Refer to #4 in Chapter 1.

MAGICIAN

Description: Performs magic acts in shows or at special events.

Time Schedule: You can set the days, weeks, or months that you will be available; however, once you have accepted a date, you must keep it.

Requirements: In addition to professional ability as a magician, you need to market yourself well or secure the services of an agent.

Compensation: You will be paid by the job. Refer to #2 in Chapter 1 for some suggestions.

MOVIE MEMORABILIA RETAILER

Description: Sells all kinds of movie-related items from a retail setting. Merchandise can include posters, photographs, costumes and props used in the movies, old scripts, and the like. Many of these items can be found in antiques stores and garage sales.

Time Schedule: Refer to #7 in Chapter 1.

Requirements: In addition to those requirements outlined in #7 in Chapter 1, you obviously need enthusiasm for movies, particularly old ones.

Compensation: Refer to #7 in Chapter 1. Because you should be able to buy some of your merchandise from garage sales, flea markets, swap meets, and so on, you may get it at reasonable cost and make a very high markup.

MOVIE AND TELEVISION EXTRA

Description: Has a nonspeaking role in television, movies, or commercials. Extras are the people who are in crowd scenes, sitting in restaurants or in theaters, running through the street as a monster is devouring a town, and so forth. Extras are chosen because they look like everyone else and do not stand out.

Time Schedule: As a freelancer, you can schedule times when you do not want to work. Then you won't show up for the "cattle calls" that invite extras to go down for casting on a specific day. Once you are accepted, however, you will have to stay at the location site until you are no longer needed; and that could be days.

Requirements: There are no special requirements—just a willingness to work and put up with the "standing around and waiting" that is the life of an extra. Because you do not speak, you do not need to belong to a union.

Compensation: You will be paid a flat rate per day based on what the going rate is in the city where you live. It is not big money. People usually perform as extras because they want to be around show business personalities and have a little excitement to tell their friends about. Many retired people and college students perform as extras.

MOVIE REVIEWER

Description: Reviews new movies for newspapers, magazines, radio, or television.

Time Schedule: Refer to #3 in Chapter 1.

Requirements: In addition to those requirements outlined in #3 (Chapter 1), you will need to appreciate and love movies. You need to know enough about motion picture production (and all its many facets) to be able to evaluate the worth of a movie. It's important to have a lively writing style, a dynamic voice, or a good screen presence so that you develop a following among your readers or listeners.

Compensation: Refer to #3 in Chapter 1.

MUSICAL INSTRUMENT INSTRUCTOR

Description: Teaches individuals how to play musical instruments. The instruction can take place at a school or out of your home

Time Schedule: Refer to #5 in Chapter 1 if you are working in a school. If you are teaching classes in your own home, you can set your own schedule.

Requirements: You need expertise in the instruments you will teach. You need all the qualities that any good teacher must have. Refer to #5 in Chapter 1.

Compensation: Refer to #5 in Chapter 1. If you are setting your own prices as an independent teacher, also refer to #1 and #2.

MUSICAL INSTRUMENT RETAILER

Description: Sells or rents musical instruments, usually from a retail setting. You might wish to give lessons if you are qualified or arrange for someone else to give them at your store.

Time Schedule: Refer to #7 in Chapter 1.

Requirements: Refer to #7 in Chapter 1.

Compensation: Refer to #7 in Chapter 1 for an understanding of how revenues in retail stores are generated; however, many music instrument stores also provide classes, and offering them can greatly increase your compensation.

MUSICIAN

Description: Plays a musical instrument, either in a band or as a soloist.

Time Schedule: If you work alone, you can generally block out the days or weeks that you don't wish to work. However, if you are with a band, then you will have to perform during its schedule.

Requirements: You'll need to be a professional musician, with much study and performance experience behind you. Many states will require that you belong to a union.

Compensation: If you work for a band, you will undoubtedly be paid a salary and possibly benefits. If you work independently, you will charge by the hour or performance. Refer to #2 in Chapter 1 for some suggestions regarding this kind of compensation.

MUSIC STORE OWNER

Description: Sells different types of music, usually from a retail store. The merchandise can include musical instruments, sheet music, videos, tapes, and compact discs. Anything having to do with music might be sold here.

Time Schedule: Refer to #7 in Chapter 1.

Requirements: You should know about all kinds of music and be aware of what kind of music is popular. Refer also to #7 in Chapter 1.

Compensation: Refer to #7 in Chapter 1.

PARTY PLANNER

Description: Plans parties and other social events for businesses, organizations, or individuals.

Time Schedule: Party planners are usually self-employed, so you would be able to set your own schedule.

Requirements: You need an imagination and a flair for putting on successful events. You must have organizational skills and know how to plan every phase of a party—designing clever invitations and party favors, selecting a theme, choosing centerpieces, booking entertainment.

Compensation: You will usually be paid by the event. Refer to #2 in Chapter 1 for suggestions.

✧ PERFORMER'S ASSISTANT

Description: Assists a performer, with professional endeavors, personal affairs, or outside business matters.

Time Schedule: You will probably be hired as an employee, so your schedule will have to complement your employer's. However, Chapter 18 gives you some suggestions on how to attain scheduling flexibility even under these circumstances.

Requirements: You will have to be competent at whatever you are being hired to do, and you need to be committed to doing a good job for your employer.

Compensation: You will probably be paid a salary and benefits, plus any expenses that you might incur in your position.

✧ PERFORMING ARTS ADMINISTRATOR

Description: Manages the business of a performing arts center. This includes bookings, scheduling, advertising, staffing, and budget.

Time Schedule: This is usually a full-time, administrative position; however, refer to #7 in Chapter 1 for suggestions on delegating some of the work.

Requirements: You'll need a business degree or background. While an understanding and love of the arts is very important, so is a good background in fund-raising and public relations.

Compensation: You will generally be paid a salary and benefits, with a possible bonus generated by profits.

PIANO TUNER

Description: Tunes pianos and does simple repairs—wherever the pianos are located.

Time Schedule: Refer to #9 in Chapter 1.

Requirements: In addition to those requirements listed in #9 (Chapter 1), you will need expertise at tuning and repairing pianos.

Compensation: Refer to #9 in Chapter 1.

PLAYWRIGHT

Description: Writes plays to be produced on the stage.

Time Schedule: Refer to #11 in Chapter 1.

Requirements: You need to know how to write plays, something that isn't necessarily learned in a classroom, although it may be. You have to be able to imagine the story you are telling as a dramatic production—something that is staged, choreographed, costumed, and lit.

Compensation: Refer to #11 in Chapter 1.

PUBLICIST

Description: Creates publicity for people and businesses in the entertainment field.

Time Schedule: As a freelancer, you will set your own hours; however, you do have to be available to meet with clients, organize events, and work with the media.

Requirements: Because a publicist has many different duties, you must be able to write press releases, organize press conferences, stage events that will bring your client to the attention of the public, and overcome any negative publicity.

Although it is possible to take formal classes in public relations, nothing will help you as much as experience, which you can get as an apprentice with a good publicist. Another way of learning this trade is to serve as a publicity chairperson for a club or civic organization. Because you are "selling" your client, you also need to think like a salesperson.

Compensation: Refer to #2 in Chapter 1.

✪ RADIO PERFORMER

Description: Performs on the radio. Positions can range from announcing the time and call letters to reading the news to having your own show (hosting a talk show or being a disc jockey).

Time Schedule: You will have to be available to perform when scheduled, although you can request that you work certain hours (such as the early morning if that fits your personal life best). Your control over your own schedule depends on your talent and your popularity with the audience.

Requirements: Although formal training in radio broadcasting definitely helps open doors, what you most need is a "radio voice" (one that sounds good over the airwaves) and a personality that radiates warmth and friendliness. All that the audience knows of you comes from your voice. If you are doing an interview show, you need to be a good interviewer; if you are a disc jockey, then you must know not only the songs that you are playing but also interesting information about the performers, the type of music, and the era the music comes from.

Compensation: The better you are and the more well known you are in your region, the more money you will make, because the more advertising you and your program will generate. All income in radio is predicated on advertising. Most performers make a salary and possibly a bonus or commission on their program's advertising. Ratings also play a very important role in how much you can demand. If yours is the most listened to program in your area during your time slot, then you can expect a higher monetary reward.

SCREENWRITER

Description: Writes screenplays for television and major motion pictures.

Time Schedule: Refer to #11 in Chapter 1. In addition, you must be available to meet with producers and perhaps be at the set during the filming of your screenplay.

Requirements: You need to know how to write screenplays—knowledge gained through formal education and a lot of practice. Writing for film or television requires a good imagination. You will need an agent to represent you, because producers do not read scripts from writers without agents. Membership in the Screenwriter's Guild is also necessary.

Compensation: You can be paid in several different ways for your screenplay. You might be paid simply for the story, and another screenwriter will be given the task of writing the finished product. You can be paid for the story and the screenplay, and then you will be paid a certain percentage of what the film makes. You may also be paid residuals every time it is re-released. Public libraries should have books explaining this business in more detail.

SET DECORATOR

Description: Decorates sets for plays, motion pictures, and television productions.

Time Schedule: During the planning stages, you can work on your own for the most part (however, you will attend a lot of meetings). Once the production begins, you will have to be there to make any last-minute changes.

Requirements: You need to be an expert in the kinds of sets that you decorate. For interior sets, you need to know about interior design, including the way houses were decorated at various times in history. If the sets you deal with are exterior, you must know about architecture, the appropriate vehicles (especially for historical pieces), street lighting and paving, natural lighting, and so on. A good imagination and the ability to visualize the finished product as it pertains to the medium you are working in is very important.

Compensation: Generally you will be paid by the project. Refer to #2 in Chapter 1 for some ideas on how to price your services. Also remember that the better your reputation, the more money you can demand.

SINGER

Description: Sings with a band or individually; in concerts, in commercials, or at any events where a singer might be used (such as weddings, funerals, birthdays, extravaganzas).

Time Schedule: You will have to be available to perform when you have agreed to; however, you might be able to block out certain months or weeks if you are not booked exclusively with one band.

Requirements: You need to have a professional singing voice and training. If you perform alone, you probably should have an outgoing, friendly personality because you will most likely be talking to the audience as well as singing.

Compensation: The better known and more talented you are, the greater your compensation. Generally, you will be paid for each appearance. If you record music offered for sale to the public, you will make a royalty on what is sold.

SOUND STAGE RECORDING EQUIPMENT OPERATOR

Description: Operates recording equipment from a sound stage. This can be something as simple as hooking up a microphone to a recorder to record someone's speech or something as complicated as producing a musical album from a live performance.

Time Schedule: As a freelancer, you can control your schedule.

Requirements: You need expertise in the operation of the assorted equipment. This can be acquired through practice and working with those who are accomplished in the business.

Compensation: You will generally be paid by the hour or by a fee based on how many hours you will work. Refer to #1 in Chapter 1 to determine how to price your work.

SPEAKER (MOTIVATIONAL)

Description: Gives motivational speeches to groups and organizations, company gatherings, and so on. The topic of the speech depends on the speaker's expertise, but it might deal with ways of improving one's efficiency, ways of getting along in a multicultural society, ways to relieve stress, and so on.

Time Schedule: You can block out certain weeks and months when you choose not to be available. However, once you have accepted speaking dates, you must be sure and honor them.

Requirements: You must be a professional public speaker who can discuss a topic in a convincing and entertaining way. You must also be able to "move your audience" by appealing to their emotions. If you can't do this, you won't be successful.

Compensation: You will be paid by the speech. Refer to #1 and #2 in Chapter 1 for ideas on how to price yourself. If you have tapes or books, selling them adds to your income.

SQUARE DANCE INSTRUCTOR

Description: Teaches square dancing to couples or groups. You might also call square dances.

Time Schedule: Refer to #5 in Chapter 1.

Requirements: In addition to those requirements outlined in #5, you obviously need an extensive knowledge of square dancing and the ability to teach it.

Compensation: Refer to #5 in Chapter 1.

SYMPHONY CONDUCTOR

Description: Conducts symphony orchestras. The orchestra might be large and well known or small and regional. For the purposes of this book, I am going to concentrate on the latter.

Time Schedule: Most orchestras play during specific seasons. This allows you some flexibility.

Requirements: You gain the skills and knowledge needed to be a professional conductor through education and experience. You must be a professional musician who has studied music for many years.

Compensation: The better and more famous you are and the larger, more prestigious the orchestra, the greater money you can command. Generally, you will be paid a salary and a commission or bonus depending on the tickets sold for your productions. Always try to get the latter as part of your compensation.

✪ TELEVISION SHOW HOST

Description: Hosts a television show. This can be for a major network's program, a regional program, or a local cable company production.

Time Schedule: Obviously you have to be available for taping of the show and any rehearsals. However, most shows are pretaped, and often several are taped in a day; as a result, more days off are possible. Also many productions shut down during certain times of the year, thus allowing you several weeks or months off.

Requirements: You need to be an entertainer, a performer. This requires a friendly attitude and a persona that will encourage people to keep on watching. If your ratings are low, you will be replaced instantly in this highly competitive business. You will have to join the Screen Actors' Guild in order to perform. It is also very important that you have an outstanding physical appearance; you must be thin because the camera adds pounds.

Compensation: Your compensation depends on the show you are on and the advertising it brings in, the time it airs, and the prestige of your name. The more famous you are and the higher your show is rated, the more money you can command. Some cable shows pay next to nothing but offer invaluable experience.

TICKET SELLER

Description: Sells tickets to all kinds of entertainment events. This can be done from a retail outlet or over the telephone.

Time Schedule: If you sell tickets from a retail outlet, refer to #7 in Chapter 1. If you work from a telephone line, someone will have to be there during specific hours to take the calls and arrange the sales. Also refer to #7 in Chapter 1.

Requirements: In addition to those requirements outlined in #7 (Chapter 1), you will need to make contacts with the various entertainment enterprises in your city in order to obtain the rights to sell certain blocks of their seats. This involves a tremendous amount of networking and marketing.

Compensation: You make money from charging a service fee above the cost of the tickets; your customers will be willing to pay the fee in exchange for the convenience of not waiting in line and not having to go to the theater, the concert hall, or the stadium to get the tickets. In our busy world, convenience has its price and people don't mind paying it.

TRADE NEWSPAPER/NEWSLETTER

Description: Writes, publishes, and sells newspapers or newsletters for a specific branch of the entertainment field.

Time Schedule: Refer to #11 in Chapter 1.

Requirements: Besides having the ability to write and market your work, you will need to be part of a network so that you can get the inside information you need for your publication.

Compensation: You will sell subscriptions for a certain number of issues. Refer to #1 in Chapter 1 for suggestions on how to price your product.

TRAINER OF PERFORMING ANIMALS

Description: Trains animals of all kinds (although in most cases a trainer will specialize in certain species) to perform in motion pictures, stage productions, circuses, or any other kind of event where performing animals are needed. The type of performance depends on the animal and the trainer's expertise. It could be a dog as multitalented as the collie that plays Lassie in a major motion picture or a cat that sits next to a box of cat food for a commercial or a live camel that walks across a stage at a Christmas pageant.

Time Schedule: As a freelancer, you should be able to control your working schedule; however, you will have to devote a certain amount of time each day to training your animals.

Requirements: You'll need knowledge and experience in training animals—which can be gained by serving an apprenticeship with trainers. You must be familiar with and obey the laws that demand the humane treatment of performing animals.

Compensation: You will be paid for the performance of your animal according to the length of the performance and its difficulty. Refer to #2 in Chapter 1 for some suggestions on pricing. In some areas, you may be required to join a union, which will affect how much you are paid. Depending on your animal's contribution to the production, you may be paid residuals.

VIDEO PHOTOGRAPHER

Description: Takes video photographs. Can be part of a camera crew for motion picture or television productions (which would include business films) or a freelancer who takes video pictures at weddings and other events.

Time Schedule: You can block out certain weeks or months when you do not wish to work; but once you have accepted an assignment, you will need to complete it.

Requirements: A professional ability to take moving pictures—usually gained from a combination of education and experience. Just taking good home movies isn't enough, but video photography isn't very difficult to learn.

Compensation: You will be paid by the hour or you will be paid a flat fee for the project (based on your hourly rate). If you work as a freelancer, you can make additional money by selling copies of the videos you have made. Refer to #6 in Chapter 1 for suggestions on how to price your services.

VIDEO PRODUCER

Description: Writes and produces videos mostly for the cable TV market, although individuals and families will also sometimes need videos produced. Your job is to oversee the project, beginning with the original idea and ending with the finished video. This could even include writing a script.

Time Schedule: As an independent operator, you have control of your schedule; but when you start working with a client, your days will probably be full and long.

Requirements: You'll need education and background in the arts. You must be able to either write scripts yourself or find people who can. You'll also have to find video photographers and performers.

Compensation: There is excellent money in this part of the entertainment business, and it is often overlooked. Refer to #1 and #2 in Chapter 1 for suggestions on how to price yourself and your service.

VIDEO RETAILER

Description: Sells video movies to the general public from a retail setting.

Time Schedule: Refer to #7 in Chapter 1.

Requirements: In addition to those requirements outlined in #7 (Chapter 1), you should love movies.

Compensation: Refer to #7 in Chapter 1. In this business, however, the bulk of your income will come from the rental fees you charge. This means that you have to develop a loyal clientele who will use you as their primary source for movie rentals. People who are successful in this business offer special prices if more than one movie is rented at the same time and offer discount cards that give a free rental after so many paid rentals. You must have better-than-average marketing and advertising skills and be able to develop a relationship with your customers because you will depend so much on repeat business.

VIDEO STORE SUPPLIER

Description: Sells videos to video stores. This is usually an outside sales job.

Time Schedule: Refer to #8 in Chapter 1.

Requirements: Refer to #8 in Chapter 1.

Compensation: Refer to #8 in Chapter 1.

VOICE TEACHER

Description: Teaches singing or speaking or both to potential entertainers.

Time Schedule: Refer to #5 in Chapter 1.

Requirements: In addition to those outlined in #5 (Chapter 1), you obviously need to be a professional singer or speaker or both.

Compensation: Refer to #5 in Chapter 1. Also realize that the better known you are, the more income you can command.

VOICE-OVER ARTIST

Description: Provides a voice for cartoon characters, narration, commercials on television or radio, educational and industrial films—anything that requires a distinctive voice appropriate to what the written words are conveying. For example, if a character in a cartoon is a baby, a tiny squeaky voice would be preferable to a low one. If a commercial is selling a well-made automobile, a man's authoritative voice is the ticket. Whenever someone on television speaks off camera, while the product is shown on the screen, a voice-over artist is at work.

Time Schedule: As a freelancer, you can determine when you do not want to work; but once you've agree to do a project, you have to work until it is completed. You might end up committing yourself for anywhere from one hour to many months if you should get on a series.

Requirements: A good voice and the ability to speak in more than one voice is also helpful. You also need an agent.

Compensation: You are paid a fee for the work. In some instances, you may also receive a residual. It all depends on how much you contribute to the production.

CHAPTER 13

The World of Caring for People

Is your greatest joy helping others? Making them feel better? Educating them? Bringing them peace and comfort? If you answered "yes" to any of these questions, then the sixty-three career opportunities described here should definitely interest you.

ACUPUNCTURIST

Description: Treats people by inserting special needles at pressure points of the body. Acupuncture is an Eastern form of medicine that claims to correct such physical ailments as headaches, musculoskeletal pain, asthma, tension, nervousness, backaches, arthritis, neuralgia, sciatica, weight gain, and nicotine addiction.

Time Schedule: Although this profession lends itself to a full-time career, it can be practiced on a part-time basis. Refer to #7 in Chapter 1.

Requirements: You'll need specialized training and the necessary state licenses. It also helps to know how to market your service.

Compensation: You will be paid a fee for the time you spend with your patients. Refer to #2 and #9 in Chapter 1 for suggestions on pricing your service.

✪ ADOPTION COUNSELOR

Description: Counsels pregnant women as well as people seeking to adopt on how to arrange adoption. This is usually done through organizations for women but can also be part of a doctor's or attorney's practice.

Time Schedule: If you work for an organization as a full-time counselor, refer to Chapter 18 for advice on turning it into a flexible job. As a freelance counselor, you can set your own schedule.

Requirements: You will need some counseling skills and, depending on whom you are working for and how in-depth your counseling, perhaps a license for your state. In this case, you would need family counseling credentials. However, some adoption counselors simply counsel women about this alternative to abortion; and once a woman has made the decision, they refer her to a lawyer specializing in adoptions.

Compensation: As a full-time employee, you will be paid a salary and possibly benefits. As a freelancer, you will be paid an hourly wage. Refer to #1 and #9 in Chapter 1 for suggestions on pricing yourself or for help in determining that what you are offered is sufficient.

✪ AIDS COUNSELOR

Description: Counsels individuals with AIDS as to medical treatment options, financial and legal help, hospice care, psychological problems related to the disease, and so on.

This most often is a position with a nonprofit organization; however, such groups do need professionals to counsel the patients.

Time Schedule: To some degree you will be able to control your own hours; refer to #2 in Chapter 1.

Requirements: You will probably need training and licensing in psychological counseling if you are going to go into this field. If you are simply giving information, you need sources for the most recent medical advances, availability of social services, and so on. The most important requirement for this position is caring for the patients whom you will meet.

Compensation: You may get a small fee depending on whom you work for and what your credentials are.

ALCOHOLISM TREATMENT COUNSELOR

Description: Counsels alcoholics on the best type of treatment to enable them to overcome their addiction. This job is usually performed in alcohol treatment centers.

Time Schedule: As a full-time employee, refer to the advice in Chapter 18 to learn how to get some flexibility in your job. Frequently, you are hired part-time or for only a few days a week or for weekends. The nature of this job makes it difficult to be unavailable for weeks or months at a time; you must be on hand to oversee the treatment of your patients.

Requirements: You will need a medical background, at least as a nurse. Depending on how extensive your counseling, you may have to be a licensed physician. You must understand the psychology and physiology behind alcoholism.

Compensation: As a full-time employee, you will probably be paid a salary and benefits. As a part-time employee or a freelancer, you will be paid an hourly wage. The amount depends on your credentials.

ASTROLOGER

Description: Gives people advice on their future as a result of studying the influence of the moon, sun, and stars.

Time Schedule: As a freelancer, you can set your own schedule.

Requirements: You'll need education and experience in the practice of astrology. This can be gained by studying with astrologers. You need to check your state and city for any licenses that you might need to have. You also need to market yourself; refer to #2 in Chapter 1.

Compensation: Refer to #2 in Chapter 1.

AUDIOLOGIST

Description: Tests and evaluates the hearing of individuals and then recommends and sells hearing aids if needed.

Time Schedule: As a professional, you can set your own hours and delegate some of your responsibilities to employees, as described in #7 in Chapter 1.

Requirements: You need the proper equipment and a knowledge of how to treat hearing problems. In most instances, state licenses will be required.

Compensation: You might charge a fee for the hearing test and evaluation, but the bulk of your income will be generated from the sale of hearing aids.

BABY-SITTER

Description: Takes care of children, including babies (thus the name), in their home for a limited number of hours so that the parents or parent can go out for an evening or run errands and take care of personal business during the day.

Time Schedule: You have total control over the days and hours that you will work.

Requirements: You need knowledge of child and baby care, which should include a knowledge of basic first aid and how to deal with emergencies. You need a pleasing personality and a willingness to play with the children.

Compensation: Refer to #1 in Chapter 1 for ideas on how to price yourself, but also check your competition to see what they are charging. This job is ideal for teenagers and senior citizens who just want to pick up a little extra money and don't want to be tied down to any other kind of job. If you can establish a group of loyal clients, you should be successful as a baby-sitter.

BARBER

Description: Cuts and styles hair, mostly for men, from a retail establishment. You might own the barbershop or simply rent your station.

Time Schedule: Refer to #7 in Chapter 1 if you own the shop. If you are renting your station and are in business for yourself, you can select the days and hours that you wish to work. However, the more hours and days you choose to be available, the more financially successful you will be.

Requirements: You'll need professional training in hair cutting and the appropriate license for your state. An ability to market yourself is also advisable, and you must have a personality so pleasing that people will return to you. The secret to being successful in this business is to get repeat customers.

Compensation: Refer to #1 and #9 in Chapter 1 for suggestions on how to price yourself.

BEAUTICIAN

Description: Cuts, colors, weaves, and styles hair; often gives permanents as well.

Time Schedule: You can plan your own schedule; however, it is difficult to take whole blocks of weeks or months off because you will lose your customers. However, this job is excellent for mothers who can work around their children's schedules.

Requirements: You have to go to a school that teaches hairdressing and, in most states, then have to pass the state board and become licensed.

Compensation: Your income is generated by what you charge for your work. In most cases, you will rent your space in a hairdressing salon and pay for your own supplies. What you make above that is your income. Refer to #1 and #9 in Chapter 1 for additional information on this subject.

BIRTHING CENTER CONSULTANT

Description: Counsels people who are contemplating having a baby in a birthing center instead of a traditional hospital. The consultant usually works for the center.

Time Schedule: If you work full-time, Chapter 18 will advise you on getting a flexible time schedule. Often you will be employed part-time and so will have more flexibility.

Requirements: Because this position may be nothing more than a sales job for the center (so that you will have to understand how the birthing center is preferable to a hospital), you probably will not need any special counseling experience. More frequently, you will need the personality and skills of a salesperson plus a great belief in what you are selling.

Compensation: It varies, but you may be paid a salary and possibly a commission on every patient whom you sign up.

BLOOD BANK ADMINISTRATOR

Description: Administers blood banks for organizations, such as the Red Cross, who collect blood and distribute it to hospitals and individuals when needed. This is mostly an administrative position, which might include public relations duties to help gain donors.

Time Schedule: If you are a full-time employee, refer to Chapter 18 for advice on making your job more flexible. You may be employed as a part-time worker, particularly if the agency you are working for is small. If this is the case, you will be able to better control your time.

Requirements: You'll need an administrative background, preferably in a hospital or medical practice. If your duties will include public relations, it would be good to have some background in that field as well.

Compensation: You will receive a full-time salary or part-time hourly wage, depending on what the job dictates.

BOARD AND CARE INSPECTOR

Description: Inspects board and care facilities, either for local government agencies or for nonprofit agencies that protect the elderly. The inspection will determine the cleanliness and safety of the facility as well as the quality of care it gives its patients.

Time Schedule: If you work for the government, you may be required to work full-time. Refer to Chapter 18 for some pointers on getting some flexibility in a full-time job. As an inspector for a nonprofit organization, you may be hired part-time or on an on-call basis. This, of course, offers a great deal more freedom.

Requirements: Depending on whom you work for, you may need a degree in medicine. Some medical background will be helpful because it will enable you to better inspect the care that the patients receive. It's important to pay attention to details and to be emotionally strong.

Compensation: You will be paid a salary if you work full-time or an hourly wage if you work part-time. Depending on whom you work for, you might also get some benefits.

BOARD AND CARE PROVIDER

Description: Provides full-time board and care for elderly or physically or mentally challenged individuals.

Time Schedule: If you live at the facility, refer to #7 in Chapter 1, which gives advice on delegating some of the work to employees. If you do not live in the facility and hire people to live and work there, then your schedule can be quite flexible.

Requirements: You will need a facility (house) large enough to accommodate patients and the people who care for them. Your state and city will also have specific licensing and possibly zoning requirements.

Compensation: Your income will be generated from what you charge your patients. Frequently you will receive their payment (a flat monthly fee that includes rental of their room and food and possibly medicines) from a government agency such as your state's welfare program and the federal social security program. Refer to #1 and #7 in Chapter 1 to learn how to establish fees after expenses.

CHIROPRACTIC INSTRUCTOR

Description: Teaches chiropractic classes to students with the intent of preparing them for the profession. This is usually done from an accredited school.

Time Schedule: Refer to #5 in Chapter 1.

Requirements: In addition to those requirements outlined in #5 (Chapter 1), you will need to be a licensed chiropractor.

Compensation: Refer to #5 in Chapter 1.

CHIROPRACTOR

Description: Treats back and leg pain; headaches; bursitis; tendinitis; hand and foot numbness; and auto, sports, and work-related injuries with physical manipulations to the body.

Time Schedule: As a professional, you can establish your own hours. Although this profession lends itself to long hours, many successful chiropractors work a reduced schedule. Refer to #7 in Chapter 1.

Requirements: You will need specialized training at an accredited chiropractic school and the appropriate internship. You will also need to be licensed in your state.

Compensation: You will be paid a fee for the time you spend with your patients. Any additional expenses, such as x-rays, are also charged to the patient. Medical insurance companies are beginning to recognize and include chiropractic treatments, which makes this an even more lucrative field to enter.

CONSULTANT ON ACCESS FOR THE DISABLED

Description: Counsels builders and businesses in creating parking spaces, ramps, special elevators, and restroom facilities so that disabled people, most generally in wheelchairs, can have access to their facility.

Time Schedule: You can control your own schedule.

Requirements: You'll need expertise in the needs and lifestyles of disabled people, which is obtained through education and experience; also refer to #2 in Chapter 1.

Compensation: Refer to #2 in Chapter 1.

COSMETICIAN

Description: Deals in cosmetics, selling or applying makeup or both. This can be done at the customer's location or from a retail store.

Time Schedule: In most cases, you can determine your own hours, particularly if you are an outside salesperson calling on people in their homes or offices. If you own a retail cosmetic store, refer to #7 in Chapter 1.

Requirements: You need training and experience in cosmetics. Check with your particular state and city regarding any licenses you may need.

Compensation: If you sell the cosmetics, your income will be generated from your sales. Refer to #8 in Chapter 1. If you simply apply makeup, you will charge a flat fee for this service. Refer to #9 in Chapter 1.

COUNSELOR FOR BATTERED PERSONS

Description: Counsels people, usually women, who have been battered by a spouse or loved one. This is usually done in a "safe shelter."

Time Schedule: You may be hired as a full-time employee, in which case Chapter 18 may be helpful. Frequently, these positions are part-time, and so you would have more flexibility.

Requirements: You need to understand the particular problems of victims of abuse. Depending on how detailed your counseling will be, you may need to be a licensed counselor. However, often what is needed is someone to give sympathy and offer the battered person some options; referrals to professionals might be part of the job.

Compensation: You may earn a full-time salary or receive an hourly wage.

COUNSELOR IN EATING DISORDERS

Description: Counsels people who have eating disorders, such as anorexia, bulimia, or bingeing. You may do so in a treatment center or weight loss center. This kind of position usually consists of explaining the program to the potential patient or customer as opposed to giving medical advice or treatment.

Time Schedule: If you are employed full-time, refer to Chapter 18. You may be a part-time employee and so have more flexibility.

Requirements: You'll need empathy for the people and their problems and a total understanding of how your center's treatment works. Refer to #8 in Chapter 1 for additional requirements that are important if you are expected to sell the service.

Compensation: You may be paid a flat salary (depending on how many hours you work). If yours is more of a sales position, you will probably receive a commission on everyone you sign up.

COUNSELOR IN SERVICES FOR THE DISABLED

Description: Provides services for the disabled in independent living (which includes an assessment of whether a disabled person can live independently) and health care; provides specially made vehicles and driving instructions for the disabled. Someone in this position also counsels businesses in sensitivity training and disability-related laws, regulations, and solutions and serves as an advocate for the disabled.

Time Schedule: If you work for the service, you can be employed as a part-time or full-time employee. Check Chapter 18 if you are the latter. If you are providing this service on a freelance basis, you can have control of your time.

Requirements: You'll need experience working with the disabled, probably as a nurse, nurse's aide, or counselor. You should have a true commitment to the cause and the ability to interact with all types of people and agencies.

Compensation: You will probably be paid a fee. Refer to #2 in Chapter 1. If you work for the service, you will earn a wage.

DAY-CARE PROVIDER

Description: Cares for people, usually children, during the day while their primary caretakers (parents) are working. In addition, elder care is becoming more common. Caregiving is usually done from your home or a facility where all of the people can be watched in one location.

Time Schedule: You will have to be available during the hours that you contract to care for the people. If you are planning on having paid workers help you, refer to #7 in Chapter 1 for ways to find and train people. This kind of business is especially good for housewives who are home with their children. Adding a few more brings in extra money.

Requirements: You'll need appropriate state or city licensing plus a facility that is safe and easily accessible for children and elderly people whom you might care for. Having a great deal of patience is very necessary—as is a sense of humor. Don't forget to learn and be able to perform basic first aid.

Compensation: Your income will come from what you charge. Before setting your prices, check your competition and refer to #1 and #9 in Chapter 1 for suggestions on how to establish a fair price.

✪ DENTAL ASSISTANT

Description: Assists dentists with patients. This includes taking x-rays, helping the dentist with surgery, and so on. In some smaller offices, it might also include cleaning teeth.

Time Schedule: If you work in a dental office, you will have to work when the dentist asks you to in order to accommodate the practice. Refer to Chapter 18 on how to convince the dentist to allow you some flexibility. You can also work for temporary employment service agencies that place you for certain periods of time in various dental offices. If you choose this path, you can determine the weeks and months that you wish to work.

Requirements: You'll need formal training in the field and any licenses that your state or city require.

Compensation: If you work for one dentist, you will be paid a salary. If you work with an agency, you will generally be paid an hourly rate. How much you can make depends on your level of education and experience in the field.

DENTIST

Description: Treats teeth. This includes orthodontia, capping, filling cavities, pulling teeth, treating gum disease—everything that affects the teeth and mouth.

Time Schedule: While this profession is usually practiced full-time, many dentists are limiting their hours in order to enjoy life more. You can limit your own hours or work on call for several dental offices for even more flexibility.

Requirements: You'll need a degree from an accredited dental school and state licensing. You also need a well-equipped office (if you are going to have your own practice); today, marketing is often important in making a dental practice successful.

Compensation: Your income will be generated from what you charge your patients, minus your costs. Refer to #1 and #9 in Chapter 1 for suggestions.

DERMATOLOGIST

Description: Treats diseases of the skin.

Time Schedule: If you are in practice for yourself, you can determine your own hours. This branch of medicine lends itself well to reduced hours.

Requirements: You'll need a degree from an accredited medical school and a license from your state, plus board certification in dermatology. Knowledge of how to market your practice is also important.

Compensation: Your income will derive from the difference between your expenses and what your patients pay. Refer to #1 and #9 in Chapter 1 for additional advice.

✪ DIVORCE MEDIATOR

Description: Offers alternatives to the high cost of divorce through legal battles and court appearances. Someone in this position works with couples on separation agreements, child support, custody, modifications, restraining orders, visitations, and so forth.

Time Schedule: If you work independently, you can establish your own hours.

Requirements: You need a legal background, either as a paralegal or as an attorney. Depending on your state, you may have to be licensed. You also need excellent communication skills and possibly a background in counseling.

Compensation: You will generally be paid a fee. Refer to #2 in Chapter 1 for suggestions on pricing your services.

✪ DRIVER FOR ELDERLY AND HANDICAPPED

Description: Provides transportation for elderly and handicapped individuals who cannot drive themselves.

Time Schedule: You can set your own schedule as far as days you choose not to work, but you will not be able to block out whole weeks or months because you will have an established clientele who will depend on you.

Requirements: You will need a special van or bus that can accommodate people with wheelchairs if you intend to transport people who use them. It will also be necessary to have special automobile insurance. Check with your city for guidelines on any other licenses you may need.

Compensation: You can charge by the mile, with a minimum fee. If you are to be successful in this business, you will want to establish a loyal clientele who will depend on you weekly to take them shopping, to the doctor's, and so forth.

DRUG ADDICTION COUNSELOR

Description: Counsels individuals seeking treatment for their addiction to drugs. This job is usually done in treatment centers.

Time Schedule: If you are hired as a full-time employee, refer to Chapter 18 for advice on making your job more flexible. You may be hired on a part-time basis and will then have more control over your schedule.

Requirements: You need to have education in the problems of addiction and experience treating it; depending on the specific job, you might need a medical background. If the job entails no more than convincing individuals that the treatment center can help them, you will need nothing more than a salesperson's requirements (see #8 in Chapter 1) plus enough understanding of drug addiction to answer questions and present the facility's program.

Compensation: You will be paid a fee if you work independently, a salary if you are an employee.

EDUCATIONAL CONSULTANT

Description: Counsels individuals on how to get college scholarships (and finds unusual ones), helps with college applications and financial aid, assesses career and education possibilities, and prepares students to do well on the PSAT and SAT tests. Also gives seminars pertaining to education and helps adults in transition. Some educational consultants specialize in helping displaced workers.

Time Schedule: You can set your own hours.

Requirements: You'll need a background in education, particularly in financial aid; experience in the admissions or financial aid office of a university is important. It's critical that you know all about the most recent changes in private and government student aid programs. Public speaking ability is very helpful. Finally, refer to #2 in Chapter 1.

Compensation: Refer to #2 in Chapter 1.

✪ ELECTROLYSIS TECHNICIAN

Description: Removes unwanted hair from an individual's body or face by using an electrified needle to remove the hair's roots. This is usually done in a beauty salon.

Time Schedule: You will be self-employed and so can set your own hours.

Requirements: You need training in electrolysis as well as the necessary equipment. Check with your state and community regarding necessary licenses.

Compensation: The fee you charge minus your expenses will generate your income. Refer to #9 in Chapter 1.

✪ EXERCISE TRAINER

Description: Teaches people to exercise and helps them maintain the discipline. This can be done through a retail outlet or in the individual client's home. If you travel to the client's home, you will be called a "personal trainer."

Time Schedule: If you work out of a gym, refer to #5 in Chapter 1. If you are a personal trainer, you can set the hours you wish to work; however, you will also have to be available to accommodate your clients.

Requirements: You'll need education in the benefits and risks of exercise, possible injuries, and the best way to set up training programs. Patience also helps. Check with your local government to learn if you need a special license.

Compensation:: Refer to #5 in Chapter 1; you may also find helpful suggestions in #1 and #9.

FAMILY/MARRIAGE COUNSELOR

Description: Counsels individuals and members of families on how to handle emotional problems that are adversely affecting their relationships. Problems commonly tackled by family/marriage counselors include children's misbehavior; inability to communicate or agree; infidelity; financial differences; substance, sexual, emotional, and physical abuse; and family interference.

Time Schedule: You can control the times and days that you wish to see patients, but it is difficult to take off for several weeks or months at a time; once you start seeing patients, you must see them frequently.

Requirements: You'll need formal education and training in family/marriage counseling, which will probably include a state license. The ability to market your service is also very necessary.

Compensation: Your income will be generated by the fees you charge your patients. Refer to #2 and #9 in Chapter 1 for suggestions.

FAMILY PLANNING COUNSELOR

Description: Works for family planning centers and women's centers dispensing information, usually on birth control. This position might also involve offering pregnancy testing and giving information on abortion services, laparoscopic sterilization procedures, and adoption counseling.

Time Schedule: You might be employed part-time or full-time. If the latter, refer to Chapter 18.

Requirements: You'll need a technical knowledge of the many options that you are recommending, plus exceptional patience and communication skills. You may need to speak a second language, such as Spanish, if the people who live near your center are not English-speaking.

Compensation: You will be paid a weekly salary if you work full-time or an hourly wage if you are a part-timer.

FIRST-AID INSTRUCTOR

Description: Teaches first aid to groups, civic organizations, and individuals. This is usually done through an agency such as the Red Cross or a fire department.

Time Schedule: If you work as a freelancer, you can establish what days and months you might not wish to work. If you are an employee with one of these organizations, refer to Chapter 18, which will advise you on how to make your job more flexible. Refer to #5 in Chapter 1 for additional suggestions.

Requirements: You'll need a professional knowledge of first aid and must hold any necessary licenses. Patience is always important in a teaching job.

Compensation: Refer to #5 if you are working independently. If you work as an employee for an organization, you will probably be paid a salary and appropriate benefits.

FUNERAL/BURIAL CONSULTANT

Description: Sells funerals and burial sites to individuals, either before they need it (called pre-need) or for a loved one upon that person's death.

Time Schedule: If you sell pre-need services, you will have the same schedule as outside salespeople; refer to #8 in

Chapter 1. Selling to people who have just lost a loved one will be done at the mortuary or cemetery. You might still be able to control your own hours to some extent.

Requirements: In addition to those requirements outlined in #8 (Chapter 1), you may need special licensing to sell funerals and cemetery plots. Check with your state. It also is very important to have understanding and empathy for people who are grieving and to be able to instill in them a feeling of confidence in you and what you suggest.

Compensation: Refer to #8 in Chapter 1.

HERBALIST

Description: Counsels and prescribes botanical and homeopathic remedies, which also include vitamins, spices, and oils for individuals' various ailments. You will usually also sell the products.

Time Schedule: As an independent practitioner, you can control your own time schedule.

Requirements: You will probably have to be licensed by your state. You will need extensive training in this field, which might be gained from science courses in universities as well as from working with herbalists.

Compensation: You will earn your income from the fees that your patients pay as well as from the markup earned on the sales of your products.

HOME HEALTH CARE PROVIDER

Description: Provides home health care for individuals who need housekeeping, companionship, and personal care. Part of the job is assessing the home and individual to determine what is needed. If you own the business, you will then provide people to fill these needs. You might also choose to work for a service.

Time Schedule: If you own the business, refer to #7 in Chapter 1 for suggestions on delegating work. If you work for a service, you can request certain blocks of weeks or days that you don't wish to work; but once you take an assignment, you will have to complete it.

Requirements: In addition to knowing how to run a business if you are the owner, you should be a registered nurse or licensed vocational nurse so that you can understand the needs of those who request your services. If you work for the service and need to provide nursing services, you too must have a medical background. However, if you are simply going to act as a companion or housekeeper, a willingness to do the work and patience are the only requirements. This can be a very emotionally demanding job, however, so you should have a commitment to it.

Compensation: Whether you own the business or work for it, your income is generated from the fees that the clients pay. This is based on an hourly rate and the amount of work required.

HOSPITAL WORKER

Description: You don't have to have a medical background to work in a hospital. There are all kinds of jobs that let you feel that you are contributing to the care of people. Some of these positions are ward secretary, admitting office clerk, housekeeping worker, kitchen helper, janitor.

Time Schedule: Although many of these jobs are full-time (in which case, check out the advice in Chapter 18), others are part-time or very flexible. And because hospitals are open every day and every hour, there are opportunities to work every day and time shift.

Requirements: Requirements vary according to position, but they are the same as they would be outside of a hospital setting.

Compensation: You will be paid a salary or hourly wage. If you are a full-time worker, you will probably receive benefits.

HYPNOTIST/HYPNOTHERAPIST

Description: Puts individuals into a sleeplike condition where consciousness is lost, yet the individual is able to respond, with certain limitations, to suggestions given by the hypnotist.

Time Schedule: As an independent contractor, you can control your own schedule. Much will depend on the number of clients you have.

Requirements: Besides the obvious training in hypnotism, you will need to know how to market your service. Most states do not require licensing of hypnotists, but hypnotherapists (who give psychological treatment through hypnosis) are generally licensed as psychologists, counselors, social workers, psychiatrists, or other members of the medical community.

Compensation: Your income will be generated from the fees you charge your patients. Refer to #2 and #9 in Chapter 1.

MANICURIST

Description: Gives manicures and applies artificial nails to clients, usually in a beauty salon setting. A manicurist might also give pedicures.

Time Schedule: As an independent operator, you can set your own schedule.

Requirements: You will need training in giving manicures and pedicures and in attaching nails. This training is usually gained through attending a trade school. Check your state regarding the need for licensing.

Compensation: Your income will be generated from what you charge your clients, minus your expenses. In most instances you will pay rent for the part of the facility you use. Refer to #1 and #9 in Chapter 1.

✪ MASSAGE INSTRUCTOR

Description: Teaches the technique of massage to people who intend to join the profession. This will usually be done from a school.

Time Schedule: Refer to #5 in Chapter 1.

Requirements: In addition to those outlined in #5 (Chapter 1), you will need to be a professional, licensed massage therapist with experience that you can pass on to others.

Compensation: Refer to #5 in Chapter 1.

✪ MASSAGE THERAPIST

Description: Uses massage to treat pain caused by muscle strain or psychological stress. This can be done from your office, or you can take your equipment (consisting of a table) to the patients' locations.

Time Schedule: You can arrange your own hours.

Requirements: You will need special training and licensing. It is also very important that you know how to market your service.

Compensation: You will receive a fee for your services. Refer to #9 in Chapter 1 for suggestions on pricing your service correctly.

MEDICAL SALESPERSON

Description: Sells medical supplies to hospitals, doctors, and pharmacists. Products include new medicines as well as equipment. This is an outside sales position.

Time Schedule: Refer to #8 in Chapter 1.

Requirements: Refer to #8 in Chapter 1; some medical knowledge is also helpful.

Compensation: Refer to #8 in Chapter 1.

MEDICAL WRITER

Description: Writes medical articles for magazines and newspapers, as well as books for the public and the profession. A medical writer might also publish a newsletter.

Time Schedule: You can control your own schedule.

Requirements: Refer to #11 in Chapter 1 for general requirements for writers. You will also need a medical background in order to understand what you are reporting.

Compensation: Refer to #11 in Chapter 1.

NANNY

Description: Takes care of babies and children in their home, by providing physical and emotional nurturing. This is usually a live-in position.

Time Schedule: Because you will be expected to live with the family and be on call for the children twenty-four hours a day, all you will have are days off—usually two in a row. Depending on your employers' schedules, you may be able to control those.

Requirements: You need to know about children and how to raise them—for that is what you will be doing. Today there are employment services for nannies, and they frequently offer training programs. If you have experience as a nurse or teacher, you would be a good nanny.

Compensation: You will be paid a wage plus board and room. This is an ideal job for a retired woman or a young woman who hasn't decided what she wants to be permanently.

NURSE

Description: Works as a medical nurse, either in a doctor's office, clinic, or hospital.

Time Schedule: If you work for one employer, such as a doctor or hospital, refer to Chapter 18 for suggestions on how to arrange flexible time. You can also work for a temporary agency specializing in medical personnel; this kind of position allows you more control over your work schedule, allowing you to block out whole weeks and months if you desire.

Requirements: You'll need a degree from an accredited nursing school, training, and experience as a nurse with the necessary state and local licenses.

Compensation: If you work as an employee, you will be paid a salary and benefits. In a hospital, you will usually also be given overtime pay. If you work for an agency, you will be paid by the hour; some agencies also pay benefits.

OPTOMETRIST

Description: Examines the eyes of an individual for farsightedness, nearsightedness, and diseases of the eye, and then determines what kind of lenses and glasses are needed to correct the problem. Some optometrists also fit glasses.

Time Schedule: You can control the hours of your own practice. Many optometrists no longer work long hours but join a practice with others so that they can enjoy a more flexible lifestyle.

Requirements: You need a degree from a college of optometry and your state's appropriate licensing. You should know how to build a practice; you'll need the appropriate equipment.

Compensation: You will charge a fee for your service and will get a markup on glasses you sell. These, minus the costs of your business, will generate your income.

PARENTING INSTRUCTOR

Description: Teaches parenting skills, usually through a school district or as part of a family counselor position. Seminars might be offered as part of the service.

Time Schedule: As an independent contractor, you can generally set your own schedule.

Requirements: You'll need formal training and education plus any necessary licenses to satisfy state requirements.

Compensation: You will charge a fee for your services. Refer to #2 and #9 in Chapter 1.

PHARMACIST

Description: Dispenses medicines from doctors' prescriptions; works from a pharmacy open to the public.

Time Schedule: Because most drugstores and their pharmacies are open every day, you can usually select the hours that you would like to work. If you own the pharmacy, you can control your own hours by taking some of the advice offered in #7 in Chapter 1.

Requirements: You'll need a degree from an accredited college of pharmacy, plus all the necessary city and state licenses.

Compensation: If you work for a pharmacy, you will earn a salary or hourly wage. If you own the business, your income will be generated on the markup you charge for the medicincs you sell.

PHYSICIAN

Description: A medical or osteopathic doctor practicing any one of a number of specialties. Usually works out of an office and hospital.

Time Schedule: Although this is a very demanding profession known for its long hours, some physicians who maintain active practices do not work long hours. I know of a woman doctor whose day starts at 7 A.M., but her office hours are over at 2 P.M. so that she can be home for her children in the afternoon. She schedules surgery for the morning.. Some doctors prefer to work for other physicians on call.

Requirements: You need a degree from an accredited school of medicine or osteopathy and all the appropriate state licenses. If you are going into your own practice, you will need all the necessary fixtures, machines, and help that make up a professional medical practice.

Compensation: Your income is generated from your fees paid either by your patients or their insurance companies, minus the costs of your business. Refer to #9 in Chapter 1.

✪ PODIATRIST

Description: A physician who treats disorders of the feet.

Time Schedule: You can control your own hours if you choose to maintain your own practice. Refer to the entry for a physician.

Requirements: You'll need the education and experience that enable you to work in your specialty and the licensing required by your state. You will also need an office and the equipment that makes up a medical practice.

Compensation: Your income will be generated from the fees that you charge, minus your costs. Refer to #9 in Chapter 1.

✪ PREGNANCY COUNSELOR

Description: Counsels individuals—frequently couples—on pregnancy-related problems or concerns. These concerns can include difficulties in getting pregnant, artificial insemination, genetic disorders, in vitro procedures, and so forth. When done in a fertility clinic, this job is frequently one where you sell the individuals on the particular services and merits of the clinic.

Time Schedule: You may be hired as a full-time employee; if so, refer to Chapter 18. If you are a part-timer, you will have more flexibility.

Requirements: If your counseling is limited to selling the service, refer to #8 in Chapter 1. If you are the counselor/physician who is supplying the service, then you will need all the medical training and experience, plus appropriate state licenses.

Compensation: You will be compensated from the fees that are paid for the service. As a salesperson, you will receive a commission. As the person doing the work, you will receive the fee, minus any costs. Refer to #9 in Chapter 1.

✪ PSYCHOLOGIST

Description: Treats individuals' emotional and psychological ailments.

Time Schedule: You can set whatever time schedule you wish for your particular practice.

Requirements: You'll need the necessary education and experience, plus a state license. You will also need an office unless you work with another psychologist.

Compensation: Your income comes from the fees you charge, minus your expenses.

✪ RAPE COUNSELOR

Description: Works with law enforcement agencies and hospitals or mental health agencies in counseling women who have suffered rapes.

Time Schedule: As an independent operator, you should be able to establish your own schedule.

Requirements: You'll need the necessary education and experience, plus state licensing. You'll need a commitment to the problem you are dealing with, and you should be able to give advice on legal options. You might have to appear as a court witness.

Compensation: Refer to #2 in Chapter 1.

✪ READING IMPROVEMENT INSTRUCTOR

Description: Teaches reading techniques to help individuals improve their reading and comprehension skills. This is usually done from a specialized school.

Time Schedule: Refer to #5 in Chapter 1.

Requirements: Refer to #5 in Chapter 1.

Compensation: Refer to #5 in Chapter 1.

RETIREMENT CONSULTANT

Description: Counsels people who are planning retirement: gives advice on where to live, what to do to stay active, how to handle finances, and so forth. Businesses generally hire retirement counselors to help their employees.

Time Schedule: You can control your own schedule. Refer to #2 in Chapter 1.

Requirements: You'll need counseling education and experience, plus particular empathy for people facing retirement. Good communication skills and patience are very important too. Refer to #2 in Chapter 1.

Compensation: Refer to #2 in Chapter 1.

SAFETY CONSULTANT

Description: Counsels businesses on safety issues mandated by federal and state law as they apply.

Time Schedule: Refer to #2 in Chapter 1.

Requirements: In addition to the requirements outlined in #2 (Chapter 1), you need to be an expert in all phases of safety, including the OSHA guidelines and regulations. You must also be a good communicator and problem solver.

Compensation: Refer to #2 in Chapter 1.

SCHOOL AIDE

Description: Aids the school in many different capacities, such as bus driver, crossing guard, cafeteria worker, classroom aide, recess helper, library aide. These are usually part-time positions.

Time Schedule: Although you will have to work the hours that the position demands, they are usually part-time; and so you will have some hours every day to do what you wish.

Requirements: Each school district has its own set of requirements, depending on the job. You'll be spending a lot of time with children, so it's an advantage if you like them.

Compensation: You will be paid by the hour. What you will be paid over minimum wage depends on the wealth of the school district and the difficulty of the job.

SCHOOL REPRESENTATIVE

Description: Represents schools, usually occupational, to prospective students. This is usually an outside sales position.

Time Schedule: Refer to #8 in Chapter 1.

Requirements: In addition to those requirements outlined in #8 (Chapter 1), you will need an understanding of the occupations the school teaches so that you can represent the careers as well as the school.

Compensation: Refer to #8 in Chapter 1.

SKIN CARE PRODUCTS SALESPERSON

Description: Sells skin-care products to the public. This can be done from a retail establishment or door-to-door as an outside salesperson.

Time Schedule: Refer to #7 and #8 in Chapter 1.

Requirements: In addition to those outlined in #7 and #8 (Chapter 1), you need an understanding of different skin types and their needs, an interest in your product, and an ability to teach and motivate others to use your products so that they will need to reorder.

Compensation: Refer to #7 and #8 in Chapter 1.

STRESS MANAGEMENT AND PREVENTION COUNSELOR

Description: Counsels individuals in managing and preventing the stresses of their jobs and personal lives. Large companies frequently hire these counselors to help their employees.

Time Schedule: Refer to #2 in Chapter 1.

Requirements: You'll need necessary education and experience, plus any mandatory state licenses. Also refer to #2 in Chapter 1.

Compensation: Refer to #2 in Chapter 1.

TUTOR

Description: Teaches certain subjects to individuals in their homes.

Time Schedule: Because you will be working independently, you will be able to control your days and hours. However, you will rarely be able to take entire weeks and months off unless you have no clients.

Requirements: You need extensive knowledge in the subjects you are teaching and the ability to teach. It also helps to know how to market your service.

Compensation: Refer to #1 and #9 in Chapter 1 for suggestions on how to price your services.

VITAMIN AND MINERAL CONSULTANT

Description: Counsels individuals in the use of vitamins and minerals to enhance their health and possibly correct health problems.

Time Schedule: Refer to #2 in Chapter 1.

Requirements: You need specialized training and knowledge in vitamins and minerals and how they interact with the body; you can get this training through working in a vitamin store or for a manufacturer; you should also check with your state about any necessary licensing. Refer again to #2 for additional recommendations.

Compensation: Refer to #2 in Chapter 1.

WEDDING CONSULTANT

Description: Helps coordinate weddings by advising the couple on clothing, music, flowers, cake, reception areas, and the like. You also need to be at the wedding to be sure that it all runs smoothly.

Time Schedule: You can establish the months or weeks when you do not wish to work. This is, however, a weekend job because most weddings take place on Fridays, Saturdays, and Sundays.

Requirements: You need to know about current and traditional customs involved in weddings; you need information on the best sources for clothing, flowers, catering, and so forth. It's essential to have patience and the ability to handle any crises calmly and professionally. You also need to know how to market your services.

Compensation: Refer to #2 in Chapter 1.

Chapter 14

The World of Religion

If you are a religious person, you might be interested in finding work with your church or work that is related to your beliefs. You don't have to be a member of the clergy to have a job in this field.

CHAPLAIN

Description: Ministers to the needs of people in jails, hospitals, colleges, armed forces.

Time Schedule: If you are hired as an employee, you will need to work specific hours. Refer to Chapter 18 for ideas on how to get more flexibility. These jobs are often part-time in nature, however, allowing you to have more free time.

Requirements: Depending on where you work, you will usually need to be an ordained and licensed member of a specific religious group or denomination.

Compensation: You will be paid a salary if you are a full-time employee; otherwise, you will usually be paid by the hour. In some instances, your compensation may come from donations. Be sure to check this latter possibility before you accept a position as a chaplain.

CHOIR DIRECTOR

Description: Leading a church choir. This job entails finding and developing the volunteer singers, the music, and any special programs the church requires.

Time Schedule: Although you will have to be available during the worship services (usually on Sunday), you can choose the times for choir practice and meetings. Many choirs take summers off because so many of their members go on vacation, so you might have that time off also. This job usually is part-time in nature.

Requirements: You usually need a formal music background, specifically in choral music. The bigger the church, the more stringent the requirements will be.

Compensation: Generally you will be paid either by the hour or will receive a salary. If you are offered a salary, be sure that it is sufficient for the hours you are expected to work.

CHURCH ADMINISTRATOR

Description: Handles all the administrative details of running a church. Duties include everything from managing personnel and budgets to overseeing the various ministries and interacting with the community.

Time Schedule: You may be hired as a full-time employee. However, since you are in charge, you can hire and train good employees to help you. Refer to #7 in Chapter 1 for some ideas.

Requirements: You'll probably need a business degree and insight into church management. This latter is best learned by being active in a church and possibly working for one in a lesser capacity. The bigger the church, the more stringent the requirements.

Compensation: You will generally be paid a salary and benefits. How much you make depends on the budget of the church and your experience.

CHURCH DESIGNER

Description: Designs churches, either the exterior (an architect) or the interior (an interior designer).

Time Schedule: Refer to #2 in Chapter 1.

Requirements: You'll need the necessary education to be a licensed architect or an interior designer.

Compensation: In addition to the requirements outlined in #2 (Chapter 11), you can make additional money by selling furnishings, such as carpeting and pews.

CHURCH FUND-RAISER

Description: Aids churches in raising funds—usually for special projects (such as new buildings or ministries).

Time Schedule: Because you will probably work as an independent businessperson, you can establish your own work schedule.

Requirements: You will need to know about the various ways of raising money and which ones will work best for the particular project and the people involved. Knowing how to motivate people and being very well organized are also important, as is knowledge of advertising and marketing.

Compensation: You may receive a retainer, but the bulk of your income will derive from a percentage of the money raised. This can be anything from 10 percent to 33 percent, depending on the scope of the project. If you supply the items to be sold, you can make a markup on that as well.

CHURCH NURSERY CARE PROVIDER

Description: Cares for children in the church nursery during worship services and other special church events.

Time Schedule: You usually will not be the only nursery care provider; therefore, you will probably be able to select times and days that you do not wish to work. This is a good part-time job.

Requirements: You need to be able to take care of children, including babies. This should include knowing how to administer first aid. You should be in good physical condition also.

Compensation: Usually you will be paid an hourly rate. How much depends on the size of the church and its budget. Occasionally, you might be paid directly by the parents. If you are asked to accept this form of payment, be sure to get a minimum guarantee.

CHURCH SECRETARY

Description: Performs secretarial tasks for the church and its staff, which most often includes the senior clergy and any assistants.

Time Schedule: You will usually have to keep specific hours; therefore, refer to Chapter 18 for suggestions on turning this job into a flexible one.

Requirements: You will need secretarial skills, and today those usually include computer skills. The ability to work with many different personality types is particularly important in this position.

Compensation: You will be paid a salary and perhaps benefits. How much depends on the wealth and size of the church.

CHURCH SUPPLIES SALESPERSON

Description: Sells supplies used by churches. Merchandise can be anything from organs to communion cups, choir robes, and so forth. This is usually an outside sales position.

Time Schedule: Refer to #8 in Chapter 1.

Requirements: In addition to those requirements outlined in #8 (Chapter 1), you need to be interested in churches and be aware of their budgets and their need to have almost all major expenditures approved by committees.

Compensation: Refer to #8 in Chapter 1.

CLERGY

Description: An ordained member of a particular religious organization or denomination. You will generally be responsible for ministering to the needs of a congregation, either as the leader of a group of clergy, as an assistant, or perhaps by yourself.

Time Schedule: Obviously you will need to be available on the day that your particular religious group meets. However, you can usually determine what days you take off and what hours you will not be available for meetings and other duties. Although this job is demanding, it still offers you better-than-average flexibility.

Requirements: In most cases, you will be expected to have formal training at a seminary or school that serves your particular religious affiliation. You may need to be licensed by your state in order to officiate at weddings. You most likely won't go into this profession unless you feel you have a special "calling."

Compensation: Your income depends on the size and wealth of the church and what your denomination might contribute. Usually you can depend on a salary, which includes normal benefits, plus auto expenses. Most clergy also receive a housing allowance or, in many instances, a church-owned house to live in rent free, with paid utilities. You can also make additional money from officiating at weddings and funerals.

MUSICIAN

Description: Performs with musical instruments or sings religious songs for television, radio, and stage productions—as well as for local concerts and religious services. You might perform your own original music.

Time Schedule: You can set your own schedule, except that you must meet your commitments to perform.

Requirements: You need excellent musical ability and training. You need all the professionalism and poise of someone trying to make it in the secular world.

Compensation: You will be paid a fee for your performance. Refer to #1 in Chapter 1.

ORGANIST

Description: Plays the organ during worship services and any other occasions where organ music is needed (such as weddings or funerals).

Time Schedule: You will have to work during the worship services, which are usually on Sunday mornings. However, you can choose other times when you may or may not wish to work.

Requirements: You'll need expertise in playing the organ.

Compensation: Usually you will be paid by the hour. How much depends on the size and budget of the church.

PUBLISHER OF RELIGIOUS BOOKS AND MAGAZINES

Description: Publishes religious books, newsletters, magazines.

Time Schedule: If you are a one-person operation, you can set your own schedule. If you run a large organization, then you will have employees working for you who should be able to give you some flexibility. Refer to #7 in Chapter 1 for ways of hiring good employees.

Requirements: You need expertise in publishing. The business and technical aspects of publishing are important, but you also need to know what will attract readers to your publications.

Compensation: You will earn your income from the sale of your publications and from any advertising that your magazines and newsletters include. If you publish only books, your income will be totally dependent on how well your books sell. That's why it is so important that you have the ability to select books that will appeal to the general public.

PUBLISHER OF RELIGIOUS NEWSPAPER

Description: Publishes news concerning what is happening in a particular religious community. The geographical area covered is larger than that of a local newspaper; readers get the paper through subscriptions. Generally this is a monthly publication.

Time Schedule: Around publication time, you will work very long hours, but at other times you can set your own schedule. If you have a staff, refer to #7 in Chapter 1 for suggestions on delegating work.

Requirements: You need to know about newspaper publishing and have the ability to find good writers and good stories. Just because your paper is religious in thrust does not mean that it shouldn't be interesting.

Compensation: Your income will be generated from your subscriptions and advertisements, minus the cost of doing business. Refer to #1 and #7 in Chapter 1 to learn how to figure business profit.

RELIGIOUS GIFTWARE SALESPERSON

Description: Sells religious giftware to retail stores. This is an outside sales position.

Time Schedule: Refer to #8 in Chapter 1.

Requirements: In addition to the requirements outlined in #8 (Chapter 1), you need to have an interest in religion and the items that appeal to religious people.

Compensation: Refer to #8 in Chapter 1.

RELIGIOUS RADIO

Description: You can own a radio station that has a religious format or work in one, performing all the various tasks that any secular radio station would need.

Time Schedule: Depending on what you do for the station, you may have a lot of flexible time or very little. If you own it, refer to #7 in Chapter 1 for information on how to find and train employees so that you have some free time. If you are an employee expected to perform a full-time job, refer to Chapter 18 for hints on making your job more flexible. If you work as a freelancer, you might be able to control your own hours.

Requirements: The qualifications needed depend on the job you are applying for.

Compensation: It all depends on the job you perform; however, in most cases, religious radio stations pay less than secular ones. If you own the station, you make your income either from the sale of advertising or from the sale of air time to ministries and people who wish to air their programs on your station.

RELIGIOUS RETAILER

Description: Sells religious items (such as books, Bibles, giftware, and rosaries) from a retail setting.

Time Schedule: Refer to #7 in Chapter 1.

Requirements: Besides those requirements listed in #7 (Chapter 1), you will need to be familiar with religious traditions, doctrines, and people.

Compensation: Refer to #7 in Chapter 1.

RELIGIOUS SCHOOL ADMINISTRATOR

Description: Handles all details of a religious school. This includes staffing, overseeing, and selecting the curriculum, the budget, and care and safety of the students.

Time Schedule: This is usually a full-time, executive position; however, if you hire capable people to help you, some flexibility might be possible.

Requirements: You need to hold college degrees and probably certificates in school administration. If you have performed this job in the secular field (as a principal for example), that will help. You must also be an adherent of the religion that the school is teaching—preferably in the same denomination.

Compensation: You will usually be paid a salary and benefits. How much depends on the enrollment of the school and your credentials.

✪ RELIGIOUS SCHOOL TEACHER

Description: Teaches certain subjects or grades in a religious school.

Time Schedule: This will probably be a full-time position. Refer to Chapter 18 for suggestions on creating some flexibility.

Requirements: In most cases, you'll need to be a certified teacher; you will need degrees in the subjects you are teaching. You might need to be a member of the religious denomination that sponsors the school.

Compensation: You will be paid a salary and benefits. How much depends on the size and budget of the school; but as a general rule, most religious schools do not pay as well as secular ones.

✪ RELIGIOUS SPEAKER

Description: Speaks at religious events, such as meetings, luncheons, retreats.

Time Schedule: As a freelancer, you can determine your own schedule.

Requirements: You have to be a professional speaker. On top of that you have to be willing to share your own religious experiences with others.

Compensation: You will be paid by the speech; your expenses will also be paid. Refer to #1 in Chapter 1 for information on how to price yourself. Generally, religious groups and churches do not have budgets as large as those of secular organizations. If you are a writer of books, you can also sell your books at speaking engagements and so increase your income.

RELIGIOUS TELEVISION PERFORMER/ WORKER

Description: Working at a religious television station doing all the same things that would be done at secular television stations. You might even be the owner.

Time Schedule: If you are expected to be a full-time employee, refer to Chapter 18, which will give you suggestions on how to turn those into flexible positions. If you own the station, you can surround yourself with competent employees who can help you. Refer to #7 in Chapter 1 for ideas.

Requirements: You will need the education and experience necessary to the position you hold. You might also need to be a member of or believer in the religion that the television station supports.

Compensation: If you are an employee, you will be paid a salary and benefits. If you own the station, your income will derive from either the sale of air time to producers who want their programs to air on your station or from advertising.

RELIGIOUS TOUR GUIDE

Description: Takes people on trips to sites of religious significance such as the Holy Land, Greece, and Rome. As a guide, you will be responsible not only for explaining the importance of the sites but also for the many details of the trip.

Time Schedule: As a freelancer, you can select those times of the year when you wish to work and those when you don't. However, many trips must be made during seasons when the weather is ideal, so you will have to keep that in mind when determining your schedule.

Requirements: You need to know the history and religious significance of the places you will be visiting and have the ability to attend to all the details involved in taking a large group of people to foreign countries. Your duties will include dealing with lodging, transportation, customs, and so forth.

Compensation: You will be paid a flat fee for each person you are taking. That should be built into the cost of their trip. Refer to #1 in Chapter 1 for suggestions on how to determine a charge that will reimburse you fairly. The trick in pricing yourself is to not charge too much or too little. (Remember, when you take on that tour, you are working intensively around the clock for quite a few days.)

RELIGIOUS VIDEO PRODUCER OR SALESPERSON

Description: Produces or sells religious videos. The videos might be designed to highlight certain religious establishments or performers—or they might be retellings of Bible stories or other religious stories.

Time Schedule: You would work as a freelancer and would be able to control your own schedule.

Requirements: You need to know about all aspects of video production if you are the producer, and you need to have a network of people whom you can call on to work for you. A salesperson needs to know all about the videos and the market being targeted.

Compensation: A salesperson could be paid as an employee or as a freelancer. If you are the producer of the videos, your income will be generated from the sale of your videos or from what you charge the religious client for producing it.

RELIGIOUS WRITER

Description: Writes religious articles or books, to be read by the religious public or specific groups of religious people.

Time Schedule: Refer to #11 in Chapter 1.

Requirements: In addition to those requirements outlined in #11 (in Chapter 1), you will need to write from a sincere belief if you are espousing a religion or religious tenet.

Compensation: Refer to #11 in Chapter 1.

Chapter Fifteen

The Sports World

Sports not only entertain us but also offer excellent sources of employment. If you would like to be part of this active, exciting world—and work when you want—then explore these twenty-five opportunities.

✪ BICYCLE REPAIRER

Description: Repairs bicycles, usually in a bicycle shop but perhaps as part of a repair service.

Time Schedule: Refer to #9 in Chapter 1.

Requirements: You must know how to repair many different brands and types of bicycles. If you are working independently, you will need to know how to market your service.

Compensation: Refer to #9 in Chapter 1.

✪ BICYCLE SALESPERSON

Description: Sells bicycles, either from a retail setting or as an outside salesperson to bicycle shops.

Time Schedule: Refer to #7 in Chapter 1 if you are working from a retail store and to #8 if you are an outside representative of a bicycle company.

Requirements: In addition to those requirements outlined in #7 and #8 (Chapter 1), you have to understand bicycling and love the sport. Participating in bicycling events will help you network.

Compensation: Refer to #7 and #8 in Chapter 1.

BILLIARD TABLE REPAIRER

Description: Repairs billiard (or pool) tables. Billiard tables must be repaired on site; therefore, this is the perfect home-based business.

Time Schedule: As an independent businessperson, you can set your own hours; however, you do have to be available often enough so that you will get work.

Requirements: In addition to knowing how to repair billiard tables, you will have to do a considerable amount of networking with billiard manufacturers, who might use your services, as well as with pool hall owners and club owners, who might have tables that could need repair. You'll need to know how to advertise and market your services.

Compensation: Refer to #9 in Chapter 1. If you can also sell pool tables, you can greatly increase your income.

BILLIARD TABLE SALESPERSON

Description: Sells billiard or pool tables, either from a retail setting or as a billiard manufacturer's representative selling to sporting goods and billiards stores.

Time Schedule: Refer to #7 and #8 in Chapter 1.

Requirements: In addition to those outlined in #7 and #8 (Chapter 1), you will need to be devoted to the sport and should attend appropriate events.

Compensation: Refer to #7 and #8 in Chapter 1.

✪ BOWLING ALLEY OWNER OR WORKER

Description: Either works in or owns a bowling alley open to the public.

Time Schedule: If you own the bowling alley, refer to #7 in Chapter 1 for suggestions on delegating some of your responsibilities to your employees. As an employee, you will probably be hired part-time; therefore, you should be able to control what hours and days you work.

Requirements: As an owner, you will need an understanding of and enthusiasm for the sport of bowling. This includes knowing how to bring people into your business. Most successful bowling alleys offer special packages for children's birthday parties and leagues with prizes at the end of the year. You should also network extensively in your community. Also refer to #7 in Chapter 1. If you are an employee, you'll need a willingness to work and a sense of responsibility as well as some knowledge of bowling.

Compensation: As an employee, you will be paid an hourly wage. If you are the owner of the alley, your income will be generated from what you charge for using the bowling alley plus rentals of balls and shoes. You then deduct your costs from this revenue, and what you have left is your profit.

✪ COACH—ALL SPORTS

Description: Coaches individuals or teams, either privately or in a school. A coach differs from an instructor in actually planning strategies and overseeing game play rather than just giving lessons in how to develop the necessary skills and techniques of the sport. A teacher can also be a coach.

Time Schedule: If you are a coach for a school, you will be expected to work certain hours. Most public schools, however, do have many holidays and summer months off, a schedule that allows you some flexibility. If you work as an independent coach, you can set your own hours as long as they accommodate your clients' schedules.

Requirements: Expertise, training, education, and experience in your particular sport. If you will be serving on a school's teaching staff, you will need your state's necessary license.

Compensation: If you are working for a school, you will make a salary and receive benefits. If you are working independently, you will be charging an hourly rate. Refer to #1 in Chapter 1 for suggestions on how to establish your fees.

EXERCISE EQUIPMENT RETAILER

Description: Sells exercise equipment to the public from a retail outlet. This can be in conjunction with other sports equipment or separately.

Time Schedule: Refer to #7 in Chapter 1.

Requirements: In addition to those requirements described in #7 (Chapter 1), you will need to know how each of the items you sell will help with weight loss, muscle building, and so forth. People have different reasons for purchasing exercise equipment, and you will need to know what equipment will help them and what might prove to be detrimental.

Compensation: Refer to #7 in Chapter 1.

FUND-RAISER

Description: Advises school and organization teams on how they can raise money and works with them to raise it.

Time Schedule: You will usually set your own hours; however, you will also have to work around the schedules of your clients.

Requirements: You will need to know how to raise money and the best way to do it in terms of the amount needed and the people (usually team members) who will be participating. You will also need significant resources for raising money and should know how to use the media to help you. Patience with children and their parents is necessary.

Compensation: Your income will be generated from a percentage of what is earned. If you supply the products to sell, you might make something on the markup of these as well.

NEWSPAPER SPORTSWRITER

Description: Writes about sporting events (professional or amateur) for local newspapers.

Time Schedule: Refer to #11 in Chapter 1. You will have to attend the sporting event you are writing about, and so team schedules could limit your flexibility.

Requirements: Refer to #11 in Chapter 1. You'll also need to know a great deal about sports, especially the ones you cover.

Compensation: If you are a full-time employee of the newspaper, you will be paid a salary; if you are a freelancer, refer to #11 in Chapter 1.

PHOTOGRAPHER/VIDEOCAMERA OPERATOR

Description: Takes photographs or videos of sporting events, either professional or amateur (such as youth leagues and school teams).

Time Schedule: Refer to #6 in Chapter 1.

Requirements: In addition to those requirements outlined in #6 (Chapter 1), you must love sports.

Compensation: Refer to #6 in Chapter 1.

PROGRAM PUBLISHER

Description: Publishes and provides printed programs for school athletic events as well as special ones for organizational sports.

Time Schedule: You can set your own schedule around the deadlines you will have to meet.

Requirements: You need to know how to publish a program. This includes selling advertising to local merchants. (You do not need to do the actual printing unless you are already a printer—then this would be an additional business opportunity). Refer to #8 in Chapter 1 for a salesperson's requirements.

Compensation: Your income will be made primarily from the sale of the advertising. If you charge for the programs, then that will be additional income. Possibly you will charge the school for the programs, and then it will take a markup in order to earn money.

RACEHORSE VETERINARIAN

Description: Serves as a veterinarian at race tracks; checks the physical condition of the horses and approves their participation in the races; attends to any injuries that might occur.

Time Schedule: You have to attend the races and be there when the track is open. Some vets work several tracks. However, when there are no races, you have a great deal of free time.

Requirements: You not only need to be a licensed veterinarian but must also specialize in racehorses.

Compensation: You will usually be paid a daily fee while you are working. Refer to #2 in Chapter 1 for suggestions on getting the fairest compensation.

REFEREE

Description: At football, basketball, field hockey, lacrosse, and soccer games, oversees the play to be certain that no rules are broken and, when they are, determines what the penalties will be and calls them. Referees are a vital part of every game, whether professional, school, or youth. For the purposes of this book, I profile referees who work in school and youth programs because they have more flexibility.

Time Schedule: As an independent contractor, you can determine days when you do not wish to work; but since each sport has a specific season, you will be busy during that time and will have the rest of the year free.

Requirements: You'll need special training in this profession and certification from the leagues that you serve. It's vital that you love the game.

Compensation: You will be paid a fee for each game. The amount depends on the level the game is played at; you'll make more for high school games than for recreational league games.

✪ SCHOOL COACH—AFTER HOURS

Description: Coaches various sports activities at the end of the school day—often at elementary and middle schools. This is usually part of an after-school care program or extracurricular activity program.

Time Schedule: Because this is a part-time job, the flexibility comes from having the rest of the day free.

Requirements: You must be able to play and teach the various sports. Depending on the program that employs you, you may need to be a licensed teacher.

Compensation: You will be paid by the hour. The amount depends on the enrollment and the budget of the program.

✪ SKATING RINK OWNER OR WORKER

Description: Runs or works in an ice-skating or roller-skating rink.

Time Schedule: If you are the owner, refer to #7 in Chapter 1. As an employee, you will usually be hired part-time, and so you can control your hours to a great extent.

Requirements: In addition to those outlined for retailers in #7 (Chapter 1), you should be able to skate well—possibly as a former professional so that you can offer lessons. If you're an employee, it will help if you're able to skate and love the sport.

Compensation: Employees receive an hourly wage; the owner's income is generated from fees charged to use the rink plus skate rentals and equipment sales, minus the costs of doing business.

SPORTING GOODS RETAILER

Description: Selling sports equipment to the general public from a retail store.

Time Schedule: Refer to #7 in Chapter 1.

Requirements: In addition to those identified in #7 (Chapter 1), you should understand and love sports and be able to network well with members of your community.

Compensation: Refer to #7 in Chapter 1.

SPORTING GOODS SALESPERSON

Description: Sells sporting goods to sporting goods stores. This is an outside sales position.

Time Schedule: Refer to #8 in Chapter 1.

Requirements: In addition to those requirements outlined in #8 (Chapter 1), you will need to know about all kinds of sports equipment and should love sports.

Compensation: Refer to #8 in Chapter 1.

SPORTS AWARDS SUPPLIER

Description: Sells sports awards, such as plaques and trophies, either from a retail store or as an outside salesperson representing award manufacturers to retail stores.

Time Schedule: Refer to #7 and #8 in Chapter 1.

Requirements: Refer to #7 and #8 in Chapter 1; you must also have an interest in your community's sports activities and be able to network with the sports groups.

Compensation: Refer to #7 and #8 in Chapter 1.

✪ SPORTS CARDS DEALER

Description: Sells sports cards to the public from a retail store.

Time Schedule: Refer to #7 in Chapter 1.

Requirements: In addition to those requirements outlined in #7 (Chapter 1), you need to be interested in sports and should network well with your community in order to generate enthusiasm for your product.

Compensation: Refer to #7 in Chapter 1.

✪ SPORTS EVENT COORDINATOR/PROMOTER

Description: Puts on sporting events for attendance by the general public. These can be professional or amateur.

Time Schedule: Refer to #4 in Chapter 1.

Requirements: Refer to #4 in Chapter 1.

Compensation: Refer to #4 in Chapter 1.

✪ SPORTS OR ACTIVITY INSTRUCTOR

Description: Gives instruction in a specific sport or activity, such as archery, baton twirling, billiards, boxing, golf, gymnastics, hang gliding, hockey, marksmanship (and gun safety), martial arts, skating, skiing, skydiving, soccer, surfing, swimming, tennis, and wrestling. This is usually done in a sports camp or school or as part of a public school program. Can also be done privately as a freelancer.

Time Schedule: Refer to #5 in Chapter 1.

Requirements: You'll need skill to play the sport—at least well enough to be respected as a teacher. You'll need teaching abilities. Unless you teach skydiving, and perhaps golf, most of your students will be children, so it helps if you enjoy being with them.

Compensation: Refer to #5 in Chapter 1.

✪ SPORTS PUBLICIST

Description: Handles public relations for sports figures and teams as well as organizations.

Time Schedule: You will be able to control most of your time; however, you will have to meet with your clients and the media. This can also be a full-time position.

Requirements: You should know how to handle the media to your advantage. This includes knowing how to write press releases that will get attention and how to set up press conferences and run them. You should have the knack for turning negative publicity into positive publicity in order to protect your clients' reputations. You will also need to know how to stage public events that will promote your clients.

Compensation: Refer to #2 in Chapter 1. If you work full-time, you'll make a salary and benefits.

✪ SPORTS SCHOOLS AND CAMPS—OWNER

Description: Offers a training school and camp in a specific sport, most often baseball, basketball, field hockey, football, lacrosse, soccer, tennis, and volleyball.

Time Schedule: During the time that the school and camp is in session, you will put in long hours; but during months when it is closed, you can have all the free time you wish.

Requirements: You'll need access to a camp setting with the appropriate sports facilities, and you'll need expertise in your particular sport. In fact, this is an ideal job for retired coaches and sports figures. You'll need to like children. The more well-known you (or your guest coaches, who might be professional athletes) are, the more successful you will be.

Compensation: Your income is based on what you charge the campers. Refer to #7 in Chapter 1 for information on how expenses affect income.

SPORTS STARS' MANAGER

Description: Manages the affairs of sports stars; can include acting as an agent and controlling their career as well as investing their money and taking care of their affairs.

Time Schedule: As an independent businessperson, you can set many of your own hours; but you will have to be available for your clients and for meetings that pertain to them.

Requirements: You must have experience in managing stars. Depending on what services you provide, you must be expert in all of them—from hiring household staff to managing money.

Compensation: You may be put on a salary or get a flat fee or retainer. Refer to #2 in Chapter 1 for suggestions on how to price your services.

UMPIRE

Description: Oversees baseball and softball games to be certain that the game is played correctly and no rules are broken. Also makes determinations regarding certain plays, such as if a runner touched the base and is safe or out, if the ball is a strike or ball, and so on. Every baseball and softball game must be conducted by umpires, whether they are professional or amateur. For the purposes of this book, I will consider umpires who officiate at amateur games.

Time Schedule: Because these sports are seasonal, you will have most of the fall and all of the winter off; depending on where you live, you could have part of the spring off as well. In spring and summer, you will be very busy, but even then you can block out days when you will not be available.

Requirements: You'll need some professional training and certification by the league that you work for.

Compensation: You will be paid a fee. The size of it is determined by the level and importance of the game.

Chapter 16

The World of Travel

The world is shrinking, and the travel industry is part of the reason. If you yearn for exotic ports and different sights, this industry may offer the perfect job and lifestyle for you.

AIRLINE QUALITY CONTROLLER

Description: Takes flights on major airlines and assesses the quality of service, the flight, and so on.

Time Schedule: This is a part-time job, and so you can determine to some extent when you are available. Most airlines give you certain dates within which they want the job done.

Requirements: You need to be very well organized and able to notice details. The airline sets you up with tickets for flights they want you to check, and you fill out an extensive questionnaire that reports the quality of the service. This is a wonderful job for people who like to travel and want to work part-time.

Compensation: In most cases, you will be paid a flat rate per flight. These jobs usually pay very well, though the amount depends on the airline and your experience.

AIRLINES/TOUR REPRESENTATIVE

Description: Calls on travel agencies soliciting business for their airline or tour. Frequently arranges special trips for the travel agents so that they can experience firsthand what the representative is selling. This is primarily an outside sales position.

Time Schedule: Refer to #8 in Chapter 1.

Requirements: In addition to those requirements outlined in #8 (Chapter 1), you will need an understanding of the travel industry, which can be gained by working as a travel agent.

Compensation: People who hold these positions are usually paid by salary plus commissions. Refer to #8 in Chapter 1.

BED-AND-BREAKFAST PROPRIETOR

Description: Receives paying guests into a private home; offers a bedroom, frequently a private bath (but a common bath is permissible), and breakfast. This alternative to staying at cookie-cutter hotels and motels is growing in popularity.

Time Schedule: Your hours will be dictated by the seasons when you get the most visitors to your area. You will certainly need to be available then. However, in off seasons, you can have total freedom. Most people who have bed-and-breakfasts live there.

Requirements: You'll need a great sense of hospitality and a willingness to open your home to strangers. This profession, although enjoyable, is filled with hard work, and so you might need some help in cleaning, changing linens, and cooking. It's advisable to have a big house with many rooms available to rent.

Compensation: Your income will be generated from what you charge your guests, minus your costs. Refer to #1 in Chapter 1 for suggestions on how you can be sure to charge enough to make it worth your while. Also check what your competition is charging.

BUS TOUR OPERATOR

Description: Drives a tour bus for tour guides and their tourists.

Time Schedule: You usually can schedule weeks off; but once you contract to drive a specific tour, you have to meet your commitment.

Requirements: You must have the necessary licenses to drive a bus, and you must be thoroughly familiar with the tour routes. It helps to be personable and a good sport.

Compensation: You will be paid either by the day or hour. If you belong to a union, you will get union wages, plus extra for overtime. However, tips from the tourists can be a welcome addition to your income, so it pays to make them like you.

COUNTRY TOUR REPRESENTATIVE

Description: Sells tours to specific foreign countries by calling on travel agencies and putting up booths in travel shows. A representative frequently offers travel agents free or very inexpensive trips to let them experience the country and its many sights so that they will suggest it to their clients.

Time Schedule: This is an outside sales position, so your time schedule will be similar to that outlined in #8 in Chapter 1.

Requirements: In addition to those requirements listed in #8 (Chapter 1), you will need to know a great deal about the country you are representing. People native to that country usually make the best representatives. A good understanding of the travel industry is also very helpful.

Compensation: You will be paid a salary and, possibly, commissions. Refer to #8 in Chapter 1.

CRUISE SHIP CHAPLAIN

Description: Serves as a chaplain on a cruise ship. Officiates at worship services and is available for spiritual counseling.

Time Schedule: You can establish the dates you wish to work; but once you're on the ship, you will have to be available almost constantly. These are usually seasonal jobs.

Requirements: You have to be an ordained member of one of the major religions (Catholic, Protestant, Jewish). It helps to be personable and approachable.

Compensation: Your major compensation is a cruise at no charge, but you will generally be paid a small fee as well. Usually the cruise is for two, so you can take your spouse.

CRUISE SHIP FEATURED GUEST

Description: A featured guest is part of the entertainment on a cruise ship but not as a performer. People chosen for this job may play bridge, act as an expert on a particular subject of interest to a number of paying guests, or be an attractive single man who will dance with a variety of female guests. Cruise ship lines feature special cruises (such as bridge tournaments) and need people to participate in them who are skilled and knowledgeable.

Time Schedule: You can determine what dates you wish to be available for work, and if the cruise line can use you, it will.

Requirements: You have to be highly skilled at whatever you do and have a pleasing personality so that the guests will relate to you.

Compensation: Your major remuneration will be a free cruise; but sometimes, depending on what you do, you might also receive a fee.

CRUISE SHIP PERFORMER

Description: Performs—sings, dances, does magic, plays a musical instrument—on cruise ships.

Time Schedule: You usually can determine the dates when you will not be available to work.

Requirements: You must be a professional musician or entertainer.

Compensation: Besides a free cruise, you will be paid a fee for your performances. How much depends on the cruise line, how famous you are, and so forth.

CRUISE SHIP WORKER

Description: Works at one of the jobs available on cruise ships. These positions include waiter, barber, gift shop clerk, and cabin cleaner.

Time Schedule: You can establish the dates that you are available to work.

Requirements: The different jobs all have different requirements, which are the same as if you were trying to get these jobs on land. On a cruise ship, however, you must be very personable and willing to please the guests. Experience working at a hotel or resort will help you get one of these jobs. It goes without saying that you must be willing to be gone from home for as long as the cruise takes. This is particularly important if the cruise line signs you on for an entire season.

Compensation: Besides the free cruise, you will be paid a salary, which is usually not large. Your best opportunity to make additional significant income is in the tips you receive from grateful guests.

FLIGHT ATTENDANT

Description: Assists people traveling on commercial airlines by helping them find their seat and buckling them into it, serving refreshments, giving basic first aid, watching over children traveling alone, answering questions, and protecting and aiding passengers in the event of an emergency.

Time Schedule: When you are new to the business and have little seniority, you will have to work whatever shifts you're assigned. As you gain seniority, you are eventually able to work and fly where and when you want. Even new flight attendants frequently have several days between assignments in which they can do what they please.

Requirements: You have to go through flight attendant school, which will be run by the airline that hires you. You must also be personable and willing to travel extensively.

Compensation: You will be paid a certain fee for each flight you work, and you will receive travel benefits that are free. The free travel is a perk that appeals to many people.

HOTEL WORKER

Description: Works in a hotel in one of many capacities: carrying luggage, making reservations, covering the front desk, serving as a concierge, supervising housekeeping, cleaning rooms, cooking, waiting on tables in the restaurant, and so on.

Time Schedule: Because many of these jobs are part-time, you can have a lot of flexibility. If you are employed as a full-time worker, refer to Chapter 18 for suggestions on turning a full-time position into one that is flexible.

Requirements: You must fill the particular requirements of the job that you are interviewing for. Those listed above require a willing attitude and the ability to learn. Although prior experience certainly does help, most hotels will train you to perform the job according to their specifications.

Compensation: You will be paid a salary or hourly wage. However, in those positions where you interact with the guests (such as concierge and housekeeper), you will also receive tips, which can be a very good addition to your income.

RESERVATIONS CLERK FOR AIRLINES

Description: Takes reservations over the telephone for airlines; usually done from airline offices.

Time Schedule: These jobs are frequently part-time, so you will have some flexibility.

Requirements: You have to be articulate and personable over the telephone. You will be trained by the airlines in how to book reservations—which is much more complicated than it seems.

Compensation: You will be paid an hourly wage that is usually significantly above minimum wage. If you work more than forty hours a week, you are usually paid time and a half or double time. You may get some benefits. Another part of your compensation is the ability to fly free—not only on your airline but on others as well. If you like to travel, this is a very attractive benefit.

TOUR DIRECTOR

Description: Plans and takes people on tours to foreign countries or specific places of interest. Sometimes you simply do the planning and leave the actual responsibility of guiding the tour to the professional guide in the particular location you are visiting. Most often, however, you will have to accompany the group.

Time Schedule: You can determine when you want to take out tours, but you will usually wish to do so during the seasons when weather is best for the area you are going to. When you are involved with a tour, you will be very busy.

Requirements: You'll need organizational and marketing ability plus a knowledge of the place or places that you are visiting. Though native professionals are available to guide the actual tour, as the tour director you need to determine where to stay, what to see, and so on. Because this job entails a great deal of responsibility, it is absolutely essential that you personally be very aware of all the pitfalls as well as delights of a particular country or city.

Compensation: Your income will be generated from what you charge for the tour, minus the costs of running it. Costs include transportation, lodging, guides, some meals (if offered as part of the tour package), and so on. Refer to #7 in Chapter 1 for additional advice on how to make profits after costs.

TOUR GUIDE

Description: Takes tourists on guided tours of cities, historical sites, and the like.

Time Schedule: You can generally work when you want, but if you are located in an area that has a tourist season, you may want to be available throughout the entire season. Once you take a tour, you are contracted to stay with it for the entire duration.

Requirements: You must be an expert on the places you are showing your tourists. Your knowledge should include local history. It is also vital that you be very personable, patient, and an interesting speaker.

Compensation: Although you will be paid a salary or fee, a significant part of your income will come from tips given to you by grateful tourists. That's why it is so important to be friendly and interesting.

TRAVEL AGENT

Description: Arranges travels for individuals—for personal or business reasons. Arrangements include booking transportation and issuing tickets, booking accommodations, and so on. This is usually done from a retail environment.

Time Schedule: Refer to #7 in Chapter 1 for suggestions on finding help from your employees. If you work at this part-time, you generally can control your own hours.

Requirements: You need to know about the travel business and be able to use the necessary computer software. A sales personality and an enthusiasm for travel are helpful. Getting repeat business is very important in this profession.

Compensation: Your income will be generated from a percentage of what you sell. The amounts vary. Another important part of the compensation is that you are able to take many trips at extremely low rates.

TRAVEL CONSULTANT/PLANNER

Description: Counsels individuals and businesses on travel, particularly if the travel is going to be used for employee prizes and/or pleasure. A consultant puts together all the details, including transportation, lodging, meals, sightseeing, and so on, but rarely accompanies the trip—leaving that to the guides and directors at the destination.

Time Schedule: As an independent businessperson, you can control your own schedule; refer to #2 in Chapter 1.

Requirements: You'll need a vast knowledge of different places of interest in this country and others. Marketing background and an understanding of the travel industry are also important; also refer to #2 in Chapter 1.

Compensation: Refer to #2 in Chapter 1.

TRAVEL LECTURER

Description: Gives lectures to the general public or special groups about travels taken. The lectures usually include the showing of slides or films that were taken during the trip.

Time Schedule: As a freelancer, you will be able to schedule your own time.

Requirements: You need to be a fairly well known traveler with a recognizable name, at least in your community. If you write travel articles or books, the lectures will enhance your writing profession. You must be an entertaining, professional speaker.

Compensation: You will be paid a fee for speaking. How much depends on how well-known you are. You can also sell your books and other publications at your engagements to increase your income. Refer to #1 and #2 in Chapter 1 to determine how to establish your rates.

✪ TRAVEL/LUGGAGE RETAILER

Description: Sells luggage and other travel-related items from a retail store.

Time Schedule: Refer to #7 in Chapter 1.

Requirements: In addition to those requirements outlined in #7 (Chapter 1), you need to know about travel and the needs of travelers.

Compensation: Refer to #7 in Chapter 1.

✪ TRAVEL NEWSLETTER WRITER

Description: Writes and markets a newsletter of travel information. The newsletter can be general or very specialized, depending on your expertise and your market.

Time Schedule: As a writer, your time is your own. Refer to #11 in Chapter 1.

Requirements: In addition to those outlined in #11 (Chapter 1), you have to be a traveler and be very adept at marketing newsletters. This is a wonderful sideline for tour directors or travel agents who have a list of happy clients.

Compensation: Your income will be generated from subscriptions to your newsletter. Refer not only to #11 but also to #1 in Chapter 1 for suggestions on pricing.

✪ TRAVEL PHOTOGRAPHER

Description: Takes travel pictures for magazines and books. You can be the photographer for a group, or you can work alone on your own projects.

Time Schedule: Refer to #6 in Chapter 1.

Requirements: Refer to #6 in Chapter 1.

Compensation: Refer to #6 in Chapter 1; if you publish a book of travel photographs, refer to #11 in Chapter 1.

TRAVEL SCHOOL PROPRIETOR

Description: Trains people to hold jobs in the travel industry. Classes are usually held in a school setting.

Time Schedule: If you own the business, refer to #7 in Chapter 1 for suggestions on maintaining a staff that can give you some flexibility. If you are a teacher working for a school, refer to #5 in Chapter 1.

Requirements: Refer to #5 in Chapter 1.

Compensation: Consult #5 and #7 in Chapter 1.

TRAVEL WRITER

Description: Writes travel articles for periodicals and books.

Time Schedule: Refer to #11 in Chapter 1.

Requirements: In addition to those requirements outlined in #11 (Chapter 1), you will need to be an avid and frequent traveler in order to get material. Be sure to look at travel from many angles—those of children, senior citizens, singles.

Compensation: Refer to #11 in Chapter 1.

Chapter 17

The World of Wheels, Wings, and Water

Jobs in the transportation field—whether air, sea, or road—offer much variety. No matter what your interests or ability, at least one of these thirty-six jobs should interest you.

AERIAL PHOTOGRAPHER

Description: Takes pictures of a variety of subjects (houses, plots of land, bodies of water) from the air. This is usually done for contractors, real estate brokers, land speculators, or newspapers and magazines.

Time Schedule: Refer to #6 in Chapter 1.

Requirements: Refer to #6 in Chapter 1.

Compensation: In addition to the compensation outlined in #6 (Chapter 1), you will have your expenses (the cost of renting the airplane or helicopter) reimbursed.

AERONAUTICAL SUPPLIES SALESPERSON

Description: Sells supplies, including replacement parts, to plane manufacturers as well as airplane dealers.

Time Schedule: As an outside salesperson, you can schedule your time according to the suggestions in #8 in Chapter 1.

Requirements: In addition to those requirements outlined in #8 in Chapter 1, you will need to know about and love airplanes. You will have to speak aeronautical language.

Compensation: Refer to #8 in Chapter 1.

✪ AIR AMBULANCE PILOT

Description: Provides ambulance service by air for people needing to be quickly transported to a hospital; also provides paramedics or other medical personnel to be with the patient in the air ambulance.

Time Schedule: If you are the only one to fly the airplane, it will be very difficult to have flexible hours. However, if you are in partnership with another pilot or work for an air ambulance service, then you should be able to arrange some flexibility.

Requirements: You will need a pilot's license and any additional licensing required by your state. If you own the airplane, you will need to have it set up with equipment necessary for an ambulance. You should have medical experience, such as a paramedic's training at the very least.

Compensation: If you work for the air ambulance service, you will probably be paid a salary or hourly wage. The amount depends on your background and expertise. As the air ambulance service owner, your income will be generated by the fee you charge, minus your costs. Refer to #7 for an explanation of how profits can be realized after costs.

AIR CARGO AND PACKAGE EXPRESS

Description: Delivers packages and cargo by airplane for quicker service. You can work for an established business or start your own in small, rural places.

Time Schedule: You might be hired as an employee by a major carrier, in which case you might be able to use the advice in Chapter 18. If you own the business, you will be able to set your own schedule, but you will have to work several times each week (for example, Monday, Wednesday, and Friday or Tuesday and Thursday).

Requirements: You will need a pilot's license and experience in flying. You'll have to own an appropriate airplane if you are going into the business and should have access to an airstrip in the rural area where you originate as well as at your destinations. You must hold any necessary licenses required by your state and community; you'll need the ability to market yourself and your service.

Compensation: If you work for a service, you will be paid a salary or fee for the work that you do. As the owner, your income will be generated from what you charge, minus your costs. Refer to #1 and #7 in Chapter 1 for some suggestions on pricing your service accurately.

ANTIQUE AND CLASSIC AUTOMOBILE DEALER

Description: Sells or arranges the sales of antique and classic automobiles; acts as a broker or consultant in matching up a buyer with a seller. A broker might also publish a catalogue with pictures of the automobiles.

Time Schedule: As an independent dealer, your time can be your own; however, you do have to be available by telephone in order to consummate the deals. It's an advantage to have a reliable employee help you.

Requirements: You'll need to know a great deal about antique and classic automobiles (most particularly their worth); it is also important to have marketing skills. Refer to #8 in Chapter 1 for a salesperson's requirements.

Compensation: You will be paid a commission on the purchase price of the cars. The percentage depends on how active you are in the marketing of the automobile. If you put a picture of the car in a catalogue that you distribute, it is appropriate to get a fee for that service from the seller.

APPRAISER OF VEHICLES

Description: Appraises automobiles, boats, trucks, and other kinds of vehicles for insurance companies or lending institutions.

Time Schedule: You should be able to control your own schedule.

Requirements: You'll need to know the market value of the vehicle you are appraising. Such knowledge usually comes from years of working in the industry and staying current on changing values. If you represent an insurance company, you will also need to know the approximate costs of repairs (body and mechanical) in comparison to the value of the vehicle in order to approve or disapprove repairs.

Compensation: You will be paid a fee for your service. Refer to #9 in Chapter 1 for suggestions on pricing your service.

AUTOMOBILE AIR CONDITIONING SPECIALIST

Description: Specializes in installing, designing, or repairing air conditioning in automobiles. You can work for a car manufacturer or dealer or from your own repair facility.

Time Schedule: If you work for a manufacturer or dealer, you will probably be a full-time employee. The advice in Chapter 18 may give you ideas on how to get some flexibility from that setup. If you own the shop, you can set your schedule, but you will have to keep some regular business hours. It will help if you have employees who can run things for you. (Refer to the suggestions in #7 in Chapter 1 on how to delegate your work).

Requirements: You'll need to understand and be able to install and repair air conditioning in many different automobile models. The ability to market your service is also very important.

Compensation: You will be paid a salary by the manufacturer or dealer. If you run your own business, your income will come from what you charge your customers, minus your costs. Refer to #7 in Chapter 1 for advice on how profits work. Refer to #9 in Chapter 1 as well.

AUTOMOBILE BROKER

Description: Sells any make and model of automobile by arranging, from an office (perhaps in the home), to buy an automobile from a dealer for slightly above the dealer's cost and then reselling it to a buyer at a markup less than the dealer would charge. The buyer simply tells the broker in advance what model of car is wanted, what color, what extra features, and so on; and the broker buys it and resells it.

Time Schedule: You will be able to control your own schedule; however, you do have to keep some regular hours (such as Monday, Wednesday, and Friday or Tuesday and Saturdays) which the public can depend on. Much of your work will be done by telephone.

Requirements: You need to know about the automobile industry and have a network of dealers whom you can do business with. You should understand how to market your business; refer to #2 in Chapter 1.

Compensation: Your income is generated from the markup you make on the automobiles you sell. If a buyer goes through you instead of a dealer, the purchase price will be less. You can charge a lower price than the dealer because you don't have overhead.

✪ AUTOMOBILE CONSULTANT

Description: Counsels individuals and businesses about the type of automobile to buy. This is particularly valuable for businesses that are considering the purchase of a fleet of cars. A consultant can recommend the right automobile for the needs and budget of the business without any of the prejudice a dealer would have. A consultant usually does not sell any automobile. This profession ties in well with another in the industry, such as newsletter writer or automobile broker.

Time Schedule: Refer to #2 in Chapter 1.

Requirements: You need to know about all the different automobile makes and models, including foreign models. You get this knowledge by working in the industry, attending trade shows, and networking with a large number of automobile manufacturers and dealers.

Compensation: You will be paid a flat fee. Refer to #2 in Chapter 1 for details on a consultant's pricing and income.

✪ AUTOMOBILE MECHANIC

Description: Repairs and services automobiles in a car dealership, from an individually owned repair station, or as an independent mobile mechanic.

Time Schedule: If you work for a car dealer or repair station, you will probably be expected to work full-time. See Chapter 18 for suggestions on how to make your job more flexible. If you own the repair station, refer to #7 in Chapter 1 for suggestions on how to train employees so that you can have some free time. If you run your own business from a mobile van or you go to the customer, refer to #9 in Chapter 1.

Requirements: In addition to the requirements listed in #7 and #9 of Chapter 1, you will need to be an expert in repairing cars of all ages and makes (unless you work for a dealer specializing in one kind of automobile). This means that you will be constantly updating your skills as cars change.

Compensation: Refer to #9 in Chapter 1.

AUTOMOBILE PAINTER

Description: Paints automobiles in an automobile paint shop.

Time Schedule: If you own the business, refer to #7 in Chapter 1. If you work in a paint shop, you may have to keep regular, full-time hours. Refer to Chapter 18 for suggestions on how to turn a full-time job into a flexible one.

Requirements: As an owner, you should have expertise in painting cars yourself; also refer to #7 in Chapter 1. If you are hired as a painter, you have to be able to do—and learn—the work.

Compensation: As an owner, you will make your income from the number of cars your business paints. Refer to #7 in Chapter 1 for suggestions on how retail business owners can realize profits. If you work for the company, you will be paid an hourly wage or weekly salary plus, perhaps, benefits. The size of this paycheck will depend on how well you know your work, the city where you live, and how successful the business is. If you are a painter for an automobile manufacturer, you will probably receive a better salary and benefits package.

AUTOMOBILE SALESPERSON

Description: Sells automobiles, new or used or both, from a retail showroom.

Time Schedule: You can probably control your days off, but this position usually requires that you work on weekends when most people shop for cars.

Requirements: You need to know about automobiles and what attracts people to certain models; refer to #8 in Chapter 1 for the general requirements for a salesperson. You really must network within your community and work to build customer loyalty because a good automobile salesperson lives off of repeat business and recommendations given by happy customers.

Compensation: The bulk of your income will be derived from commissions on what you sell. The dealership where you work may give you a base salary or draw, but commissions are what makes this profession a good-paying one.

AUTOMOBILE SECURITY SYSTEMS—SALESPERSON AND INSTALLER

Description: Sells and installs security systems for automobiles. Combining sales and installation works well in this business. With theft increasing no matter where you live, this business can be very profitable. It can be run from a home office because you can go to the customer's location to make the sale and install the system.

Time Schedule: Whether you sell the system or install it or both, you will have some control of your time; however, you will have to be available at least part of every week. When people decide they want or need a security system, they want it immediately and will not wait for you to return to work.

Requirements: Knowledge of the different security systems and how to install them. This is a fast-changing industry, and so you will have to keep current.

Compensation: Your income will be generated from the markup you charge for the security system and what you charge to install it. Refer to #7 and #9 in Chapter 1 for suggestions on pricing your service and marking up your merchandise for a profit.

✪ AUTOMOBILE SUPPLY REPRESENTATIVE

Description: Sells automobile parts and supplies to automobile supply retail stores. This is an outside sales position.

Time Schedule: Refer to #8 in Chapter 1.

Requirements: Refer to #8 in Chapter 1.

Compensation: Refer to #8 in Chapter 1.

✪ AUTOMOBILE SUPPLY RETAILER

Description: Sells automobile parts and supplies from a retail store.

Time Schedule: Refer to #7 in Chapter 1 to learn how to delegate some of the work to your employees.

Requirements: In addition to those requirements outlined in #7 (Chapter 1), you will need an extensive inventory of the most requested parts for many makes and models of automobiles. For this reason, starting up this business can be expensive.

Compensation: Refer to #7 in Chapter 1.

AUTOMOBILE WRECKER AND SALVAGE YARD PROPRIETOR

Description: Buys old cars for parts and sells the parts, usually in a salvage yard; dismantles car wrecks and hauls them away.

Time Schedule: Because you will usually have a retail operation (such as a salvage yard) where the public or mechanics can come to find a part, you will have to be open at specific hours every day. The best way for you to gain some flex time is by taking the advice in #7 in Chapter 1, which outlines how employees can be trained to help you with your responsibilities.

Requirements: Besides having the necessary equipment (a tow truck and wrecker), you will need a place large enough to keep your inventory. It's also very important to market your business by advertising and networking with mechanics and others who repair automobiles of all ages and makes.

Compensation: Your income is generated from selling still-good parts, minus your costs. Refer again to #7 in Chapter 1. You can also make some money from selling the smashed vehicles to recycling companies.

BALLOON RIDES—PILOT OR OWNER

Description: Provides rides in hot-air balloons for individuals and groups. These flights take place over undeveloped areas and are very scenic and relaxing. They are also safe as long as the equipment is properly cared for. This business can be operated from a home office.

Time Schedule: If you are a pilot for a balloon ride operator, you can usually control your own schedule. As the owner, you too can have some flexibility if you have employees to help you (refer to #7 in Chapter 1).

Requirements: You need a pilot's license and FAA approval. You must adhere to all the public utility regulations and restrictions of your community as well as gain permits from landowners to land on their property. On top of that, you need an understanding and knowledge of marketing and advertising. And, of course, you need good equipment.

Compensation: You will charge a flat fee for each individual. Most flights take about an hour, but you also have to pick up the people and return them to the pick-up point after they have landed. Most balloon rides include picnic lunches so that the whole experience takes about three hours. Your profit is generated after your costs are deducted from the fees you collect. If you work for a balloon ride service, you will be paid a fee for the flight. This will be determined by the length of time you are expected to work and your background.

BOATING INSTRUCTOR

Description: Teaches boating to individuals who own their own boats; this can be done in conjunction with a boat dealer, through boating organizations, or through the Coast Guard.

Time Schedule: Refer to #5 in Chapter 1.

Requirements: In addition to those requirements outlined in #5 (Chapter 1), you may need special licenses and other credentials (depending on whom you are working for).

Compensation: Refer to #5 in Chapter 1.

BOAT MECHANIC

Description: Repairs boats, usually at the marinas where they are stored.

Time Schedule: Refer to #9 in Chapter 1.

Requirements: Refer to #9 in Chapter 1.

Compensation: Refer to #9 in Chapter 1.

BOAT SALESPERSON

Description: Sells boats, usually from a retail boat dealer's showroom.

Time Schedule: You may arrange this position to have certain days off and perhaps even part-time hours. Also, in some parts of the country, boating—and consequently sale of boats—is a seasonal activity, so you may find yourself not working for several winter months.

Requirements: In addition to those requirements outlined in #8 (Chapter 1) for salespeople, you need to love boating yourself so that you can sell the product knowledgeably and passionately.

Compensation: Most of your income will be generated from commissions on your sales. You may receive a small base salary or advance also.

BOAT STORAGE PROVIDER

Description: Stores boats in marinas during the boating season or in dry dock in the off-season. You must have water space or an enclosed building in order to run this business.

Time Schedule: Depending on which kind of storage you supply, you will work during that period. The rest of the year you will be free to do what you wish. If you have both the marina and the dry dock, then you should refer to #7 of Chapter 1 for suggestions on training employees to help you.

Requirements: Besides having the space required, you need marketing skills and extensive networking within the community. An understanding of boats is also important because you will be watching over them for people who have entrusted you with their expensive possession. Check with your state and city regarding any special licenses and requirements.

Compensation: Your income will be generated from the rental of the storage spot. Refer to #9 in Chapter 1 for additional suggestions.

CARGO AND FREIGHT CONSULTANT

Description: Sells space in containers for shipment on steamship lines. These spaces are priced per cubic foot. This is an outside sales position.

Time Schedule: Refer to #8 in Chapter 1.

Requirements: You'll need an understanding of this business plus the mathematical ability to figure container spaces. Refer to #8 in Chapter 1.

Compensation: You will be paid a salary plus commission; refer to #8 in Chapter 1.

DRIVING INSTRUCTOR

Description: Teaches people how to drive automobiles through automobile driving schools.

Time Schedule: Refer to #5 in Chapter 1.

Requirements: In addition to those requirements outlined in #5 (Chapter 1), it helps if you can speak more than one language, particularly if you live in a metropolitan area.

Compensation: Refer to #5 in Chapter 1.

FLIGHT INSTRUCTOR

Description: Teaches people how to fly airplanes—usually through flight schools.

Time Schedule: Refer to #5 in Chapter 1.

Requirements: Refer to #5 in Chapter 1. It also helps to know how to fly more than one kind of aircraft. Check your state laws regarding state and federal licensing.

Compensation: Refer to #5 in Chapter 1.

LIMOUSINE DRIVER

Description: Drives limousines for people who are going to special events (such as weddings or school dances) or who need transportation to or from an airport. Sometimes people who are highly successful in entertainment or business use limousine services to drive them to and from work. A limousine driver usually works for a limousine service.

Time Schedule: Generally you will be treated as an independent contractor; therefore, you should be able to have some control over your schedule. However, you will want to make yourself available during times when limousines will be used often, such as during prom time or the wedding season or when something is going on in your community (such as the Academy Awards in Los Angeles). If you don't do this, you will miss out on the chance to make a lot of money.

Requirements: A good, safe driving record is a must. Check with your state to see if you need more than a standard driving license. It also helps to be attractive and very personable so that you will make good tips. Reliability is another important requirement, along with knowing your way around the city.

Compensation: You will be paid an hourly wage by the limousine service; but your big income will be generated from tips given to you by people who appreciate your hospitality and pleasing personality.

MOTORCYCLE MECHANIC

Description: Repairs and services motorcycles, usually from a dealership or repair station.

Time Schedule: If it is your own business, refer to #7 in Chapter 1 for suggestions on how to train your employees to take some of the responsibility off of you. If you work for an employer, refer to Chapter 18 for advice on turning a full-time job into a flexible one.

Compensation: If you own the shop, your income is generated by how many motorcycles you service and repair. Refer to #7 in Chapter 1 for advice on how to realize profits. If you work for a repair station or dealer, you will be paid an hourly wage or weekly salary plus, possibly, some benefits. How much depends on your experience and the size and success of the business.

MOTORCYCLE RETAILER

Description: Sells motorcycles, new and used, through a retail motorcycle dealership.

Time Schedule: If you own the dealership, refer to #7 in Chapter 1 for suggestions on how to use your employees to help give you a flexible work life. If you work as a salesperson for the dealership, you can probably schedule your own days off, but normally you will have to work some weekends.

Requirements: In addition to those outlined in #7 and #8 (Chapter 1) for salespeople, you will need to be enthusiastic about motorcycles and able to build a following of loyal customers.

Compensation: As a salesperson, you will earn the bulk of your income from commissions. If you are an owner, refer to #7 in Chapter 1.

SAIL MAKER

Description: Makes and repairs sails for sailboats. You can work for a sailboat manufacturer or yourself—it all depends on what your community's needs are.

Time Schedule: As an independent operator, you can establish your own hours; but remember that people who want their sails repaired or replaced want the work done immediately. If you work for a sailboat manufacturer or someone else, refer to Chapter 18 for suggestions on turning full-time positions into flexible ones.

Requirements: You will need expertise in your craft. If you run your own business, you will also need to know how to market your service.

Compensation: Your income will be generated from what you charge for your service. Refer to #1 and #9 in Chapter 1 for suggestions on proper pricing. As an employee, you will be paid a salary and possibly benefits.

SKY WRITER

Description: With the use of a specially devised airplane, "writes" advertisements in the sky over large groups of people, such as those attending a sporting event or enjoying the beach. The message can be displayed by flying the plane in the form of letters so that a special chemical in the exhaust leaves visible words (more dramatic and costly to the advertiser) or by pulling a long banner containing the advertisement behind it.

Time Schedule: As a freelancer who owns the business or as the pilot doing the work, you can probably determine much of your own schedule.

Requirements: You will need the proper aircraft and other equipment in addition to necessary licenses and city and state permits. You will also need to know how to market yourself and your business. An understanding of advertising and networking with advertisers is also very important.

Compensation: You will be paid a fee for the service if you own the business. Refer to #9 in Chapter 1 for suggestions on pricing this service. If you work for the service, you will be paid an hourly wage. The amount depends on your background and expertise.

TAXI DRIVER

Description: Drives people to specific destinations in a taxicab.

Time Schedule: Because most taxi drivers rent their taxis from the cab company, they are free to set their own schedules. If you should be an employee of a cab company, then your opportunity to have a flexible work schedule is significantly decreased. If you are an employee, refer to Chapter 18 for advice on making your job more flexible.

Requirements: You must know how to find your way around the community where you work. Being pleasant will earn you bigger tips.

Compensation: If you rent your taxi, all the money you collect constitutes your income after, of course, your expenses (gas, oil, insurance—and the taxi rental). If you work as an employee, you will receive a percentage of the fares. You may or may not receive a salary or base pay.

TEST DRIVER

Description: Drives test models of new vehicles (automobiles, trucks, boats, airplanes) for manufacturers. Tests handling and safety, including speed.

Time Schedule: You will have to be available to do the work when it is required of you, usually when the new models are ready for testing before they are made available to the public. Other times of the year, your time belongs solely to you.

Requirements: You'll need a better-than-average ability to handle the vehicle you are testing and an understanding of its mechanics (because you will be expected to make judgments and recommendations on it). It helps to be somewhat fearless because you will be testing in some dangerous situations. A good reputation, gained by being reliable and through extensive networking, is also important.

Compensation: You will generally be paid a fee that should be very generous, depending on your reputation.

TOW TRUCK DRIVER

Description: Uses a truck to tow automobiles that can no longer run to a repair shop or other location. You might work in a gas station that offers this service or be an independent towing service. For the purposes of this book, I am going to profile an independent service.

Time Schedule: As an independent operator, you can control your own time; but you will need a pager and should be available most of the time—or else you won't be successful. Your best chance at running this business and still having a lifestyle with some freedom is to have a partner or someone who will work when you don't want to. Or else you can limit your service to weekends, when many towing services are not available.

Requirements: You must have a tow truck that is reliable, and you'll need the ability to market your service. Refer to #9 in Chapter 1 for additional suggestions.

Compensation: Your income will be generated by the fees you charge for your service. Refer to #9 in Chapter 1.

TRANSPORTATION EXPO PRODUCER

Description: Produces a show or expo that features special modes of transportation such as automobiles and boats.

Time-Schedule: Refer to #4 in Chapter 1.

Requirements: In addition to those requirements outlined in #4 (Chapter 1), you will need a fascination with transportation in order to attract manufacturers and plan an advertising campaign that will attract attendees who also love it.

Compensation: Refer to #4 in Chapter 1.

TRUCK DRIVER

Description: Hauls freight for companies of all kinds—over several states or within one state or area. You can either work for a trucking company or run your own firm. For the purposes of this book, I am going to profile a small business run by an individual—who might own only one truck.

Time Schedule: To a certain extent, you can schedule specific blocks of time when you might not wish to work; however, the longer you are away from your business, the more risk you run of having someone else take your customers.

Requirements: In addition to having the necessary equipment (a large covered truck) and licenses (for yourself and your vehicle), you need the ability to sell your service to businesses that might contract with you. Then you must be reliable and trustworthy so that you can get their repeat business.

Compensation: You will be paid by the job. Refer to #9 in Chapter 1 for advice on pricing.

TRUCK MECHANIC

Description: Repairs and services trucks—any kind of truck or just commercial vehicles. You can work in the service department of a truck dealer or in your own repair station.

Time Schedule: If you work for yourself, refer to #7 in Chapter 1 for suggestions on how to delegate some of your work to trusted employees. As a full-time employee, you might want to check the advice in Chapter 18 on how to turn that job into a flexible one.

Requirements: You'll need training and experience in repairing and servicing trucks. This background can be gained from working with other mechanics or working for the truck manufacturers. You will also need to know how to market your service.

Compensation: As an employee, you will be paid a salary or hourly wage and possibly benefits. If you own your business, your income will derive from what you charge for your service, minus your costs. Refer to #9 in Chapter 1 for advice. Be sure to check what your competition charges.

TRUCK RETAILER

Description: Sells trucks, either small ones to be driven by individuals or commercial ones to be used by trucking companies. This is a sales job most often done from a showroom.

Time Schedule: As a salesperson, you will probably have some flexibility; but, depending on the type of truck you sell, you might have to work on weekends to accommodate the shopping habits of the public.

Requirements: In addition to those requirements outlined for salespeople in #8 in Chapter 1, you must know about the trucks that you are selling and how they will help your customers.

Compensation: You will make a salary and commission as described in #8 in Chapter 1.

Chapter 18

Keep the Job You Have but Work When You Want

Perhaps you're different from most of the other people who have read this book. You already have a great job in a field that you enjoy. The only problem you have is that you are stuck in the 8-to-5 grind we've been trying to avoid.

"If only I had more time to enjoy life but could still keep my job," you moan to yourself.

This chapter will advise you on how to make that good job of yours more lifestyle-flexible. Let's start by exploring all the ways that you can rearrange traditional full-time jobs.

Flexible Time

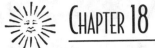

If you are presently working in an 8-to-5 job and would like to be home by 3 P.M. (when the kids come home or just to have more daylight time to "do your thing"), assess your job with the idea of rescheduling the hours to run from 6 A.M. to 3 P.M. Do you interact with national or international customers as a customer service representative, receptionist, or secretary? Has your boss considered how it would benefit the company by having you at the phones when people in other parts of the country or world are already at work? It always amazes me, as I communicate with companies doing business nationwide, how few have people at the telephones during business hours other than their own. Or maybe you'd like to start later in the day (you're one of those Owls we talked about in the introduction) and work into the early evening? The same justifications apply.

But perhaps you don't deal with others in different time zones. Maybe you're a clerk in a store or a legal secretary or an accountant. But you'd like to be at the job for only seven hours—not eight. Consider swapping your lunch hour for a quick snack at your desk while you work. Would it really matter to your employer if you did that?

Are you in a position where you could cut the day into thirds? You could work mornings and evenings but be off during the afternoons. This alternative works very well for positions in retail stores, which need people during all three periods of the day.

The Six-Day Work Week

If your job can accommodate it, try a six-day work week consisting of six hours each instead of the standard eight. You would have to cut out or shorten your lunch hours. And you would have to be willing to work six short days.

The Four-Day Work Week

The other side of the six-day week is the shorter week with longer days. Of the two, more businesses are choosing a four-day week where everyone works ten hours each day. People I have talked to who work this schedule love it after the initial period of getting used to it. Yes, it is true that the day is longer; but once you're at work, it's not so difficult to work a little longer to have the luxury of those three-day weekends. Most businesses allow half their workforce to work Tuesday through Friday while the others work Monday through Thursday.

Working At Home

With traffic getting more and more snarled in urban cities and the cost of utilities and work stations rising, many businesses are allowing some of their clerical, administrative, or creative staffs to work one to two days a week from home. If you have a fax machine, computer, and everything else that your company requires, why not try telecommuting, as it's called? Usually people who work from home get more accomplished than they do in the office—possibly because interruptions from telephones, visiting colleagues, and so forth are almost nonexistent.

Think About Part-Time Work

But perhaps there is no way that you can turn your full-time job into one with flexible and still full-time hours. Consider, then, working part-time.

You may be surprised to learn that you can afford it—particularly if you are paying a baby-sitter or if your salary has moved your family income into a much higher tax bracket. Add up how much of that full-time wage you really net after paying all of your working expenses (including lunches). If you then decide that working half the time (and cutting out half or more of your expenses) could work for you financially, you might want to consider the following options.

The Buddy System

Also called piggy-backing or job sharing, the buddy system allows you to share your single, full-time job with another person and work half of the normal day. You might work in the morning, your buddy in the afternoon. Some people alternate weeks. One person works for a week and has the next week off while the "buddy" works.

Employers like this setup because it gives them the comfort of knowing that the job will always be done; if one employee is sick or out on vacation, the other puts in a full day (and vice versa). Also if one should quit, work does not stop until the position is filled.

If you want to try the buddy system and are in charge of finding your buddy, you must be certain that he or she is as skilled as you are. If you are not both equal in abilities, your employer will not continue to support the program. You will both need to be committed to this type of work schedule. Don't let someone take the job only to leave for a full-time one. That would be counter-productive. Be sure that you are both similar in personality—both extroverts, hard workers, and so forth. You don't want your employer to have a favorite and choose to dismiss the other.

If a buddy system in any form won't work for you, think about self-employment.

Your Own Home-Based Business

Is it really so important that you continue to be your employer's employee? Could you serve the business just as well (and with more flexibility for you) by becoming an independent contractor or consultant?

Think seriously about this because I know that chances are you have never considered it.

By contracting with you to do your job (as an accountant, marketing manager, advertising executive, salesperson, company trainer, or whatever), your employer will save substantial costs of employment. Those costs include workers' compensation, the business's share of your social security and medical insurance, paid vacation time, paid sick leave, and so forth. You, on the other hand, have the basis for your own business, with a flexible lifestyle and possibly the opportunity to add other clients if they are not competitors of your present employer.

Today, with the cost of business becoming more and more prohibitive and with downsizing at an all-time high, more businesses are looking at this alternative. If your colleagues are being forced to take early retirements or positions are being eliminated, and if you even suspect that you may be next, take the initiative and put together a consultant program for your employer—where you will work independently for the same salary (or nearly the same salary) but without the benefits. If you do make this suggestion, however, try to get at least a one-year contract so that you will have the opportunity to find other clients and make your business grow.

As you consider these ideas for making your full-time job more flexible, be sure to present your recommendations from your employer's point of view. This means that you should outline the advantages to your employer of what you propose. For example, using the buddy system means that the business will always have a worker on the job; flex hours mean that someone will always be available by telephone to all the customers; telecommuting and four-day work weeks mean that fewer parking spaces and work spaces will be needed; turning employees into consultants will cut down the costs of employment.

I always advise people to remember that *the employer is primarily interested in what's best for him or her and the company.* Present your proposal with this in mind and you will be more likely to get what *you* want.

Chapter 19

Now That You're Working When You Want and Still Making Money, What Are You Going to Do with the Rest of Your Life?

Congratulations! You've found a good job where you make the money you need and—best of all—you have free time left over to do what you want.

Be careful! Don't squander your newfound time. Crazy as it seems, doing what you want to do isn't easy—especially if you are part of a family or have lots of contact with other people. The reason is obvious. People, even those you love, can and do make lots of demands, and it's hard to say "no."

Therefore, it's important to make plans for your life which will insure that you get what you want out of it and which will let you make the best use you can out of the free time you've earned from your flexible career.

These ten steps will help you.

1. Set Your Life's Priorities

Psychologists tell us that worthwhile, satisfying lives are fulfilling in four different realms—in the realms of the spiritual, the family, career, and leisure time.

Assuming you've got the work part taken care of, what do you want to do in the other three? Spend more time with the family? play golf? help your fellow human beings? Make a list and be specific.

2. Set Measurable Goals For Areas Of Your Life Not Related To Work

It's not enough to *say you want to do something with your family or leisure*—you have to plan what that is, then figure out how and when you're going to do it.

3. Learn To Say "No"!

It's bound to happen! When the people around you learn that you're not a slave to a time clock, they'll start asking you to join this, do that, go here, help there. And if you don't say "no," you'll be even busier and more short of time than if you had an 8-to-5 job.

A good way to determine if you should agree to the request is to ask yourself these questions:

- Is it *absolutely* necessary to the well-being of the requester and will it *truly* adversely affect my relationship with that person? (Note the key words here are "absolutely" and "truly"—not "maybe" or "might.")
- Can anyone besides me do this? If the answer is "yes," you know what to do.
- Will I feel angry, bitter, aggravated, martyred, resentful, or in any other way unhappy if I do this? If you say "yes" and fulfill the request anyway, don't blame anybody but yourself. You are your own worst enemy!

4. Schedule Time To Do Something You Really Want To Do And Stick To That Time Commitment

Why are we so good about scheduling work-related appointments and so bad about scheduling the pleasurable things that we wanted a flexible job to be able to do? Don't let time escape you. *Schedule* the fishing trip, the lunch with a friend, the trip to the museum, the time to read a book, and so on.

5. Take Good Care Of Your Physical Self

Exercise and eat right so that you'll live long enough to enjoy yourself. A simple walk around the block and cutting back on sweets will do if you're not the "physical" type. Those of you already into working out don't need this pointer. Just keep on keeping on.

6. Learn Something New Every Single Day

It doesn't have to be a big lesson. Simply learning the name of your neighbor, where a new store is located, a mystery of nature—something new about your spouse or child. (By the way, the tragedies on the evening news do not count.)

7. Occasionally, Take Inventory Of Your Life

What are you doing with it, where are you going, what are its blessings? That will keep you focused.

8. Every Day Give Someone Or Something A Touch Of Love

Kiss your loved ones, hug your dog, pet your cat, smile at a grim-looking stranger. It will make you feel even better than it will them.

9. Once A Month Be Totally Spontaneous

Throw the schedule away and do what you woke up *wishing* you could do. It won't matter to the world if you take a day off but it *will* matter to you.

10. Once A Week For One Hour *Do Absolutely Nothing*

That's right—I did say *do nothing*. Don't sleep, read, watch television, talk, think. Simply find a quiet place—your front porch, a shade tree, a brook, the bathroom—any place where you can be uninterrupted and *just sit*. Empty your mind of all thoughts and just carefully and completely absorb what life brings your way.

The results will surprise you! (Yes I know you can hear the flapping of hummingbird wings!)

Now—go forth and really enjoy the rest of your life!

Index